TILOPA'S MAHAMUDRA UPADESHA

Tilopa's Mahamudra Upadesha

The Gangama Instructions with Commentary

Sangyes Nyenpa

TRANSLATED BY

David Molk

SNOW LION
BOSTON & LONDON
2014

Snow Lion
An imprint of Shambhala Publications, Inc.
Horticultural Hall
300 Massachusetts Avenue
Boston, Massachusetts 02115
www.shambhala.com

9 8 7 6 5 4 3 2 1
First Edition
Printed in the United States of America

⊚ This edition is printed on acid-free paper that meets the
American National Standards Institute z39.48 Standard.
♲ Shambhala makes every effort to print on recycled paper.
For more information please visit www.shambhala.com.

Distributed in the United States by Penguin Random House LLC
and in Canada by Random House of Canada Ltd

Designed by Gopa & Ted2, Inc.

Library of Congress Cataloging-in-Publication Data
Saṅs-rgyas-mñan-pa X, Rin-po-che, 1964–
[Phyag chen gangama'i 'grel pa dam pa'i źal gyi man ṅag. English]
Tilopa's Mahamudra Upadesha: the Gangama instructions with commentary /
Sangyes Nyenpa; translated by David Molk.—First edition.
pages cm
The oral instruction of Sangyes Nyenpa Rinpoche given to the monks
and nuns of Benchen Monastery, Pharping, Kathmandu, Nepal in 2001.
Includes bibliographical references.
ISBN 978-1-55939-426-0 (pbk.: alk. paper)
1. Meditation—Tantric Buddhism. 2. Tillopāda, 988–1069. Phyag rgya
chen po'i man ṅag. I. Molk, David, 1953– translator. II. Title.
BQ8939.5.S2613 2014
294.3'4435—dc23
2013028406

CONTENTS

May this publication of the teaching of the *Gangama Mahamudra,* given and transcribed by Sangyes Nyenpa Rinpoche at Yangleshö Benchen Drubkang, open wide the doors of pure virtue and goodness.

Karmapa Ogyen Trinley
6 May 2008

PREFACE

—————

T HIS *Discovery of Sacred Secrets on the Banks of the Ganges: A Commentary to Tilopa's Gangama Mahamudra Instructions* is intended primarily
for great meditators. Since there is so much to learn and we don't know how
long we may live, it would be a shame if those who are doing essence-practice
for the sake of ultimate aims could not learn the tantric dohas, the spiritual
songs of realization that escaped the lips of the supreme mahasiddhas of
India. I would regret, however, if such precious instructions were shown to
any who would misuse them for worldly aims. Therefore, I ask those of highest faculties who rely on discerning insight to practice it without mistaking
what is beneficial for this and future lives. An important point to note is
that I would ask uninitiated readers to temporarily not read "How to Dispel
Obstacles," from the middle of verse nineteen onward, as this deals only with
tantric techniques. First train in the preliminaries. Then, in conjunction with
receiving the oral instructions from the guru, in accordance with how one
studies, vast benefit is certain to emerge.

Nyenpa

TRANSLATOR'S INTRODUCTION

THIS COMMENTARY to the Ganges Mahamudra is the oral instruction of Sangyes Nyenpa Rinpoche given to the monks and nuns of Benchen Monastery, Pharping, Kathmandu, Nepal in 2001. The root text was given as a doha, a spontaneous song expressing spiritual realization, by the mahasiddha Tilopa[1] to the pandit Naropa[2] on the banks of the Ganges River about a thousand years ago. Naropa passed them on to the Tibetan Marpa Lotsawa,[3] who translated them and brought them to Tibet. Sangyes Nyenpa Rinpoche has added an outline of his own composition, here presented as the titles to the chapters, in order to facilitate the practice of the instructions. It is only thanks to the irreversible faith, great devotion, and perseverance of Naropa, Marpa, Milarepa,[4] Gampopa,[5] and so on—all of the illustrious masters of the Kagyu, the "Lineage of Transmission"—that we are fortunate to have these instructions and the transmission of sudden enlightenment that accompanies them intact and fully potent to the present day.

These instructions present, in an essential and condensed form, the ultimate path and result of Buddhist meditation: realization of the ultimate nature of oneself and all phenomena. Rather than analyzing self and other phenomena individually, however, the Mahamudra approach derives understanding of the ultimate nature of phenomena by considering their relationship to mind, in particular the very subtle mind of "clear light." Mahamudra, "great seal," refers to this ultimate nature that can be experienced and realized through meditation. Not a simple negation, it is a primordial union of luminous awareness and emptiness that is identified in the *Ornament of Stainless Light* commentary to the Kalachakra tantra:

> The primordial mind is a very subtle mind, and when manifest,
> it takes as its objects phenomena such as the complete absence
> of any limiting conceptual elaboration, the direct cognition of

emptiness. It has the ability to create every quality of a buddha, and it has dwelt in the continuum of every sentient being since beginningless time without interruption. When it is purified it becomes the dharmakaya.[6]

When Buddha said that all living beings have buddha nature he was referring to this luminous core of consciousness that becomes a buddha. It is a pure, completely nonconceptual blissful awareness that underlies and is the source of all consciousness yet is empty of all grosser levels of awareness. Referred to as *sem-nyi* in Tibetan, often translated as "mind-itself," I have coined the term "elemental mind" to attempt to describe this irreducible, unpolluted element of consciousness.

Mahamudra meditation is an eminently practical approach to Buddha-dharma because it focuses attention directly on our buddha nature as the main path to manifesting it; the mind itself is taken as the path. Without using many technical terms that could possibly obscure it further, clear light mind, empty of all grosser levels of awareness, is caused to manifest by focusing directly on the essence of the present moment of awareness. By not fueling thoughts of past or future, grosser levels of awareness such as strong delusions of attachment and aversion are disempowered and allowed to subside. If it can be accessed directly, no other practice is necessary, and it is considered to be a separate tantra that did not require initiation.[7] If that is not possible, however, generation and completion stage tantric practice of deity yoga is necessary, for which tantric initiation is required.

When meditation "heats up," it is like a fire that can consume ignorance and delusion. Mahamudra meditation makes watching the mind, both in and out of meditation, the primary focus that is never to be lost. It is like keeping a strong flame burning under a pot so that the water quickly boils. Instead of getting lost in projections of mind as if they were real, Mahamudra meditation reins them in by noting that they are the mind's own products, and focuses continuously and directly upon their source, the mind itself. Without this constant mindfulness of all mental activity, one will be occasionally distracted and revert to habitual reification of thought processes and memories, especially between periods of meditation. This is like trying to boil water with an intermittent flame. Mahamudra meditation brings intensity to practice very quickly because it focuses firmly on elemental mind itself, abandoning distraction. It is like a final assault on the ultimate. It "ignites" the buddha nature to the point that it blazes up and manifests immediately, in this very lifetime. It is not comparable to initial levels of practice when, to purify negative karma and accumulate merit, virtuous thought must be encouraged and negative thought attenuated. Rather, it is an advanced level of practice in which subtlest awareness is emptied of all grosser levels, the "true path" of highest tantra, the most powerful force for purification and accumulation, itself the highest of virtues.

THE LINEAGE OF THE INSTRUCTIONS IN BRIEF

The spiritual biographies of the Bengali mahasiddha Tilopa by the Third Karmapa Rangjung Dorje, translated in this volume's first appendix,[8] and by Dorje Dze Ö,[9] translated by Khenpo Könchog Gyaltsen,[10] follow the same fourfold outline as the earliest known biography by Marpa Lotsawa, which has been translated by Fabrizio Torricelli and Acharya Sangye T. Naga[11]—Tilopa's life as a human being, his renown as an emanation of Chakrasamvara,[12] his renown as Chakrasamvara himself, and his renown as an emanation of all buddhas. There is little presentation of any chronological timeline because his life was miraculous and inconceivable. Even the account of his human life mainly reveals how he came into direct contact with Vajradhara, Buddha's immortal enjoyment body. It is said that he only demonstrated having human gurus to give others a more accessible object of faith. Yet to understand how he received teachings from Nagarjuna, who is generally accepted to have lived during the second century, does indeed require faith in the miraculous ability of enlightened beings to manifest outside of linear time! The biographies by Karmapa Rangjung Dorje and Dorje Dze Ö list his four human gurus as Charyawa, Nagarjuna, Lawapa, and Dakini Samantabhadri, while another biography by Padma Karpo[13] lists four human gurus in addition to Nagarjuna: Matangi, Lalapa, Dakini Samantabhadri, and Nagpopa. The Dorje Dze Ö and Padma Karpo biographies both assert that Nagarjuna enabled Tilopa to become a king and to miraculously defeat invading armies.

According to Padma Karpo's biography, Tilopa met Nagarjuna's female disciple, Matangi, when he sought to find Nagarjuna again and discovered that he had already passed away. Tilopa received Guhyasamaja teachings on illusory body from Matangi, Mahamudra and Chakrasamvara teachings on clear light from Lalapa, Hevajra teachings on *tummo* from Dakini Samantabhadri, and Chakrasamvara teachings from Nagpopa before being instructed by Matangi to work as a sesame oil maker[14] and as servant to a prostitute named Dharima. This, she said, was to destroy Tilopa's last traces of class arrogance from having been a king. After twelve years of absorption in continuous meditation while doing this work, Tilopa attained full enlightenment and blessed Dharima with high realization as well. He and Dharima floated into the sky, Tilopa still grinding his sesame seeds with mortar and pestle. He then sang of his discovery of primordial awareness in the mind, using the metaphor of extracting sesame oil from the seeds.[15] He sang, from the Dorje Dze Ö biography,[16]

> Pounding the shell of sesame
> Releases its essence;
> Likewise, the meaning of suchness
> Is revealed by the Lama's instructions.

This is very descriptive of the Mahamudra practice. Although the same realization may be reached through gradually deepening analysis and experience, Mahamudra practice depends upon immediately and directly observing one's own mind under the direction of a qualified lama. By simply being introduced to the coemergent, that is, the innate, unborn clear light wisdom of one's own being, realization may occur, with all concepts gradually or instantly collapsing into it. One then dwells in that awareness, experiencing it directly. Tilopa compares the process to pounding away the shell of mind to extract the oil of dharmakaya clear light within.

The uncommon biographies also tell of Tilopa subduing eight disciples with miracle powers, and of his early career as a monk who was renowned to be an emanation of Chakrasamvara. The story of Tilopa's principal disciple, Naropa, is not usually told in his biographies because it is covered in such detail in Naropa's own. An exception is the biography of Tilopa by Gampopa, which I've translated in appendix 2. In it, Gampopa says almost nothing about Tilopa's life, and focuses instead on Naropa's relationship with Tilopa.

Naropa was also a prince who, like Buddha Shakyamuni, renounced married life and his kingdom. He received lay ordination in Kashmir and mastered the five fields of knowledge.[17] He then took full ordination as a monk and tantric practitioner and stabilized his practice while living at Pullahari Monastery, near Nalanda Monastery. He became the recognized bearer of the teachings and the chancellor of Nalanda. He gave ordinations and teachings, and as protector of the northern gate of the monastery, defeated all challengers who came to debate the sangha.

The appearance of a dakini and other visions, however, revealed to him that he understood no more than the letter of the teachings, and that he should seek a master named Tilopa to receive instructions on Mahamudra. He developed deep renunciation and all the pandits of Nalanda could not dissuade him from leaving. He endured twelve minor hardships in his search for Tilopa, and twelve major hardships during his twelve years of training.[18] Repeatedly Naropa sacrificed life and limb, with Tilopa reviving and healing him each time. With each of the major trials he received further tantric instructions that finally culminated in Tilopa's Mahamudra instructions on the banks of the Ganges.

Before Tilopa gave the instructions, Naropa offered a mandala[19] to Tilopa made with his own blood. Tilopa responded by saying,

> Your own awareness is transcendent wisdom realizing things
> as they are!
> Tilopa has nothing at all to teach!

Naropa, however, continued to prostrate, circumambulate, and request instructions. Tradition has it that Tilopa then slapped Naropa with his sandal. Gampopa writes that Tilopa spat in his palm and then slapped Naropa's forehead. Naropa fainted. When he revived, the meaning of the instructions and all the tantras poured into his mind. Naropa went on practicing, eventually exhibiting immeasurable realized qualities and miraculous capabilities.

According to *The Blue Annals,*[20] Tilopa prophesied Marpa to Naropa, saying, "Remove the darkness of ignorance in the Tibetan and encompass him with the light of wisdom!" From a young age Marpa strongly wished to become a translator and studied Sanskrit with Drogmi Lotsawa. He was inspired to seek teachings in India, and went to Nepal where he stayed for three years while adjusting to the heat and receiving tantric teachings from the Nepalese master Chiterpa.[21] *The Blue Annals* states that the Nepalese Bendapa[22] then took him to Pullahari Monastery to be introduced to Naropa. Naropa was pleased with him and gave him Hevajra teachings. He studied Guhyasamaja with Jnanagarbha and Kukuripa in West India and then returned to Naropa for more teachings on Guhyasamaja and Mahamaya before returning to Tibet. It was at Pullahari that Marpa translated and confirmed his translation of the *Gangama* Mahamudra instructions.

In those days great wealth was offered for teachings. Marpa saved gold from offerings before again going to India to seek Naropa. This time Naropa had left, so Marpa received instructions from other teachers before again seeking Naropa in East and South India. During his journey he met and received instructions from many other siddhas such as Kasoripa. Finally he found Naropa and offered him his gold but Naropa threw it away. Marpa was upset by this but Naropa touched his big toe to the ground and the whole earth transformed into gold. He said, "This all is a golden island!" Then he disappeared.

Marpa returned to Tibet to settle down and marry Dagmema, his ninth wife.[23] He later heard of Maitripa's greatness and returned to India a third and final time.[24] He found Maitripa in East India and received essential Mahamudra instructions and other tantric teachings from him. He would later say about Maitripa,

> Through the great Venerable Lord I have realized the fundamental Nature as nonorigination and have grasped the relative nature of the Mind. Since then my doubts were removed.[25]

Next in the lineage, Milarepa is the most famous of Tibetan yogis. His disciple Gampopa also held Atisha's Kadampa lineage and was the first to preserve the Kagyu teachings in textual form. If the reader is not already familiar with or deeply immersed in this tradition of the golden garland of Kagyu masters, most illustrious lineage of mahasiddhas on earth, I would highly recommend learning more because it is wondrous and inspiring. The most important qualities necessary for receiving and understanding these instructions fully are faith, conviction, and devotion to the lama as a fully enlightened buddha. These attitudes are not difficult to develop when one's masters are mahasiddhas with miracles at their fingertips!

ORAL INSTRUCTIONS

The most concrete evidence we have of these miraculous beings' lives is the transmission of the instructions that they have bequeathed to us, which still flourish today. Traditionally, a text such as this is used as a support for oral instruction. Transmissions of dharma from Buddha's time onward were always living transmissions of energy that were only symbolized by the written texts that recorded them. In the Tibetan tradition, if the lineage of transmission of a sutra or commentary is interrupted, the text can no longer be taught. Rinpoche may seem strict by what he says in his preface, but we must understand that the lineage he speaks of is not just a communication of words. It is a living experience of enlightenment that must be fully transmitted by one master to the next in the lineage. It cannot be understood through written words alone, and certain aspects of the instructions were never even allowed to be set to paper; they only pass from the lips of the lama to the ears of the trainee. Rinpoche's strict adherence to the commitments of the lineage is the quality that has preserved its purity and potency through the generations. We should take it as an indication that we need a living teacher to understand these instructions in their fullest sense. In a traditional context a student might not even look at the written words until they had received, or were receiving, the oral transmission. Still, Rinpoche felt it would be beneficial to have a translation of his commentary made available. I feel that the instructions are so rich with his flowing eloquence, citation of scripture, and pith instructions that no one, from beginning to advanced, could fail to appreciate them. They can support practice for those who have already received the instructions, and inspire others to practice the preliminaries to receive them directly.

General Preparation

The most practical and extensive way to prepare for Mahamudra practice is by means of a *lamrim,* a stages of the path to enlightenment such as Gampopa Dagpo Rinpoche's *Jewel Ornament of Liberation.* In that text Gampopa summarizes the path to enlightenment in six points: the substantial cause of enlightenment, buddha nature; the basis of enlightenment, precious human birth; the condition for enlightenment, the *kalyanamitra,* the virtuous spiritual friend; the method for enlightenment, their instructions; the result, full enlightenment; and the activities of enlightenment, deeds benefiting beings. From this an understanding of the entire structure of the path to enlightenment can be gleaned. I will briefly outline the first four of these points.

As Gampopa asks in his *Ornament,*

> Why would we not attain enlightenment by practicing with effort, because we, and all sentient beings, possess the cause of enlightenment, which is tathagatagarbha?[26]

Sangyes Nyenpa Rinpoche emphasizes that it is only because we have the buddha essence, tathagatagarbha, that our efforts of listening, contemplating, and meditating on the teachings can bear fruit. It is very heartening to contemplate this point. In the middle wheel of Buddha's teachings we learn that sentient beings are not inherently bad, but they are not inherently good, either. This is descriptive of the space-like experience in meditation realizing nonduality, in which good and bad do not exist. The third turning of Buddha's teachings makes it clear, however, that sentient beings are intrinsically good. No matter how bad things get we can remember that we and all beings have an amazing treasure within us that will manifest when it has the chance. Its presence is the motivating force behind our wish to be free and to develop ourselves to our full potential. As Rinpoche says,

> When we know that there is this amazing quality present within our own mind that enables us to attain enlightenment in our very lifetime, we develop awe and esteem for that quality, which in turn gives us a joyful wish to practice. . . . Without devotion to that ultimate quality, we will not have devotion for the conventional lama who teaches us.

In the science of mind which is Buddha's teachings, the mental factors of faith, conviction, and devotion are of crucial importance. Three types of faith are explained: belief, clear faith, and aspiration. While not considered an incontrovertible or "valid" way of knowing anything, Buddha said that faith is the mother of knowledge. It is only when we believe we see benefit or truth in something that we will pursue it and delve into it sufficiently to fathom it fully. If someone believes it would be good for them to become a doctor, for instance, they may put in the years of study necessary to become qualified. Faith fulfills this role in everyday life. Faith is conviction in something positive, as well as clear admiration and aspiration for it. Faith is said to be a part of every virtuous state of mind. With a guru, conviction that the guru is a buddha catalyzes progress along the path.

The mental factors of esteem and devotion[27] take faith to a more personal and emotional level. By contemplating one's good fortune to be cared for by the guru and contemplating the endless suffering in samsara that would be the alternative, one develops an intense feeling of gratitude and reverence. Along with faith that the guru is a buddha, esteem and devotion are the catalyzing forces for realization. There is a saying in the lineage: with little esteem and devotion, little realization results; with middling esteem and devotion, middling realization results; with great esteem and devotion, great realization results.

On the second point, Gampopa says in his *Ornament,*

> The base is the supremely precious human rebirth. If all sentient beings have the buddha essence, can hell beings, pretas, and all five forms of life attain buddhahood? No they cannot. They must necessarily have the facilitating condition of what is called a precious human rebirth: a body endowed with the two aspects of leisure and endowments, and a mind of threefold faith.²⁸ This is the indispensable excellent base that is the special life form suited for the attainment of buddhahood.

Contemplating this gives great encouragement and determination. Gampopa cites Chandragomin:

> That, which attained, bestows liberation from endless rebirth,
> Or even virtues that plant seeds of supreme enlightenment,
> Its qualities far surpassing those of a wish-fulfilling jewel,
> That is the human form. Who would waste it fruitlessly?

The third and fourth points are the condition—having the spiritual guide—and the method, the instructions received from them. In the *Ornament* Gampopa says,

> Even though we have the perfect base, without the urging of a spiritual friend, since we are already accustomed to previous bad activities, the power of our habituation makes it difficult for us to enter the path to enlightenment.... The spiritual friend is like our guide when we don't know the way; like our escort when we need to go through a dangerous region; like the ferryman when we need to ford a powerful river.

It is not enough just to have a spiritual guide, we must receive instructions from them. The first of the four reliances²⁹ advises us to rely not upon the person but upon their teachings. The best way to rely upon a spiritual teacher is to emphasize the practice of listening, contemplating, and meditating on their teachings. Out of all ways of serving and making offerings, this pleases a virtuous spiritual guide most of all.

Gampopa divides the instructions into four parts: meditation on impermanence, meditation on karma and the faults of samsara, meditation on love and compassion, and the bodhichitta teachings, including instructions on the entire path to enlightenment. The instructions dispel four obstructions to enlightenment: attachment to things of this life, attachment to the happiness of samsara, attachment to the happiness of nirvana, and not knowing the method to attain buddhahood. Meditation on impermanence counters attachment to things of this life, meditation on karma and the faults of samsara counters attachment to the attractions of samsara, while meditation on love and compassion counters attachment to the bliss of nirvana, and the bodhichitta teachings act as the antidote to not knowing the method to attain buddhahood.

If you sense that there is something important to discover about life, perhaps a feeling of bliss or connectedness you've had glimpses of before; if you are concerned that time is limited and you see your life passing before your eyes; if you are tired of feeling that you are wasting your time, running a race that seems to be going nowhere; if you would like to turn away from inconsequential things to develop ultimate qualities of immeasurable love and inner peace that are everlasting, then I would highly recommend taking Rinpoche up on his offer to receive these precious instructions while the opportunity lasts. Long-time students of Rinpoche, as well, welcome to this attempt to bring forth his rich, erudite, compassionate, mellifluent, teasing, wrathful, mahasiddha voice!

May all beings enjoy this work, treasure, practice, and benefit greatly from it!

David Molk
Big Sur, California
Buddha's Birthday, 2013

THE GANGAMA MAHAMUDRA OF TILOPA

The Root Text in Tibetan and English

༄༅། །གྲུབ་ཆེན་ཏེ་ལོ་པའི་ཕྱག་རྒྱ་ཆེན་པོ་གངྒཱ་མའི་གཞུང་བཤུགས་སོ།།

༄༅། རྒྱ་གར་སྐད་དུ། མ་ཏུ་སྲུ་ད་ཨུ་པ་དེ་ཤ །
བོད་སྐད་དུ། ཕྱག་རྒྱ་ཆེན་པོའི་མན་ངག །

དཔལ་རྡོ་རྗེ་མཁའ་འགྲོ་ལ་ཕྱག་འཚལ་ལོ། །

དགའ་བ་སྤྱོད་ཅིང་བླ་མ་ལ་གུས་པ། །
ཕྱག་བསྐལ་བཟོད་ལྡན་སྒྲོ་ལྡན་ནུ་རོ་པ། །
སྐལ་ལྡན་ཁྱོད་ཀྱིས་བློ་ལ་འདི་ལྟར་བྱོས། །༡།

ཕྱག་རྒྱ་ཆེན་པོ་བསྟན་དུ་མེད་ཀྱིས་ཀྱང་། །
དཔེར་ན་ནམ་མཁའ་གང་གིས་གང་ལ་བསྟེན། །
རང་སེམས་ཕྱག་རྒྱ་ཆེ་ལ་བརྟེན་ཡུལ་མེད། །
མ་བཅོས་བཅུག་པའི་ངང་དུ་སྒྲོལ་ལ་ཞོག །༢།

བཅིངས་པ་སྐྱོད་ན་གྲོལ་བར་ཐེ་ཚོམ་མེད། །
དཔེར་ན་ནམ་མཁའི་དཀྱིལ་བལྟས་མཐོང་བ་འགག་པར་འགྱུར། །
དེ་བཞིན་སེམས་ཀྱིས་སེམས་ལ་བལྟས་བྱས་ན། །
རྣམ་རྟོག་ཚོགས་འགག་བླ་མེད་བྱང་ཆུབ་ཐོབ །།༣།

In Sanskrit the title is *Mahamudra Upadesha.*
In Tibetan it is *Chag-gya Chen-pö Men-ngag,*
Mahamudra Instructions.

Prostration to Shri Vajradakini!

Intelligent Naropa, you who have undergone austerity
Bearing suffering with devotion to the guru,
Fortunate one, pay attention to this! [1]

There is no "teaching" of Mahamudra,
Yet an example is space: upon what does it rely?
Our mind Mahamudra, likewise, has no support.
Not remedying anything, relax and settle in the unborn
     primordial state. [2]

If bonds are relaxed, we are liberated, without doubt.
Just as looking into space stops our sight of visual forms,
If mind looks into mind,
Thoughts cease and unexcelled enlightenment is attained. [3]

དཔེར་ན་ས་རྡུངས་སྟིན་ནི་ནམ་མཁའི་དབྱིངས་སུ་དེངས། །

གར་ཡང་སོང་བ་མེད་ཅིང་གར་ཡང་གནས་པ་མེད། །

དེ་བཞིན་སེམས་ལས་བྱུང་བའི་རྟོག་ཚོགས་ཀྱང་། །

རང་སེམས་མཐོང་བས་རྟོག་པའི་ཆུ་རླབས་དྭངས། ༑ །༨།

དཔེར་ན་ནམ་མཁའི་རང་བཞིན་ཁ་དོག་དབྱིབས་ལས་འདས། །

དཀར་ནག་དག་གིས་གོས་ཤིང་འགྱུར་བ་མེད། །

དེ་བཞིན་རང་སེམས་སྟིང་པོ་ཁ་དོག་དབྱིབས་ལས་འདས། །

དགེ་སྡིག་དཀར་ནག་ཆོས་ཀྱིས་གོས་མི་འགྱུར། ༑ །༧།

དཔེར་ན་གསལ་དྭངས་ཉི་མའི་སྟིང་པོ་དེ། །

བསྐལ་པ་སྟོང་གི་མུན་པས་སྒྲིབ་མི་འགྱུར། །

དེ་བཞིན་རང་སེམས་སྟིང་པོ་འོད་གསལ་དེ། །

བསྐལ་པའི་འཁོར་བས་སྒྲིབ་པར་མི་ནུས་སོ། ༑ །༦།

དཔེར་ན་ནམ་མཁའ་སྟོང་པར་ཐ་སྙད་རབ་བཏགས་ཀྱང་། །

ནམ་མཁའ་ལ་ནི་འདི་འདྲ་བརྗོད་དུ་མེད། །

དེ་བཞིན་རང་སེམས་འོད་གསལ་བརྗོད་གྱུར་ཀྱང་། །

བརྗོད་པས་འདིར་འདྲར་གྲུབ་ཅེས་ཐ་སྙད་གདགས་གཞི་མེད། ༑ །༥།

Clouds of vapor ascend in the sky.
They don't go anywhere, nor do they remain.
Similarly, when we see that thoughts are our own mind,
The rising waves of thought will clear. [4]

The nature of space is beyond color and shape;
It does not stain light or dark, does not change.
The essence of our mind is also beyond color and shape;
It is not stained by light or dark, good or bad phenomena. [5]

The brilliant clear essence of the sun
Is not obscured by the darkness of a thousand eons.
Likewise, the clear light essence of one's mind
Cannot be obscured by eons of samsara. [6]

For example, we use the term "empty space"
Yet there is nothing in space to which the term refers.
Likewise, we say, "our own clear-light mind"
Yet there is nothing that is truly a base for the designation. [7]

དེ་ལྟར་སེམས་ཀྱི་རང་བཞིན་གདོད་ནས་ནམ་མཁའ་འདྲ། །

ཆོས་རྣམས་ཐམས་ཅད་དེ་རུ་མ་འདུས་མེད། །

ལུས་ཀྱི་བྱ་བ་ཡོངས་ཐོངས་རྣལ་འབྱོར་དལ་བར་སྡོད། །

ངག་གི་སྨྲ་བརྗོད་མེད་དེ་བྲག་ཆ་སྟོང་བར་ཆའད། །

ཡིད་ལ་ཅི་ཡང་མི་བསམ་ལ་བླའི་ཆོས་ལ་ལྟོས། །

ལུས་ལ་སྙིང་པོ་མེད་པ་སྨྱུག་མའི་སྟོང་པོ་འདྲ། །

སེམས་ནི་ནམ་མཁའི་དཀྱིལ་ལྟར་བསམ་པའི་ཡུལ་ལས་འདས། །

དེ་ཡི་རང་ལ་བཏང་བཞག་མེད་པར་སྟྱོངྡ་ལ་ཞོག །༦།

སེམས་ལ་གཏད་སོ་མེད་ན་ཕྱག་རྒྱ་ཆེན་པོ་ཡིན། །

དེ་ལ་གོམས་ཤིང་འདྲིས་ན་བླ་མེད་བྱང་ཆུབ་འཐོབ། །༧།

སྔགས་སུ་སྨྲ་དང་ཕ་རོལ་ཕྱིན་པ་དང་། །

འདུལ་བ་མདོ་སྡེ་སྡེ་སྣོད་ལ་སོགས་པ། །

རང་རང་བཞུང་དང་གྲུབ་པའི་མཐའ་ཡིས་ནི། །

འོད་གསལ་ཕྱག་རྒྱ་ཆེན་པོ་མཐོང་མི་འགྱུར། །

ཞེ་འདོད་བྱུང་བས་འོད་གསལ་མ་མཐོང་བསྒྲིབས། །༡༠།

Thus, mind's nature has always been like space.
There is no phenomenon that is not included in it.
Giving up all physical activity, the yogi sits relaxed.
Vocal expression does not exist. Why? It is like empty echoes.
Without a thought in mind, look at the moon of Dharma!
Body has no essence, like a plantain tree.
Mind, like being in space, is beyond objects of thought.
Without discarding or placing, relax and settle within that state. [8]

If mind is without fixed reference point, that is Mahamudra.
Meditating and familiarizing with that, unexcelled enlightenment is
    attained. [9]

Practitioners of Mantra, and of the Paramitas,
Vinaya Sutra, the Pitakas, and so on,
Will not see clear light Mahamudra
By way of the tenets of each of their scriptures.
Because of their assertions, clear light is obscured, not seen. [10]

རྟོག་པའི་སྒྱུར་རྟོམ་དམ་ཚིག་དོན་ལས་ཉམས། །

ཡིད་ལ་མི་བྱེད་ཞེ་འདོད་ཀུན་དང་བྲལ། །

རང་བྱུང་རང་ཞི་ཆུ་ཡི་པ་རྦ་འདྲ། །

མི་གནས་མི་དམིགས་དོན་ལས་མི་འདའ་ན། །

དམ་ཚིག་མི་འདའ་སྒྲུན་པའི་སྒྲོན་མེ་ཡིན། ༔ །༡༡།

ཞེ་འདོད་ཀུན་བྲལ་མཐའ་ལ་མི་གནས་ན། །

སྡེ་སྣོད་ཚོས་རྣམས་མ་ལུས་མཐོང་བར་འགྱུར། ༔ །༡༢།

དོན་འདིར་གཞོལ་ན་འཁོར་བའི་བཙོན་ལས་ཐར། །

དོན་འདིར་མཉམ་བཞག་སྡིག་སྒྲིབ་ཐམས་ཅད་བསྲེག །

བསྟན་པའི་སྒྲོན་མེ་ཞེས་སུ་བཤད་པ་ཡིན། །

དོན་འདིར་མི་མོས་སྐྱེ་བོ་བླུན་པོ་རྣམས། །

འཁོར་བའི་ཆུ་བོས་རྟག་ཏུ་འཁྱེར་བར་ཟད། །

དན་སོང་སྡུག་བསྔལ་མི་བཟད་བླུན་པོ་སྙིང་རེ་རྗེ། །

མི་བཟད་ཐར་འདོད་བླ་མ་མཁས་ལ་བསྟེན། །

བྱིན་རླབས་སྙིང་ལ་ཞུགས་ན་རང་སེམས་གྲོལ་བར་འགྱུར། ༔ །༡༣།

Conceptual vows degenerate from the meaning of samaya.
No activity in the mind, free of all desire,
Naturally arisen, naturally extinguished, like designs on water,
If we do not leave the meaning of nonabiding and nonobservation,
We don't transgress samaya and are a lamp in the darkness. [11]

Free from all desire, if we do not abide in extremes
We shall see all teachings of the three pitakas. [12]

If we mount this meaning, we will be liberated from samsara.
Absorbed in it, all harm and obscuration will be burned.
We are said to be a lamp of the teachings.
Silly beings, uninterested in this meaning,
Are always carried away by the river of samsara and finished.
How pitiful, silly beings suffering unbearably in the worse realms.
If we are unable to bear it, want liberation, rely upon a skillful guru,
And their blessings enter our heart, our mind will be liberated. [13]

གྲུ་ཕྱི་འཁོར་བའི་ཆོས་འདི་དོན་མེད་སྲུག་བསྒྱལ་རྒྱུ། །

བྱས་པའི་ཆོས་ལ་སྙིང་པོ་མེད་པས་དོན་ལྡན་སྙིང་པོ་སྐྱོས། །

བཟུང་འཛིན་ཀུན་འདས་ལྟ་བའི་རྒྱལ་པོ་ཡིན། །

ཡེངས་པ་མེད་ན་སྒོམ་པའི་རྒྱལ་པོ་ཡིན། །

བྱ་རྩོལ་མེད་ན་སྤྱོད་པའི་རྒྱལ་པོ་ཡིན། །

རེ་དོགས་མེད་ན་འབྲས་བུ་མངོན་དུ་འགྱུར། ། །༡༤།

དམིགས་པའི་ཡུལ་འདས་སེམས་ཀྱི་རང་བཞིན་གསལ། །

བགྲོད་པའི་ལམ་མེད་སངས་རྒྱས་ལམ་སྣ་ཟིན། །

བསྒོམ་པའི་ཡུལ་མེད་གོམས་ན་བླ་མེད་བྱང་ཆུབ་འཐོབ། ། །༡༥།

ཀྱེ་མ་འཛིག་རྟེན་ཆོས་ལ་ལེགས་རྟོག་དང་། །

བརྟག་མི་ཐུབ་སྟེ་སྒྱུ་ལམ་སྒྱུ་མ་འདྲ། །

སྒྱུ་ལམ་སྒྱུ་མ་དོན་ལ་ཡོད་མ་ཡིན། །

དེས་ན་སྐྱོ་བ་བསྐྱེད་ལ་འཛིག་རྟེན་བྱ་བ་ཐོངས། །

འཁོར་ཡུལ་ཆགས་སྡང་འབྲེལ་པ་ཀུན་ཆོད་ལ། །

གཅིག་པུར་ནགས་འདབས་རི་ཁྲོད་གནས་པར་སྒོམས། །

སྒོམ་དུ་མེད་པའི་ངང་ལ་གནས་པར་གྱིས། །

དཔེར་ན་ལྐྲུན་ཞིང་སྐྱོང་པོ་ཡལ་ག་ལོ་འདབ་རྒྱས། །

རྒྱ་བ་གཅིག་བཏད་ཡལ་ག་ཁྲི་འབུམ་སྐྱེས། །

དེ་བཞིན་སེམས་ཀྱི་རྩ་བ་བཏད་ན་འཁོར་བའི་ལོ་འདབ་སྐྱེས། ། །༡༦།

Kye ho! These samsaric things are the cause of meaningless suffering.
Since fabricated things lack essence, look at the essential meaning!
Beyond all subject-object duality is the king of views.
If we have no distraction, it is the king of meditations.
If we exert no effort, it is the king of action.
If we lack hope and fear, the fruit will manifest. [14]

Beyond observed objects, mind's nature is luminous.
With no path to travel, keeping to the buddha path,
Accustomed to no object of meditation,
One attains unexcelled enlightenment! [15]

Kye ma! Worldly things cannot be well checked
Or analyzed, like illusions or dreams.
Dreams and illusions do not exist in actuality,
So, disillusioned, give up worldly activity.
Sever attachment and aversion to entourage and land.
Staying alone in the forest, meditate in retreat.
Abide in the state of nonmeditation.
A tree grows with trunk, branches, and foliage;
If its single root is cut, the hundreds of thousands of branches will dry up.
Likewise, if the root of mind is cut, the foliage of samsara will dry up. [16]

དཔེར་ན་བསྐལ་སྟོང་བསགས་པའི་མྱུན་པ་ཡང་། །

སློན་མེ་གཅིག་གིས་མྱུན་པའི་ཚོགས་རྣམས་སེལ། །

དེ་བཞིན་རང་སེམས་འོད་གསལ་སྐད་ཅིག་གིས། །

བསྐལ་པར་བསགས་པའི་མ་རིག་སྲིག་སྒྲིབ་སེལ། ༎ །༡༡།

ཀྱེ་ཧོ་བློ་ཡི་ཆོས་ཀྱིས་བློ་འདས་དོན་མི་མཐོང་། །

བྱས་པའི་ཆོས་ཀྱིས་བྱར་མེད་དོན་མི་རྟོགས། །

བློ་འདས་བྱར་མེད་དོན་དེ་ཐོབ་འདོད་ན། །

རང་སེམས་རྩད་ཆོད་རིག་པ་གཅེར་བུར་ཞོག །

རྟོག་པ་དྲི་མའི་ཆུའི་དྭངས་སུ་ཆུག །

སྣང་བ་དགག་སྒྲུབ་མི་བྱ་རང་སར་ཞོག །

སྤང་ལེན་མེད་པར་སྣང་སྲིད་ཕྱག་རྒྱར་གྲོལ། །

ཀུན་གཞི་སྐྱེ་བ་མེད་པར་བག་ཆགས་སྲིག་སྒྲིབ་སྤོང་། །

སྐྱེམས་བྱེད་ཚིས་གདབ་མི་བྱ་སྐྱེ་མེད་སྙིང་པོར་ཞོག །

སྣང་བ་རབ་སྣང་བློ་ཡི་ཆོས་རྣམས་ཟད་དུ་ཆུག །

མུ་མཐའ་ཡོངས་གྲོལ་ལྟ་བའི་རྒྱལ་པོ་མཆོག

མུ་མེད་གཏིང་ཡངས་བསྒོམ་པའི་རྒྱལ་པོ་མཆོག །

མཐའ་ཆོད་ཕྱོགས་བྲལ་སྤྱོད་པའི་རྒྱལ་པོ་མཆོག །

རེ་མེད་རང་གྲོལ་འབྲས་བུའི་མཆོག་ཡིན་ནོ། ༎ །༡༢།

For example, darkness accumulated over a thousand eons,
That whole mass of darkness, is dispelled by a single lamp.
Likewise, our own clear-light mind instantly dispels
Ignorance, harm, and obscuration amassed over eons. [17]

Kye ho! Intellectual Dharma does not see what transcends intellect.
Fabricated Dharma does not realize what "nonactivity" means.
If you wish to attain "transcendence of intellect" and "nonactivity,"
Cut the root of your mind and leave awareness naked.
Immerse conceptual thoughts in that bright stainless water.
Do not approve or reject appearances; leave them as they are.
Not abandoning or adopting, all of existence is liberated in Mahamudra.
In birthless alaya—"foundation of all"—imprints, harm, and obscuration
    are abandoned.
Don't be proud and calculating; settle in the essence of birthlessness.
Since appearances are reflexive, we run out of mental creations.
Freed from boundaries and limits is the supreme king of views.
Boundless, deep and vast, is the supreme king of meditations.
Cutting extremes, unbiased, is the supreme king of conduct.
Without hope, naturally liberated, is the supreme result. [18]

ལས་ནི་དང་པོ་གཅོང་རོང་ཆུ་དང་འདྲ། །

བར་དུ་ཆུ་བོ་གཙང་དལ་ཞིང་གཡོ། །

ཐ་མ་ཆུ་རྣམས་མ་བུ་འཕྲད་པ་འདྲ། །

བློ་དམན་སྐྱེས་བུ་རང་མི་གནས་ན། །

རླུང་གི་གནད་བཟུང་རེག་པ་བཅུད་ལ་བོར། །

ལྟ་སྟངས་སེམས་འཛིན་ཡན་ལག་དུ་མ་ཡིས། །

རིག་པ་རང་ལ་མི་གནས་བར་དུ་གཅུན། ། ༑ །༦༩།

ལས་རྒྱ་བསྟེན་ན་བདེ་སྟོང་ཡེ་ཤེས་འཆར། །

ཐབས་དང་ཤེས་རབ་བྱིན་རླབས་སྟོམས་པར་འཇུག །

དལ་བར་དབབ་ཅིང་བསྐྱིལ་བཀྲོལ་དྲངས་བ་དང་། །

གནས་སུ་བསྒྱལ་དང་ལུས་ལ་ཁྱབ་པར་བྱ། །

དེ་ལ་ཆགས་ཞེན་མེད་ན་བདེ་སྟོང་ཡེ་ཤེས་འཆར། ། ༑ །༢༠།

ཚེ་རིང་སྐྲ་དཀར་མེད་ཅིང་ཟླ་ལྟར་རྒྱས་པར་འགྱུར། །

བཀྲག་མདངས་གསལ་ལ་སྟོབས་ཀྱང་སེང་གེ་འདྲ། །

ཐུན་མོང་དངོས་གྲུབ་མྱུར་ཐོབ་མཆོག་ལ་གཞོལ་བར་འགྱུར། ། ༑ །༢༡།

ཕྱག་རྒྱ་ཆེན་པོ་གནད་ཀྱི་མན་ངག་འདི། །

འགྲོ་བ་སྐལ་ལྡན་སྙིང་ལ་གནས་པར་ཤོག ། ༑ །༢༢།

At first, it's like racing mountain rapids.
In the middle, it moves slowly like the River Ganges.
At last, all rivers meet the sea, like the meeting of mother and child.
If those of little intelligence cannot abide in this state,
Apply breathing techniques and cast awareness into the essence.
Through mode of view, holding the mind, and many branches,
Persevere until you abide in awareness. [19]

By having karmamudra, bliss-void wisdom will dawn.
Blessings of method and wisdom join in union.
Elements slowly falling, spinning, drawn back upward,
Are brought into the places and made to pervade the body.
Without attachment to it, bliss-void deep awareness dawns. [20]

Long life without white hair, waxing like the moon,
Luminous complexion with the strength of a lion,
Common siddhis quickly attained, we mount the supreme. [21]

May these pith instructions of Mahamudra
Abide in the hearts of fortunate living beings! [22]

ཕྱག་རྒྱ་ཆེན་པོ་སྒྲུབ་པའི་དབང་ཕྱུག་དཔལ་ཏེ་ལོ་པ་ཆེན་པོའི་ཞལ་སྔ་ནས་མཛད་པ་ཁ་
ཆེའི་པཎྜི་ཏ་མཁས་ལ་སྒྲུབ་པའི་ནཱ་རོ་པས་དཀའ་བ་བཅུ་གཉིས་མཛད་པའི་རྗེས་ལ་ཆུ་བོ་
གངྒཱའི་འགྲམ་དུ་ཏི་ལོ་པས་གསུངས་པ་ཕྱག་རྒྱ་ཆེན་པོ་རྡོ་རྗེའི་ཚིག་རྐང་ཉི་ཤུ་རྩ་གསུམ་པ་
ཚོགས་སོ། །ནཱ་རོ་པ་ཆེན་པོའི་ཞལ་སྔ་ནས་དང་། དེ་ནས་ནཱ་རོ་པ་ཆེན་པོས་
པོད་ཀྱི་ལོ་ཙཱ་བ་ཆེན་པོ་སྒྲ་བསྒྱུར་གྱི་རྒྱལ་པོ་མར་པ་ཆོས་ཀྱི་བློ་གྲོས་ཀྱིས།
ཞང་ཕུལླ་ཧ་རི་བསྒྱུར་ཅིང་ཞུས་ཏེ་གཏན་ལ་ཕབ་པ་ཚོགས་སོ།
ཨི་ཐི། དགེའོ། ༕༢༣༕

This completes the twenty-three vajra verses on Mahamudra taught by the sovereign of Mahamudra siddhas, Tilopa, to the learned and accomplished Kashmiri pandit Naropa on the banks of the River Ganges. Great Naropa then taught it to the Tibetan lotsawa, Great King of Translators Marpa Chökyi Lodrö, who translated it and made it definitive at Naropa's northern abode of Pullahari. ITHI! May all be virtuous! [23]

Discovery of Sacred Secrets on the Banks of the Ganges

A Commentary to Tilopa's Gangama Mahamudra Instructions

INTRODUCTION TO THE COMMENTARY

Guru Karmapa, glorious Vajradhara, pervasive lord of all lineages,
Yidam Yogini, source of all mandalas, glory of samsara and nirvana,
Dharmapalas Bernagchen and Chamdrel, controlling all agents of action,
This yogi bows to you with single-pointed devotion!
Please care for us inseparably with compassion!

PLEASE STUDY THIS with a bodhichitta motivation, thinking, "I shall
set all sentient beings equal to space into the state of omniscient buddhahood! It is for this purpose that I shall practice the profound Mahayana
Dharma of the instructions on Mahamudra."

As for the sacred Dharma we will be studying, it is that of the Mahasiddha Tilopa. All of the Kagyu lineages trace back to him. In particular, it is
an uncommon lineage of the guru's oral instructions coming through that
Tibetan sovereign of Mahamudra, Marpa, and his disciples—that liberated
path of Mahamudra through which enlightenment is attained during the
brief moment of this lifetime, in this very body. It is this uniquely excellent
lineage of the actual realizations that was passed from Mahasiddha Tilopa
to the great Pandit Naropa, and so on, that we are receiving.

We are always talking about Mahamudra. There have been many commentaries on Mahamudra composed by Indian and Tibetan masters, and
commentaries to those commentaries, as well. Many are composed in the
style of oral instructions or oral commentaries. Many take into consideration
possible objectors' positions and cite numerous scriptural sources, making it
very difficult, however, to cohesively delineate the actual instructions. Mahasiddha Tilopa's Mahamudra, the *Gangama,* on the other hand, is a short
scripture with a presentation embellished by oral instructions and precepts
alone, rather than extensive scriptural and dialectical elaboration. It is a holy
instruction that is convenient even for beginners to practice, convenient for

those of middling capacity to practice, and extremely convenient for the
practice of those of highest capacity. The *Gangama* is a source of the Marpa
Kagyu, one of the eight great practice lineages[1] included in the *Treasury of
Instructions*. I received it from Kyabje Vajradhara Dilgo Khyentse Rinpoche.[2]

Generally speaking, I have no practice of Mahamudra at all and would not
dare to write a commentary. Still, what we call the "blessings of the lineage"
is very sacred; and I thought it would be good if I gave an easily understandable instruction especially for the monks and nuns who are beginning practitioners. It is solely with this motivation and for the sake of the lineage that
I offer this commentary.

It is because Tilopa taught this to Naropa on the banks of the Ganges, that
river of the East, that it is called the Ganges Mahamudra. To consider this
in terms of words and meaning, just as the Ganges River flows without
interruption, for those yogis and yoginis to whom clear light awareness
has dawned, the experience of Mahamudra flows throughout the day and
night, without interruption. Since all concepts that arise also cease within
that clear light awareness, since all instances of awareness of objects by the
six consciousnesses arise from and collect back into this ultimate reality of
elemental mind; and again, since Mahamudra clear light mind experience
flows without interruption throughout the day and night, it is like the River
Ganges. Thus, in terms of the name, Tilopa's teaching was so called because it
was taught on the banks of the Ganges; and in terms of the meaning, the title
symbolizes the fact that Mahamudra practice flows without interruption.

1. THE MEANING OF THE NAME

In Sanskrit the title is *Mahamudra Upadesha*.

"Upadesha" means instructions.

**In Tibetan it is *Chag-gya Chen-pö Men-ngag,
Mahamudra Instructions*.**

IT IS SAID that the *chag* of "Chag-gya" means *shunyata jnana,* the transcendent knowledge or awareness of emptiness; and that *gya,* "seal," means not passing beyond that. Generally speaking, in this context *chag* is nondual clear light and emptiness. What is nondual clear light–emptiness? To take the direct meaning of the words in this context, nondual clear light–emptiness refers to the nature of our present thought of this very moment of awareness. There is no nondual clear light–emptiness awareness other than or separate from our present moment of awareness. As it is said,

> This mere present illuminating clear awareness
> Is the actual nature of all conventional truth.
> Also, if one understands that it is unfabricated,
> Just that is their ultimate truth.

Thus, if we do not examine our own positive or negative thoughts and just leave them as they are, they become causes for samsara. If, in reliance upon such thoughts we can investigate them and meditate upon their actual nature, if we can recognize the actual entity of our thoughts, they are seen to be transcendent wisdom and become causes for the attainment of nirvana. Therefore, the root of all of samsara and nirvana is the clear light mind of

Mahamudra. What should we identify as clear light Mahamudra? Our own clear light mind realizing emptiness nondually.

So, again, *chag* refers to empty transcendent wisdom. Mahamudra oral instructions explain that its entity is shunyata, its nature is luminous, and it appears in various aspects. *Gya* carries the meaning that this mind of nondual, luminous, empty transcendent wisdom pervades all phenomena of samsara and nirvana without exception. Lower phenomena of samsara are the nature of mind, the nature of luminous empty transcendent wisdom. Higher phenomena of nirvana are also the nature of luminous empty transcendent wisdom. It is not the case that nirvana is sealed, or pervaded, by luminous empty transcendent wisdom while samsara is not. All phenomena of samsara and nirvana whatsoever are the play of luminous empty transcendent wisdom. They are the creative energy or nature of luminous empty transcendent wisdom; the display of its energy, of its nature. Thus, *gya* means that they do not pass beyond that. There is no phenomenon of samsara or nirvana that is not subsumed by nondual luminous empty transcendent wisdom.

That is why, in the context of Tantra as well, there is the practice of yuganaddha, the "unified pair" of luminosity and emptiness, the unified pair of bliss and emptiness, the unified pair of awareness and emptiness, the practice of the four emptinesses and four blisses: these terms are used in connection with anuttara or unexcelled highest yoga tantra. In the present context of these Mahamudra oral instructions, the understanding is the same.

When we speak of *men-ngag,* the "oral instructions" of Mahamudra, we are speaking of the lineage of oral instructions that are passed on from master to disciples who show signs of having the good fortune to be able to hold that lineage which is the actual experience of the meditation, the very essence of the practice, of Mahasiddha Tilopa. That is what is referred to as oral instructions, not just an explanation that is given to any disciple whatsoever. Some disciples, just a few with the good fortune, those of highest faculties, are taught with sign language, nonverbally, or with secret methods; this is also the oral instructions. These oral instructions are so profound, such an excellent method that, if they are practiced, buddhahood can be attained in a single lifetime; and if they are not, one is certain to take birth in samsara.

2. Marpa the Translator's Homage

Prostration to Shri Vajradakini!

THE TERM "Shri Vajradakini" here we understand to mean the mandala of ultimate truth. The translator is prostrating to Shri Vajradakini as the mandala of ultimate truth. In general, the term "Vajravarahi" or "Vajradakini" conventionally refers to the deity in her aspect with body and limbs that we see. Ultimately her entity is that of Prajnaparamita, the Perfection of Wisdom, Mother of All Buddhas, while in aspect she is the nature of Vajravarahi. She can serve as the basis for all *arya* attainment.[3] "Vajravarahi" is a name that we give to the mandala or sphere of ultimate truth.

In Tibetan, *Vajravarahi* is "Dorje Pagmo." *Pag* means "pig" in English. In general it refers to that which can destroy conceptual subject-object duality while displaying the appearance of a pig. Usually we consider pigs to be filthy, right? But nothing is clean or filthy to a pig! The pig's head symbolizes abiding by means of nondual transcendent wisdom once the snare of dualistic conceptuality has been destroyed. That is what her boar's head symbolizes.

Vajradakini in this context means the mandala of ultimate truth. What we mean by *vajra* includes the body, speech, mind, qualities, and activities of all buddhas. We also speak of five vajras: vajra body, vajra speech, vajra mind, vajra qualities, and vajra activities. Another set, of four vajras, is vajra body, vajra speech, vajra mind, and vajra jnana transcendent wisdom. So, what is a vajra? It is a name given to that quality of the inconceivable secrets of all buddhas. *Vajra* is a name given to inconceivable qualities, to inconceivable transcendent wisdom.

Dakini symbolizes the sphere of emptiness. How does such inconceivable transcendent wisdom arise? Since it does not pass beyond the sphere of the union of appearance and emptiness, the union of luminosity and emptiness, the union of bliss and emptiness, the union of awareness and emptiness, it is called "dakini" to symbolize the sphere of emptiness. When we explain how the vajra develops within such a sphere of emptiness, we must introduce inconceivability of body, speech, mind, qualities, and activities; thus *vajra* is an understanding of inconceivable qualities. On what basis are such inconceivable qualities realized? It is on the basis of the four great blisses: one is introduced to identifying the union of appearance and emptiness, the union of luminosity and emptiness, the union of bliss and emptiness, and the union of awareness and emptiness. It is a very profound method.

Prostration to Shri Vajradakini! So this Vajradakini, is she someone separate from ourselves whom we must think of and prostrate to? No. She belongs to us. We must prostrate with the recognition that we are prostrating to something which exists within ourselves. In this context we do not think of ourselves as prostrating to a Vajradakini separate from ourselves as we would normally think when prostrating. We must prostrate recognizing the existence of that which does in fact exist within ourselves. As it is said,

> To that which is primordially enlightened,
> With a nature knowing that it exists,
> I go for refuge until enlightenment.

The way things appear, conventionally and deceptively, is that we and all sentient beings experience continual suffering in samsara. In actuality, however, we are never separate from this quality of Vajradakini. Apart from recognizing or not recognizing this quality of Vajradakini that exists naturally within all of us, all sentient beings are buddhas. As it is said,

> Discerning all specific phenomena in an instant,
> Instantly, one attains full enlightenment.

Thus, recognizing the existence of Vajradakini within ourselves is what distinguishes liberation from deception. Therefore we prostrate to Shri Vajradakini. We prostrate thinking about the fact that we have naturally had such a quality within us primordially, from beginningless time.

Next comes the admonition for Naropa to listen.

3. The Promise to Impart the Essence Instructions

**Intelligent Naropa, you who have undergone austerity
Bearing suffering with devotion to the guru,
Fortunate one, pay attention to this! [1]**

H ERE, THE MENTION of the great siddha Naropa as one who has *undergone austerities with devotion for the guru* indicates that Naropa took Venerable Tilopa as his guru and, in so doing, had to go through twenty-four different major and minor hardships.[4] Through undergoing these hardships, he attained resultant Kechara Yuganaddha[5] in that very lifetime. It makes these instructions so sacred that the disciples surpass their masters, as Venerable Milarepa said; it really is an inconceivable lineage in which the disciples even surpass their gurus; in which, by practicing its profound meaning, buddhahood can be attained in a single lifetime, in this very body.

These instructions inform us that we have been under the control of karma and delusion in samsara since beginningless time up to the present. We have willingly volunteered for meaningless suffering. Then we have remained suffering incessantly in worse realms of existence. Yet there has been no benefit; it has not been fruitful for us. This time, we have the opportunity to practice the shortcut path of Secret Mantra Vajrayana, these instructions of Mahamudra, the heart-essence of all teachings of Sutra and Tantra. If we can practice it with real faith, joy, and devotion to this lineage, we will have the opportunity to benefit all of our aged mother sentient beings of the six realms throughout space. It was because of having inexhaustible joy and insatiable perseverance for this practice that Naropa went through such hardships. This does not mean just working as hard as we can throughout the day and night. It is continual perseverance applied on the basis of joy and reverence for the practice. The fact that we have this uninterrupted actual lineage of the Kagyu coming from Vajradhara is due solely to the kindness of Venerable Naropa. That is the significance of his austerities.

Devotion for the guru refers to having the perception that the guru is an actual buddha; it is not just having ordinary devotion for the guru. If we can realize that the guru is at the center of our heart and that the ultimate guru and conventional guru are inseparable, that is the principal practice of devotion for the guru. In this context, the ultimate guru is present within our own mind. Since the ultimate guru's presence in our own mind does not develop without the conventional guru who points it out to us, and since there is an indispensable need for the conventional guru to introduce us to the ultimate guru of our own mind, that is why we speak of "devotion to the guru."

Here we are mainly referring to devotion to the ultimate guru—the ultimate mode of existence of our mind, its union of appearance and emptiness, union of awareness and emptiness, union of bliss and emptiness, that incredible nature of our own mind just as it is. When we voluntarily delight in devoting ourselves to the ultimate guru, by force of that we can also naturally develop devotion for the holy guru who reveals it to us. There is this connection. However, generally speaking, we will not develop faith in the ultimate guru by developing faith in the conventional guru who reveals Dharma to us. When we know that there is this amazing quality present within our own mind that enables us to attain enlightenment in our very lifetime, we develop awe and admiration for that quality, which in turn gives us a joyful wish to practice. When we feel such aspiring faith, by force of that we will seek out a lama who can reveal it to us. There are certain qualities and qualifications that this lama must have. Thinking about this we will naturally develop devotion for a lama who has such qualities and qualifications. So without the devotion for the ultimate quality, we will not have devotion for the conventional lama who teaches us.

Therefore, to be devoted to a qualified guru, even if we do not understand all of their qualities and qualifications at first, we must be interested in ultimate truth. We must aspire to truth, pray for truth. Out of aspiration and devotion to truth we will develop devotion for the lama who has qualities and qualifications. That is why we have devotion for the guru. Once we have devotion for the guru, if the guru tortures us, beats us or scolds us, gives us difficult tasks, even body- and life-threatening tests, we will be able to bear it. We won't be able to get enough of it. We will want to volunteer for it. We will see that suffering as delightful. It was out of seeing the purpose in bearing such suffering that Naropa had the capacity to bear it.

We speak of *bearing suffering*. Generally speaking, when we bear the suffering of the lower realms of existence, we have no choice but to do so, and it serves no purpose at all. But it is different with difficulty encountered for the sake of Dharma, for the sake of such instructions as these of Mahamudra by which enlightenment can be attained in this lifetime, in this body. If we think about it, such difficulty serves great purpose; it is very meaningful. We understand that there is benefit in undergoing such difficult tasks. When we understand the meaning and purpose of undergoing such austerities, we are able to bear them.

What, first of all, is the reason we must bear suffering? It is because of our joyful enthusiasm, the delight we take, in the quality of the ultimate, the quality of the incredible secret. If we do not know such delight we will be unable to bear suffering. So notice that there is this connection, this relationship, between earlier and later levels of understanding and development.

Intelligent Naropa, you who have undergone austerity: Who is it who has undergone austerities? It is intelligent Naropa. Intelligence means having discerning wisdom—having wisdom with the ability to discriminate between right and wrong, between faults and positive qualities. It means having the intelligence to discern the distinction between causes of samsara and causes for liberation from samsara. Great Pandit Naropa was endowed with such wisdom. Tilopa was saying that this is the reason Naropa had the good fortune to receive these instructions.

Fortunate one, pay attention to this! He was saying, Set your mind like this! It does not mean that he was proposing to instruct Naropa just because he could bear austerities, have devotion for the guru, and put up with suffering. The purpose of austerities in the context of devotion to the guru is to develop devotion that is present no matter what the guru does. How does such devotion originate? There are conventional and ultimate explanations regarding the purpose of bearing suffering, as explained above. Mahasiddha Tilopa is addressing Great Pandit Naropa who is endowed with such qualities of wisdom, and telling him to pay attention to the instructions.

4. BEGINNING THE ACTUAL INSTRUCTIONS: MAHAMUDRA TRANSCENDS THE SPHERE OF TERMS AND CONCEPTS

There is no "teaching" of Mahamudra,
Yet an example is space: upon what does it rely?
Our mind Mahamudra, likewise, has no support.
Not remedying anything, relax and settle in the unborn
    primordial state. [2]

WHAT WE CALL Mahamudra is free from all extreme projections. As it is said,

"Seeing space" best describes it in the words of living beings.
How do you see space? Think about what those words mean.
Although the tathagatas have seen Dharma as it is,
They cannot find another metaphor better than "seeing space."

Thus, there is nothing that can illustrate or demonstrate Mahamudra. There is no symbol that can reveal it. It cannot be illustrated by skillful means. We give instructions about it, but no matter how skillful we are in describing it, Mahamudra cannot really be exposed or displayed. Buddha Shakyamuni himself said that the inconceivable nature of dharmata, ultimate truth, was not revealed in the past, is not being revealed at present, and will never be revealed in the future by any buddha. He even said that no past, present, or future buddha has ever seen it. This is what we mean by the "great seeing of nonseeing."

There is no teaching Mahamudra. In *Entering the Middle Way (Madhyamakavatara)*, it is also said, "Yet this secret of yours is not to be found!" Generally speaking, all presentations of emptiness explain in detail why all phenomena lack self-nature. Included in that is detailed explanation of personal selflessness, the lack of self-nature of living beings. So all phenomena are established as empty and selfless. Yet when speaking about it, glorious Chandrakirti says, "This secret of yours is not to be found!" If you have to explain the mode of existence of this inconceivable secret, it is beyond articulation. It is beyond words, beyond metaphors, beyond objects, so it cannot be explained.

Uttaratantra states,

> Since it is subtle it is not something to hear.
> Since it is ultimate it is not something to think.
> Because dharmata is profound,
> It is not an object of mundane meditation.

Buddha is saying that because it is extremely subtle it cannot be heard by mundane hearing; since it is extremely ultimate it is beyond mundane thinking; and because dharmata is extremely secret and inconceivable, extremely profound, it is not an object of mundane meditation.

When we say there is no teaching of Mahamudra, this does not mean that a teaching exists but we cannot give it. That would indicate an unfortunate lack of skill in means. Rather, it means that the ultimate itself is beyond being taught, beyond articulation, beyond words, beyond metaphors.

In the context of chöd practice we praise the Mother of Jinas with the words,

> Beyond speech, thought, expression, Wisdom Gone Beyond,
> Unborn, unceasing, with a nature like space . . .

Saying it is beyond speech, thought, or expression, again, does not mean that there exists a way to say it but we cannot; or that there exists a way to think it but we cannot; or that there exists a way to express it but we cannot. It is because Prajnaparamita itself is beyond speech, thought, or expression that we praise it in this way.

In the context of Mahamudra as well, the ultimate is beyond the four extremes, beyond the eight extreme projections.[6] It cannot be the object of a mundane state of mind. As said in the *Guide to the Bodhisattva's Conduct (Bodhicharyavatara),*

> Ultimate truth is not within the sphere of intellect.
> Intellect is said to be a conventional state of mind.

As Shantideva says, ultimate truth is not within the sphere of comprehension of the intellect. Intellect consists of our current mundane thoughts, thinking that is controlled by delusion, by attachment and aversion, by karma. It is compulsive thinking that lacks free will. It is thinking that causes us to enter samsara. It has grosser and subtler forms. It doesn't help to identify its grosser forms. That will not help to get rid of its very subtle form, which is innate self-grasping ignorance. How could we who are so thoroughly enmeshed in the subtle and vast three realms of samsara be able to see what is referred to as Mahamudra? It cannot be revealed or displayed even to those bodhisattvas who are of the highest good fortune, capacity, and wisdom.

> Like visual forms to the blind,
> Infants have never seen it before.
> Like an embryo that has never seen the sun,
> Even aryas ...

This is from *Uttaratantra*. A baby born today, when seeing the sun for the first time, will see light but not recognize the form of the sun. Similarly, it is said that even aryas who have attained the various stages of realization get only an inkling of the ultimate inconceivable secret; they cannot see it clearly.

Therefore, there is no teaching of Mahamudra; what we mean by Mahamudra is beyond examples and metaphors. This is why, as Tilopa smacked Naropa in the head with his shoe,[7] he said,

> I, Tilopa, have nothing to teach!
> If you see yourself, you will be free!

There is nothing to teach. If we talk a lot we will be fooled by the words. If we teach many meanings we will be deceived about meanings. Once we are distracted by words and meanings, we cannot go beyond them. Mahamudra is beyond the expression of words. It is beyond meanings that can be expressed, beyond objects of philosophy, beyond imagined objects, beyond objects of meditation. There is nothing more ultimate.

Thus, *there is no teaching of Mahamudra*. There is a great deal that can be understood by these words. Again, it does not mean that Mahamudra can be taught but we cannot manage to teach it; rather, it is that Mahamudra itself is beyond metaphors, beyond words, beyond objects of expression.

In *Uttaratantra* there are six reasons given:

> Because it is not an object of speech, because it is included in
>   ultimate truth,
> Because it is not an object of thought, because it is beyond
>   metaphors,
> Because it is unexcelled, because it is not included in samsara or
>   nirvana,
> An object of buddhas, it is inconceivable even to arya beings.

Because it is not an object of speech, it is inconceivable. Because it is included in ultimate truth, it is inconceivable. Because it is beyond speech and included in ultimate truth, it is not a source, not an object of mundane thought. The network of mundane thought cannot realize it.

Then, "Because it is not an object of thought, because it is beyond metaphors": Even if one had to give an example to describe it, it is beyond exemplifying. No example can symbolize it. We say it is unexcelled, because it is supreme sacred knowledge, the supreme of realized qualities. It is unexcelled because there is no realized quality or qualification, no view or meditation that surpasses it. Because it is unexcelled, it is inconceivable. Because it is not included in samsara or nirvana, it is not subsumed by the faults of samsara or the qualities of nirvana. It is beyond samsara and nirvana. Since it is beyond both samsara and nirvana, because it is not an object of speech, because it is included in the ultimate, because it is not an object of thought, because it is beyond exemplification, because it is unexcelled, since it is not included in samsara or nirvana, it is an object of buddhas that is inconceivable even to arya beings. Buddha is saying that even arya beings cannot realize it. So just knowing how to sit cross-legged and join our hands in meditation position is not going to help a bit. Saying, "I'm meditating" and being very emphatic about it will not help. That is why it is very important to proceed by way of knowing what is essential. What is essential? The essentials are what come with the guru's quintessential instructions. It does not help to be extremely intelligent. It does not help to be very persistent. Great intelligence alone cannot realize it. Great perseverance alone will not help. The essentials can only be realized on the basis of both great wisdom and great perseverance and the oral instructions of a real lama. What are called the lama's oral instructions can only be received when one perceives the guru as an actual buddha. One cannot receive oral instructions of Mahamudra with the perception of the lama as just an ordinary person; they won't be understood.

Therefore, on the basis of awe and aspiration and seeing a good lama as an actual buddha, the oral instructions can be understood when they are given. The lama cannot express everything they have realized, but they use words, expressions, and explanations as best they can, and we must develop meditative ascertainment on the basis of joyful effort. Why is it that we can recognize our object of meditation on the basis of enthusiasm? With nothing to be taught, when we meditate, what sort of recognition can we develop? The Mahamudra instructions and the ultimate nature of the mind are beyond words and examples. The fact that we can understand by meditating is just the nature of ultimate truth. That is because the Dharma that cannot be taught exists in relation to our own mind. That Dharma, which cannot be taught, has naturally existed in our mind forever. That meaning of Mahamudra, which cannot be taught, has primordially naturally existed in our own mind. No matter how much our mind has been controlled by delusion, no matter how much we have been subjected to suffering, Mahamudra in our mind never deteriorates. No matter how much our realized qualities develop, Mahamudra in our mind does not improve or increase. Buddhas cannot improve it and sentient beings cannot harm it: that is the unceasing ultimate nature of our own mind's Mahamudra. Since it is our own, we are simply manifesting something that exists within us. The lama does not, in reliance upon indications and instructions, give us something that we never had before.

It is said that there is no teaching Mahamudra, and this is a very profound point. There is no teaching Mahamudra, but why do we say that? We have no choice but to use metaphor when speaking to ordinary beings. We have no choice other than to reveal a meaning on the basis of a parallel analogy; there is no solid object that can be directly handed over. So we must make use of examples. Mahamudra is beyond them in actuality, but conventionally we need them.

An example is space: upon what does it rely? What do we mean by space? When we say that its entity is empty, we mean that the nature of space does not rest upon anything. The nature of space is clear. Its characteristics are unceasing. It pervades all realms. Space pervades all of us, pervades everything. It even pervades excrement. It would be incorrect to assert that it does not pervade the washroom. It pervades the washroom. Space also pervades the deity's inconceivable celestial mansion. Space pervades both samsara and nirvana. Space pervades all places.

In a similar way, Mahamudra pervades all phenomena of samsara and nirvana. Just as space pervades all worlds, Mahamudra pervades all phenomena of samsara and nirvana. It would not be correct to say that its pervasion excludes all sentient beings who are under the control of karma and delusion and includes only buddhas who are liberated from all of the faults of samsara.

Thus it pervades all of samsara and nirvana, like space whose defining characteristic is "absence of obstructive contact." We may come and go and perform actions; space does not stop us. In all actions whatsoever, going or staying, acting well or badly, lifting objects up or setting them down, space puts up no resistance. Openness is the very defining characteristic of space. In a similar way, within the expanse of Mahamudra, the various emanations of samsara and nirvana can appear. Within the expanse of Mahamudra can appear all of the faults of samsara and all of the qualities of nirvana. Whatever faults or qualities of samsara or nirvana occur, they arise from the expanse of Mahamudra and cease in the expanse of Mahamudra.

Therefore, the whole illusory mechanism of thoughts arises from the expanse of Mahamudra, no other way. The same exact thing is said in Dzogchen. It speaks again of thought being the emanation, the display, of our own mind's ultimate true nature, dharmata.

Karmapa Rangjung Dorje says in his *Mahamudra Prayer*,

> It does not exist—even jinas[8] do not see it.

If we ask whether the ultimate mode of being of our mind exists or not, it does not. It is not something existent. In saying this we do not mean that is it completely nonexistent. But it does not exist in the manner that a worldly intellect would conceive of it as existing. If we say that something exists we think of something solid, something that everyone can see. It does not exist like that. It is recognized only on the basis of practice and meditation; it cannot be shown to you by anyone else. That is the import of the words, "It does not exist; even jinas do not see it." So does this mean it is nonexistent? No. As the *Prayer* continues,

> It is not nonexistent—it is the basis of samsara and nirvana.

Thus, circling in samsara is a result of not realizing the ultimate mode of existence of our mind. Nirvana is a case of realizing the mind's ultimate mode of existence. Recognizing it we are liberated. So there is the possibility of liberation through recognizing Mahamudra, the ultimate mode of existence of our mind, and the possibility of continuing to be deceived by not recognizing it. So whether we are liberated or deceived is rooted in whether we realize the ultimate mode of existence of our mind or not. It is as Saraha says in one of his dohas,

> Homage to wish-fulfilling jewellike mind
> Which grants bestowal of all desired fruits
> Whether of samsara or nirvana.

So as for space, its essence is empty. The nature of Mahamudra is also emptiness. Space is clear by nature. Various appearances such as that of the sun and moon can appear in it. Similarly, in Mahamudra all of the phenomena of samsara and nirvana can be illuminated. The defining characteristic of space is its absence of obstructive contact. Likewise, the expanse of Mahamudra is characterized by absence of obstruction. Space pervades all spheres of existence; Mahamudra also pervades all phenomena of samsara and nirvana. This is why Saraha sings,

> What we call Mahamudra
> Is like viewing the nature of space.

When we view space, when we say, "Look at space!" we say that we are looking at it, but in fact we are not really looking at space in its actual nature. Blue is not space, it is a color, right? When we see blue, we are not "seeing space," are we? There is no seeing of space. Again,

> "Seeing space" best describes it in words of living beings.
> How do we see space? Think about what those words mean.

If we say we have seen space, we say, "I saw space." How did we see space? If we say we saw the stars, the stars are not space. The sun and the moon are not space. Clouds are not space. So how have we seen space? In everyday language, however, we do say, "I saw space." We can say that; it is acceptable language. Similarly, seeing the ultimate mode of existence of the mind is synonymous with "nonseeing," the highest sacred seeing. There is no actual seeing of the ultimate mode of existence of the mind. It is said that this "nonseeing" itself is the supreme sacred seeing. That is what we are talking about here, not seeing some kind of looming bright light; that is not seeing the ultimate mode of existence of the mind. If sentient beings see the ultimate mode of existence of their own minds, they can easily, naturally become buddhas. But just seeing whatever thought happens to be going through our mind is not what we call seeing the "ultimate mode of existence" of our mind.

So is the ultimate mode of existence of our mind realized by simply stopping all thought? No. That mental state also exists in the formless realm of samsara, where the minds of beings are focused on nothing at all. Just stopping thought is of no benefit.

So what does this mean? There is an important point here, a pith essential: the fact that we must have the sacred instructions of the holy guru. If you look at the ultimate mode of existence of the mind, which has such importance, it is not to be found. Sought with awareness, it is not to be found. No matter how much we meditate upon it, it cannot be seen. Without the blessings of the lineage there is no way to engage it. That is what we mean when we speak of the blessings of the lineage. We say, "Please give me a blessing. Please give me the blessing of the lineage. Please give me the transmission. Please give me a commentary." That is not what is meant here. What is meant is that whether we will be able to realize the meaning of the instructions on Mahamudra or not depends upon whether we have the blessings of the glorious root guru or not. As it is said,

> Inexpressible by others, innate within us,
> A "nonfinding" no matter where we search,
> But when the time comes, taught through methods by the guru,
> And to be known because of arising from merit.

This is something very important. Upon what does space depend? On who or what does space rely? According to what is said in *Uttaratantra,* earth, water, fire, wind, and so forth all depend upon space, but space does not in turn depend upon earth, water, fire, or wind. So, upon what does space depend? Space does not depend on anything.

There is no revealing of space. It is said,

> That which is called Mahamudra
> Should be viewed as the nature of space.

So, what are we talking about? Saraha sang,

> One's mind of Mahamudra does not rely on any object.
> Meditating, there is nothing outside to meditate upon.
> Distracted, there is nothing inside to wander back to.
> It is just that unfabricated primordial state.

Considering this, when we say we are meditating, there is nothing that we can present as that which we are meditating upon. And regarding wandering, there is nothing to come back to. If we relax and settle on the basis of unfabricated mind, this is what we refer to as our "own mind of Mahamudra."[9] We say that our mind of Mahamudra does not rely on any object. Mahamudra does not depend on any object at all. It doesn't need to depend on samsara "below" or nirvana "above." It relies on nothing at all. It need not depend on land or houses, good thoughts or bad thoughts. Therefore, equipoise in our unfabricated primordial state is what we call "Mahamudra" or our "own mind Mahamudra."

As said,

> Since nondistraction is meditation,
> Bless us to not part from our object
> Fixed right on the unfabricated
> Original nature of all that appears.

The *Prayer* speaks of nondistraction.[10] Someone who is undistracted knows what it is to be mindful. If we ask what this is like, it is similar to asking a mute person to describe the taste of sugarcane. When they eat it for the first time, it is sweet; they are surprised and want to eat more. But if asked what it is like, how could they indicate it with their hands, eyes, or voice? There would be no way for them to really express it. Yet they are still experiencing the taste, aren't they? The instructions on Mahamudra are like that, it is said.

"Fixed right on the unfabricated original nature of all that appears." *So ma*—"original," "new," "pristine"—refers to the unfabricated state. We have been to lower realms of existence but this nature has not been altered by the suffering there. We have been to liberated states as well and this nature has not been altered by that either. The resultant buddha nature that is even now present in the minds of sentient beings is just what it is; there is no improving it. So that is what is being referred to by the word "original," *so ma*. When we say, "fixed right on the unfabricated," this indicates the absence of any need for fabricating or changing anything: equipoise in a state free from hope for improvement and fear of worsening, free from hoping certain thoughts will not arise and fearing that others will arise. Equipoise in that state free from hope, fear, and all dualistic clinging is what is called our "own mind Mahamudra" that is "without support." Thoughts are not rejected or affirmed, they are not given any energy or effort. Even if they develop we allow them to arise. They are left with equanimity in their own nature, their own entity. If we gently relax and poise ourselves naturally in the unfabricated state, that is what is called our "own mind Mahamudra free of support."

5. Meditation within the Unfabricated State

―――――――――

Tilopa says, *Relax and settle within the unproduced primordial state.* When he says this, it is like the words,

> If we gently release entangling thoughts
> We will be free.

At present, we proceed with difficulty in dependence upon our six consciousnesses because our thoughts bind us as if by chains. Bound by concepts, when we are now introduced to the ultimate nature of our own mind in dependence upon the holy guru's instructions and, on that basis, settle in the unfabricated state, when we are introduced to Mahamudra, that is when the idea of "gently relaxing" those concepts comes into play. We naturally soften or relax them. They are relaxed in bliss, lightly set to rest. Therefore, when Tilopa says, "Relaxing, settle within the unproduced primordial state," there is actually nothing to relax. The word "relax" is not used here with the sense of there being something to loosen or relax. Up to now, we have been bound in beginningless samsara by karma and delusion and the net of conceptuality; we are not free of this net. At present, when we meditate and see the nature of thoughts, we give it the name "relaxing thoughts." "Relaxing" means just seeing the nature of the thought and leaving it at that; it doesn't mean abandoning or annihilating thought. There is no abandoning of thought. In particular, as these Mahamudra instructions are given in connection with highest yoga tantra, there is only advice to willingly accept thought; there is no instruction to abandon thought. In the context of these teachings, thought is "taken onto the path," incorporated into the spiritual path. We have to make it the path. We take appearances as the path, dream as the path. In connection with that, Jamgön Lodrö Taye in his *Chöd: Taking Appearances on the Path,* says,

> I prostrate to my mother hell beings.
> I prostrate to my mother pretas.
> I prostrate to my mother animals.
> I prostrate to my mothers with attachment.
> I prostrate to my mothers with hatred.
> I prostrate to my mothers with jealousy.
> I prostrate to my mothers with ignorance.
> I prostrate to my mothers in worse states of existence.

This prostration must be made when we arrive at the unfabricated primordial state; otherwise it would be strange to be prostrating to attachment, right? Attachment is to be abandoned, not prostrated to. However, when we see the entity or nature of attachment, when we understand the character of attachment; when we see the entity or nature of hatred, when we understand the character of hatred; then the entity of attachment is discriminating transcendent wisdom; the entity or nature of hatred is mirrorlike transcendent wisdom; the nature of pride is equalizing transcendent wisdom, and so on. The nature of the five poisons is the five transcendent wisdoms, the five jnanas. It is with this knowledge that prostration is made.

Furthermore, to be able to relax as instructed in the unfabricated primordial state we must be introduced, with the aid of the guru's oral instructions, to the entity of our own mind Mahamudra and then make this prostration; otherwise, just saying that the nature of attachment is discriminating wisdom and that you should prostrate to attachment will not bring any benefit whatsoever. It may bring increase of hatred, we don't know; that wouldn't help. So we definitely need experience regarding this essential point. But even if we do not have direct experience of it, we should keep that meaning in mind. That is very important. Lord Buddha said that in the future during the final five-hundred-year period of his teachings, if someone could actually practice his teaching of Prajnaparamita, the Perfection of Wisdom, that would no doubt be best; but that if someone even suspects that the Prajnaparamita teachings are valid, it ends samsara. These teachings have such incredible qualities.

What we call Prajnaparamita is the Sutra name; in the context of Tantra the same meaning is given the name Yum Chenmo, Mahamaya, the Great

Mother. These Mahamudra instructions teach a view that combines the two in a union of Sutra and Tantra. Moreover, when the perfect wisdom, as explained in the Sutra path, is merged with the great bliss taught in Tantrayana, Dagpo Rinpoche[11] referred to it especially as "Mahamudra of uncommon unified Sutra-Tantra view."

For the venerable Sakyas, if practice of Mahamudra instruction is not preceded by conferral of the four initiations, it is impossible to realize Mahamudra. In Dagpo Rinpoche's system that is not a prerequisite. This Mahamudra is the sacred instructions by which someone with heavy bad karma can be forcefully enlightened. That is part of this system; there is no indispensable requirement to receive the four initiations to practice it. With the sacred method of the holy guru's instructions, when a guru who has realized experience of Mahamudra practice gives commentary, even if the recipient has very bad karma, there is profound means for them to be forcefully enlightened in these Mahamudra teachings of ours. Our excellent lineage maintains that there is no need to receive the four initiations as is the case in the Sakya system; you need have no doubt that it grants liberation, nevertheless. This concludes explanation of the line *Not remedying anything, relax and settle in the unborn primordial state.*

If bonds are relaxed, we are liberated, without doubt.

If, for example, there were someone in prison who was bound hand and foot and could not move, when they were released, they would feel very happy, right? Knowledge that we have been released from court or prison would make us very blissful and happy, wouldn't it? Like that, "If bonds are relaxed, we are liberated, without doubt." Even if someone is an ordinary being with heavy bad karma, no need to mention if they were doing a qualified practice of Mahamudra, even if they just understand the character of the practice, great bliss will come. Tilopa says, if bonds are relaxed, we are liberated, without doubt.

The fact is that we are now bound under the control of delusion and karma. All within the entire three realms of samsara are controlled by karma and delusion. It is said that if a person who is bound with heavy bad karma and delusion can be so benefited by merely attending to the general meaning of these instructions, then what need is there to doubt the fruit of practicing them correctly? If we develop the wisdoms arisen from hearing, contemplation, and meditation, and, in particular, rely upon wisdom arisen from meditation; and if we make repeated, insistent supplication to the guru with driving intensity,[12] never relaxing in our conviction and devotion to the guru and developing deeply felt devotion that is beyond tightening and loosening, then certainly we can be liberated. As a central principle, in the context of Mahamudra practice, it is said that just a single line of reasoning will not benefit us. It will not help us just to have vast wisdom arisen from hearing, contemplation, and meditation: here we need sublime esteem and devotion for the guru. It is said,

> Since aspiration and conviction are the head of meditation,
> Bless us with the great meditators'
> Unfeigned faith, always praying
> To the guru who reveals the instructions!

The *Prayer* says that aspiration and conviction are like the head of meditation.[13] Thus, when we practice Mahamudra, the meaning here is that we who are caught in the net of samsara, bound by the six root delusions, in dependence upon applying ourselves to the practice of these Mahamudra instructions and then correctly meditating and practicing them, will be liberated.

We free ourselves from bondage of our own making. It is not as if we are bound and we need someone else to come save us. It is said that it is like when a knotted snake is thrown into the sky. Who knotted the snake? The snake knotted itself. We don't need to go untie the snake's knots, do we? The snake can untie its own knots. So the snake that is thrown into the sky tied itself up and must untie itself. Although this ultimate mode of mind is present within us, we don't recognize it. We are distracted by objects that have never existed. Out of ignorance we are deceived into conceiving of reflexive awareness as a self; and then because of clinging to duality we are bound in samsara. In this way we bind ourselves; there is no one else binding us.

So who frees us? We free ourselves.

> Saying "it is this" cannot portray it,
> Saying "it is not this" does not stop it.
> May I realize my own true nature, unproduced,
> Beyond intellect, ultimate perfect truth.

When we see this incredible secret quality of mind that is beyond intellect that discriminates between existence and nonexistence, there is no doubt that we will free ourselves. That is what is being said. If we make the supplication with driving intensity to understand these instructions and practice them from the depths of our heart and bones, there is no doubt that we will be liberated. This is not just something that used to happen in the old days!

6. How to Settle in the Original State without Modification

Just as looking into space stops our sight of visual forms,

WHEN WE WANT to look at space, there are no sights, sounds, scents, tastes, or tactile objects, nothing at all to see. There is a cessation of sights. Colloquially, when we say "look at space," we look at space and there is really nothing to see. Sights cease. When we say that we see something, it normally means we see something like a form: I saw a beautiful form; I saw an unpleasant form. We talk about seeing *something,* right? When we look into space we do not see anything. That is why Tilopa says, "Looking into space stops our sight of visual forms." Space is being used to exemplify the characteristic of being free of projections.

Why is space being presented as an analogy? It is the best example we have in the world. Free of all projections, beyond limit, beyond characteristics, impossible to exemplify: space is the best example we have. So again, "By looking into space, visions cease." When we look into space there is nothing at all about which we can say, "I see it; I know it," is there? Therefore, "by looking into space, visions cease." It is free of all projections, beyond all characteristics, beyond all happiness and suffering. That is why Tilopa says, "looking into space stops our sight of visual forms."

If mind looks into mind,

The root of all phenomena is the sphere of one's own elemental mind. It is said that the sphere of one's own elemental mind is the root of all phenomena of samsara and nirvana. Because of that, Saraha sang,

> Elemental mind is the seed of all,
> That which emanates samsara and nirvana.

Homage to wish-fulfilling jewellike mind
Which grants bestowal of all desired fruits!

In saying that elemental mind alone is the seed of all, what do we mean? What is the "seed of all"? In dependence upon this elemental mind come all of the faults of samsara "below"; and in dependence upon this root elemental mind come all of the qualities of nirvana "above." Therefore, if we know the nature of elemental mind we attain nirvana, and if we do not know it, samsara is the result. The distinction between deception and liberation lies in whether we understand the ever-present nature of our own mind or not. In Mahamudra, that's the whole thing. Knowing our own face is liberation; not knowing our own face is samsara. This is not something far distant from us. The difference is made in a single instant. In Dzogchen it is said this way:

Looking out is samsara;
Looking within is nirvana.

"Looking out is samsara" means that if we cling and are attached to the objects of our six sense faculties, this is samsara. "Looking within is nirvana" means that if we gather the six consciousnesses within and look with the transcendent wisdom of natural awareness, this is nirvana. To say "Looking out is samsara, looking in is nirvana" is to place the dividing line between deception and liberation at whether or not we abide in our ever-present primordial mind. There is not a great deal to explain. It does not require things like setting forth reasons and syllogisms like, "The subject, sound, is impermanent because of being a product." Setting forth logical statements does not help in this case. It will just take us on a journey wandering through endless mountain valleys and passes. After a while we will lose the meaning in the words. Changkya Rolpay Dorje said,

These days, some of us with new ideas
Leave looming appearances just as they are
While seeking some other horned object of negation;
I suspect our old Mother will escape.

What he is saying is that within the Gelug there are some who do not question appearances that arise, saying that a cup, for instance, must be left just as it is. But then, what is empty? Something is absent on that basis. They seek something else, some "horned object" called "true existence" to negate, and say that all phenomena are empty of being truly existent, but feel that the present appearance is not empty. Then someone needs to tell them it is empty of inherent existence; emptiness is identified as something additional. When something like this happens, Changkya Rolpay Dorje "suspects our old Mother will escape." What is this about? He is saying that the Great Mother is being lost at that point, that the Great Mother Perfection of Wisdom is far from being understood. One is distracted in mere verbiage. This is an example of being bound by projections.

Then, regarding mind looking at mind, when we speak of mind looking at mind, it is like the eye looking at itself. In *Ocean of Definitive Meaning of Mahamudra* it is said,

> When we speak of the eye looking at the eye, how can the eye
> look at itself?

We cannot look at our eyes with our own eyes. Yet we need some kind of view. It is not good to force it. Is there such a thing as eyes looking at themselves? No. Yet it is being said that our view should be like the eye looking at the eye. What is this telling us? When we speak of looking at the mind with the mind, we might say, "Okay, now I am going to look at my mind." We sit down cross-legged, close our eyes, and look, wondering if there is something to see. But, there is nothing at all to see. If there was something to see everyone would see it, wouldn't they? There is nothing to see. So what we need here is an absence of seeing. "The sacred seeing of nonseeing is supreme." Buddha was saying that this is the supreme of realized qualities. It is a "nonlooking." Mind look at mind! Mind must look at mind in a manner in which there is no object nor action of looking. It is beyond there being an object that is viewed or a mind that views. If we settle in equipoise on the unfabricated nature that is beyond all projections of an action or object of viewing, that is what we call "looking at the mind." On the basis of this "looking at mind" that is beyond all projections of viewed object and viewing mind, with mindfulness and introspection in the unfabricated state, with mindfulness on guard, by simply not wandering, if we gently relax in equipoise, this is what we call "seeing the mind." Otherwise, in actuality, mind is only awareness, clear awareness. It is not the case that there is a viewer that looks at the mind.

Thoughts cease and unexcelled enlightenment is attained. [3]

What benefit is there to mind looking at mind after having ceased all collection of concepts? If mind looks at mind we will see the nature or entity of the mind. When we say "look at the mind" we are not talking about a viewing mind looking at a viewed object. We see our elemental mind—mind, itself. *Thoughts cease and unexcelled enlightenment is attained.* If we look at the mind with mind, all conceptual thought will cease. Tilopa is not saying that it stops because we look at the mind, but that thought is naturally pacified. For example, if a large fire is burning, when the burning wood is used up, the fire will naturally go out, right? If you add more wood, the fire will continue burning. Similarly, when there are many thoughts arising and subsiding in our mind, by following them and adding many more thoughts to their number, they are perpetuated.

Therefore, without adding more thought, when a thought arises, let it arise; don't make anything of it. Don't approve it or reject it. If we leave thought as it is, we will have less and less thought. At some point when we have developed the sacred power of the antidote, the more thoughts arise, the more they provide support for the yogi's realization; they become an aid to realizing Mahamudra, the ultimate mode of existence of the mind. The more thought arises, the more a yogi with such Mahamudra realization will develop higher and higher meditative experience. They can raise the level of realization. If there is a big fire in a forest, the more wind there is, the more the fire will spread. Likewise, for the yogi who takes appearances on the path, the yogi who has reached a secure level of realization, the more thought arises the more realization will occur.

So what does "cessation of thought" mean in this context? Cessation of thought means a natural pacification of thought. We must understand what these words mean. The whole collection of thought is naturally pacified. There is no need to stop thought. We cannot stop thought. So "cessation of thought" does not mean that thought is actively stopped. It is like Jetsun Milarepa said to a tantrika from Kuthang in the early community of Dragkya Dorje Dzong:

This movement of mind cannot be stopped even by putting it into an iron container.

That is coming from a lord of yogis who knew thought to be empty! Say we put thought into an airtight iron container. Thoughts get through it in an instant. Even huge armies outside with arrows and spears, knives and guns, cannot stop the movement of thought. If we say that you are not about to have a thought, you can still have many more thoughts; we cannot stop thoughts at will. There is no stopping of thought. Yet, in the context of Madhyamaka, in general it is said that we can bring a cessation to our ignorance grasping the true existence of phenomena. Even so, this cessation of ignorance grasping the true existence of phenomena is a rejection of true existence on the basis of wisdom realizing its absence, the emptiness of true or inherent existence of all phenomena. It is not a case of appearances being intentionally stopped. The Svatantrika Madhyamaka in particular points out many contradictions to the assertion that thought can be intentionally stopped.

So thought cannot be stopped. What is it that is stopped? Remember that the word "stop" here carries the connotation of being naturally pacified. When we know the nature of thought, thought is released in its ultimate nature. When we know the nature of thought, thought becomes an aid to meditation. When we know the nature of thought, thought becomes a dawning of meditative experience. When we know the nature or entity of thought, thought can become of the nature of meditation. Thus it is taught. What we call "taking thought onto the path" means it can become an aid to the yogi's ability to attain unexcelled enlightenment. Tilopa is saying that if we can reach that realization, with the cessation of concepts we will attain unexcelled enlightenment.

7. How the Movement of Thought Is Purified on the Spot

Clouds of vapor ascend in the sky.
They don't go anywhere, nor do they remain.
Similarly, when we see that thoughts are our own mind,
The rising waves of thought will clear. [4]

FROM WHERE does thought first arise? A place where thought first arises cannot be found. Where does a thought go when it is over? There is no finding of a place where thought ceases. If we search for the current location of thought in our flesh, skin, and blood, inside and outside our body, we will not find it. For instance, vapor rising from the ground we call clouds. When a cloud forms in the sky, where does it come from at first? From where does a cloud first arise? We don't find it. We don't know where it disappears, either. We say the cloud ascends into the sphere of space. In any case, it disappears into the sphere of space without a trace. But if we have to show where the cloud first came from and where it went, there is nothing for us to show.

Similarly, if we seek our present mind, the teachers of seeking the mind[14] ask if it has color, if it has shape; ask, "Where did it first come from?" "Where does this mind go afterward?" "Where is this present mind—outside or inside our body, or someplace in between?" The teacher of seeking the mind gives this instruction. What does this accomplish? Basically, we will understand that mind has no color, no shape, no characteristics. Yet we need to seek it. We have strong clinging. So, just as we cannot say where a cloud has gone, no matter what sort of thoughts arise in our mind, no matter what kinds of thoughts we have—good thoughts, bad thoughts—there is no finding their point of origin, no tracing where they have gone. In order to say a current thought exists, we must present some basis for it inside or outside our body, or in between; yet there is nothing we can show.

Therefore, our present thoughts are like clouds; clouds are taken as a metaphor: *Clouds of vapor ascend in the sky. They don't go anywhere, nor do they remain. Similarly, when we see that thoughts are our own mind, the rising waves of thought will clear.* In general, clouds that arise in vapors from the earth arise in dependence upon rain. Rain doesn't fall without clouds either. So are the two, clouds and rain, one and the same? No, they are not. Are they completely separate and different? No, not that either. Neither is separate from the other. What we call water comes only in dependence upon rain; without rain there would be no water. It comes from rain, but if there were no clouds there would be no rain. Before clouds there was no rain. Thus, clouds and rain are neither one nor simultaneous.

All thoughts that arise in our mind are simultaneous, concomitant with Mahamudra. No matter how many thoughts there are in the mind, we must understand that they are simultaneous with Mahamudra. This ultimate mode of the mind has naturally existed forever. It is just from the presence of Mahamudra, the ultimate mode of existence of the mind, that thoughts occur. Thoughts arise together with it. The two, thought and Mahamudra, are simultaneous, concomitant, of the same age.[15] Just as we have naturally had the true nature of mind primordially within ourselves, we have also had thought at the same time. It comes no matter what we do. Thought is the energy of Mahamudra. Thought is the play of Mahamudra. Thoughts emanate from and re-collect into Mahamudra. They are its function, its activity, its emanation.

Therefore we do not think of thought as something bad. Problems arise only from clinging to thought, not from its mere presence. Thought is allowed to exist. So what is the problem? The problem is that we connect more thought to the aftermath of thoughts, the "tracks" left by thoughts. We make thought continuous, uninterrupted. On that basis we cling to thought as if it were truly existent. We cling tightly to thought. Clinging to thought, we circle in samsara. Apart from that, thought itself is not a problem. Thought must occur. Thought exists. Why does thought exist? Because Mahamudra exists. The ultimate mode of existence of our mind is Mahamudra. There exists this transcendent wisdom of nondual luminosity-emptiness. If this transcendent wisdom of nondual luminosity-emptiness exists, thought will occur. Thought is the "miracle emanation" of the mind, no matter what. Thought is the "magical emanation" of Mahamudra. Thought is the energetic display of Mahamudra, itself. Thought emanates from and re-collects into Mahamudra. Therefore, those two, Mahamudra and thought, have a big connection; I've been saying they are simultaneous, right? Because of not recognizing Mahamudra, sentient beings wander in samsara.

Now, Tilopa is saying that when we see our elemental mind, waves of thought clear up, disappear. When waves of thought arise, abiding as great bliss, discriminating wisdom realizes them to be elemental mind, Mahamudra. It is very important for us to see our elemental mind. If we see our mind, how do we see it? As I was saying before, we call it "seeing the mind" if we settle in equipoise in the ultimate state beyond examples, words, and meanings. Not engaging in much fabrication, without fabricating many expressions and expressed meanings, there is a primordial Mahamudra that is the ultimate mode of existence of our mind. We settle in equipoise upon it with the help of the holy guru's oral instructions. We settle in the unfabricated, gently relaxing. If we are conscientious, we will see our mind. When we see our mind, waves of thought are cleared away. When they arise we realize them to be nondual great bliss and realize Mahamudra discriminating wisdom. Thus it is said.

8. THE ESSENTIAL MODE OF EXISTENCE IS NOT SOMETHING OR NOTHING

The nature of space is beyond color and shape;
It does not stain light or dark, does not change.
The essence of our mind is also beyond color and shape;
It is not stained by light or dark, good or bad phenomena. [5]

WE SPEAK ABOUT the sky or space quite a bit in ordinary conversation. Saying, "I see the sky," or "Look at the sky," we look at the sky. But if we ask what the nature of space is and look with correct objective mind, or if we investigate with correct wisdom, if we investigate with logic on the basis of what is considered factual or objective in the world, no matter what name we give it—whether we say light space, dark space, yellow space, green space; whether we call it formless, invisible, ineffable, open, closed—that name cannot signify space. When we write "space" in Tibetan there are five characters, five letters. Those letters cannot signify space, cannot signify actual space. It cannot be expressed in such ways; however, we do arrogantly assume expressions for the inexpressible, conceive of and cling to conventional terms. We engage objects in the world on the basis of these conventional terms. We talk about space. We talk about what to abandon and what to adopt. That which heals disease we call medicine; that which takes life we call poison. These are all imputed by concepts, mental constructs. What we call space, for instance, is not white, yellow, black, green, nor blue; not open, closed, nor unimpeded. No matter how much we use these words, the nature of space is beyond color, beyond shape, beyond characteristics. Because space's nature is beyond agent and object of expression, it cannot be signified. It is beyond shape, characteristics, color; beyond "natures." White, yellow, black, green, blue; being open, being closed: these cannot change space; none of these can stain or color space. As explained in *Uttaratantra,* no matter how much air or water is polluted, it cannot pollute space itself. Similarly, the essence of our mind is beyond color and shape. We set forth an analogy, and the meaning should follow, correct? What meaning is being symbolized? In this context it is what is being called the "essence of our mind," and here, when we speak of essence and mind, these are two different things. When we use the term "mind," we are speaking of a basis of deception. In the general Dzogchen context, *sem*, "mind," and *rigpa*, "awareness," are differentiated. When mind and awareness are differentiated, mind is posited as the basis of deception and awareness as the liberated result. "Mind" is the term used on occasions of impurity, and "awareness" on occasions of purity. In the context of Mahamudra, both of these are spoken of as well, with the terms "mind" and "awareness" sometimes being distinguished as different, and sometimes not.

As it is said,[16]

> Since thought's essence is dharmakaya,
> Not being anything but appearing as anything . . .

When thought's essence is taught to be dharmakaya, thought and its essence are being distinguished as two different things. When we say that the essence of thought is dharmakaya, we are not saying that thought is dharmakaya, are we? When we speak of the nature or essence of thought we are distinguishing something different from thought. In this context it is a factor that is separate from thought that is being termed "dharmakaya."

Sometimes, however, mind and awareness are not differentiated. In his doha, Saraha says,

> Elemental mind is the seed of all,
> That which emanates samsara and nirvana.
> Homage to wish-fulfilling jewellike mind,
> Which grants bestowal of all desired fruits!

Saraha refers to mind as the wish-fulfilling gem, the basis of emanation of all fruits of samsara and nirvana, free of all projections of samsara and nirvana, agent of all. He calls that "mind." In Chittamatra, three terms—mind, awareness, and consciousness—are all considered synonymous. All three are asserted to refer to the same thing. In any case, this is the conversation of scholars of tenet systems. Here, using terms that are freed from tenet systems, there is nothing to be confused about. We don't wonder, "Are mind and awareness the same or not?" When the teacher of mind-investigation introduces us to the meaning of mind, in Jigme Lingpa's *Yeshe Lama,* the question is asked three times: "What is mind? What is mind? What is mind?" As the guru asks a qualified disciple, What is mind? the guru, directly, with skillful means, introduces the disciple to none other than this present awareness to which every sort of thought appears. "Look at this present awareness!" This "present awareness" refers to our current transitory awareness. Past mind has already ceased and is nowhere to be seen. Future mind has yet to arise and does not exist at present. When we say, "present awareness," it is a momentary awareness, an instant of awareness, that we are referring to. Present awareness only exists when we don't check or examine it because, if we examine it, present awareness does not exist either. When previous moments of awareness have already receded into the past, and future moments have yet to arise, there is no present awareness to be found. It disintegrates every moment.

Therefore, "mind" is introduced directly when the instruction "Look at the mind!" is given. To give an example, Jamyang Khyentse Wangpo's previous incarnation had an attendant. There was a tea service of Jamyang Khyentse Wangpo Rinpoche that was considered very sacred, even in the old days in Tibet. Because it was so sacred this attendant developed a lot of clinging attachment to it. If there was the slightest indication it might fall and break he would gasp with such horror that he would almost suffocate, like his throat was stuffed with tsampa![17] They say that he would suffer terribly. Then, at some point, instructions on mind and mental factors were given, but he did not seem to have really received the introduction. He seems to have been thickly resistant to transformation. Nothing could be done. Later on, a moment for skillful means presented itself when the tea service was on a table among many people during a large teaching. As the attendant was pouring the tea, the auspicious cup fell. As it fell the attendant gasped with terror, at which time Jamyang Khyentse Wangpo miraculously saved it from breaking. The tea did not even spill out and was still in the cup. At the very moment the attendant thought it was broken, Jamyang Khyentse Wangpo instructed him, "Okay, you! Now, look at your mind!" The attendant looked at his own mind, recognized its true nature, and in that very instant became a yogi, it is said. That is what it is like when mind looks at the essence of mind.

So, in the general Mahamudra context, when we are introduced to the nature of mind, it is the present moment of our awareness, whether good or bad, that we are talking about. Apart from that, if we ask what the essence of mind is, we do not need to say that its nature is luminous and assert many more qualifying characteristics. If we talk about it that way our words will become contradictory, will take us in the wrong direction—which we don't need.

What is mind? It is that which is thinking something. It is that which is aware. We don't need to learn all the definitions and divisions of mind. In his *Praise of the Teachings on Mind and Mental Factors,* the great Khenpo Tsultrim Gyamtso Rinpoche, in his expression of homage at the beginning, says,

> With movement of mind and mental factors purified at the base,
> Homage to awareness that is beyond mind, that is nondual from
>   emptiness, actual Manjushri!
> Homage within nonduality of mind and transcendent awareness,
> That mind's deception may be purified on the spot.

This is extremely profound. In the first line—"With movement of mind and mental factors stopped at the base"—mind and mental factors refers to main mind, five omnipresent mental factors, and the rest of the fifty-one mental factors. Being purified or stopped at the base refers to the so-called naturally abiding lineage, the tathagatagarbha, the buddha nature. No matter how much we are released or deceived by mind and mental factors, it is said that, at base, we are liberated. When we say, "purified at the base," it means that, without having to rely upon effort or anything, mind is pure by nature.

"Homage to awareness that is beyond mind, that is nondual from emptiness, actual Manjushri!" When he speaks of "awareness beyond mind," he differentiates between the two terms, "mind" and "awareness." In this twofold division, mind is necessarily conceptual, the principal basis of deception of samsara. It is understood as alayavijnana in Chittamatra. When we pay homage to such a transcendent mind of "self-risen wisdom" as "actual Manjushri" so "that mind's deception may be purified on the spot," mind and awareness are being differentiated for the sake of beginners who cannot recognize their nonduality. When mind and awareness are differentiated in this way, "mind" refers to the impure side and "awareness" to the pure side. The words "that mind's deception may be purified on the spot" indicate a practice for a beginner, one who has not realized the indivisibility of mind and awareness.

Having said that, how do we pay homage to it, practice it? How do we actually internalize it on the basis of our own true nature? How do we develop realization on the basis of a view that cuts through reification? He says we pay "homage within nonduality of mind and transcendent awareness." He is saying we must prostrate within a state of mind and awareness being nondual. So now they are in the same class again.

In short, when we speak of the "essence of mind," "mind" indicates the impure, and "essence" is understood as mind's "nature" or "entity," as when we say, "Since thought's essence is dharmakaya . . ." So sometimes we call this essence of mind "mind"; sometimes we call it "awareness"; sometimes, "consciousness." We call it different names. We call this present awareness of ours "mind," "awareness," "consciousness," but even if we give it a hundred names, a thousand names, none can illustrate or represent our mind's ultimate mode of existence. More names only add up to more distraction and confusion and cannot make us know the actual mode of existence of things. Even in the context of pramana, valid cognition, it is said that generic names cannot illuminate specifically characterized phenomena, actual "things." When we speak on the basis of concepts, as when we say "vase," mind's conception of it fulfills the function of a vase, but as for the actual, specifically characterized vase, the conventional term does not reach, does not engage, the object.

It is excellent to apply this understanding to these terms as well. Although we apply the names *mind, awareness, consciousness* to the essence of our mind, what we call "mind" is still not something easy to understand. There is nothing substantial to grasp, no sphere, no cube, no springtime color, no color or shape at all, no characteristic. "Likewise, space is beyond color and shape." Just as space lacks color, shape, or characteristic, even if we keep repeating "present mind," "mind," "mind," it does not become some spherical or block-like object. Neither does it come to have any color or shape. Therefore, since it is beyond shape, it is completely nonestablished.

The mind is like space in these respects. For example, when we create virtue, the essence of our mind does not become virtuous; and no matter how serious the nonvirtue we commit, the five heinous crimes and so on, the essence of our mind, our mind in its deepest mode of existence, does not become stained by nonvirtue. The true nature of our mind is beyond virtue and nonvirtue; it is not colored by virtue or nonvirtue. Even if virtue and nonvirtue cease, this phenomenon does not. In dependence upon it we, and all sentient beings, have forever been buddhas. This is the reason that all sentient beings have always been buddhas: on the basis of mind's true mode of being, the nature of all beings' minds has always been beyond faults, and all realized qualities are spontaneously present. Therefore, although strongly deluded sentient beings are controlled by delusion and experience continual suffering, the true nature of the mind, its deepest mode of being, does not degenerate. No matter how much positive qualities are heightened, no matter how much we practice the wisdoms of learning, contemplation, and meditation, the quality of mind's true nature is not improved at all.

So what does this mean? When we look right at the fundamental nature of our mind, if we see it the way it is, we become a buddha, it is said. That is the fact. *Uttaratantra* states,

> There is nothing to illuminate,
> Nothing at all to set forth.
> Perfectly look at perfect truth!
> If you see it perfectly, you are free.

> Minds differentiating characteristics,
> Adventitious, see the elements.
> But nondifferentiating minds,
> With unexcelled Dharma, do not see.

Thus, this "nonseeing" fundamental nature of the mind, this unexcelled Dharma, cannot be improved upon by buddhas, cannot be damaged by sentient beings. This fundamental nature naturally present in the mind of all sentient beings does not need to be created by remedies; it can liberate us just by recognizing it.

"Looking outward, samsara; looking inward, nirvana!" It is the six consciousnesses that we are speaking of turning inward. If we can apply this advice to the essential thing, to our own reflexive deep awareness, that itself will liberate us. Otherwise, while our awareness continues to be bound by clinging to objects engaged by the six consciousnesses, it will not help no matter how hard we cling to a remedy. We remain deceived. Therefore, the basis on which liberation and deception are distinguished is whether awareness is bound by strong antidotes or not. The ultimate nature of mind is not stained or "clothed" by color, shape, black, white or anything, so no matter what we say, no matter what terms we use, verbal expressions cannot signify the essence of our mind.

When we recite, "Beyond speech, thought, expression, wisdom gone beyond / Unborn, unceasing, with a nature like space . . . ," why is space put forth as an example? One reason is that, first of all, it is unproduced; in the meantime, it does not "abide" at all; and finally, it does not cease. Since space is convenient and easy to understand, it is put forth as the illustration. But just saying, "Unborn, unceasing, with a nature like space..." cannot convey our own reflexive deep awareness. There is no way to really portray it.

But if we were to say, "If the essence of our mind is beyond color and shape, it does not matter if we practice the instructions on the true nature of our mind," that is incorrect. We need to practice them because, as it is said, "It is not stained by phenomena, virtue, nonvirtue, darkness, light." We need to actually understand this reason; it doesn't help just to verbalize it, even if we keep repeating "it is beyond color, it is beyond shape." How is it beyond color? How is it beyond shape? What is this special quality in the essence of our mind that makes it unaffected by virtue, nonvirtue, dark, light, and so forth? When we investigate, it is realized through the wisdoms of learning, contemplation, and meditation. We develop a confidence that cannot be undermined by others; definite understanding that cannot be taken away from us by others. Even if all the buddhas and bodhisattvas of the ten directions were to come to the space before us and say, "You are mistaken about this ultimate mode of existence of your mind!" we would be able to understand that it is only a provisional statement, not a definitive one. It is when this level of definite understanding arises that we actually "see the ultimate mode of existence of our mind."

We need analogies, however. Without analogies there is no way to indicate the object. We need names as well. As it is said,

> If he did not name it
> The world would remain ignorant.
> Therefore, to dispel ignorance
> Buddha gave it a name.

The reason examples are used is because ordinary beings are caught up in a net of concepts. To destroy that net, they cannot understand it if you introduce them directly to the true nature of their mind, its deepest mode of existence. However, to symbolize it, to exemplify it, numerous analogies are necessary. That is why, in the context of our tantric practice, we cannot realize completion stage immediately; generation stage must be taught first. There can be no completion stage without generation stage. Without having skillful means there can be no union arisen from skillful means. Therefore, in Tantra, generation stage is taught first. In generation stage, deity practice is explained—the deity of the inconceivable celestial mansion, the mandala, recitation of mantra, syllable letters, and so on—in brief, the way of generating the deity and mandala through the five manifest enlightenments.[18] All of this is conventional, provisional explanation. What is called a "deity" does not in fact exist. But even if we do not speak about deities, if we just consider it in terms of developing good or bad thoughts, we are taught to develop good thoughts, right? Just because of negative thought patterns, with ignorance acting as the main cause and delusions and karma acting as the contributing conditions, the six realms' beings have to take rebirth in samsara and experience the sufferings of the worse realms of existence. It is only the fault of senseless negative thoughts. If we had to try to destroy them directly by immediately teaching completion stage, there would be no way to destroy concepts. That is because our predisposition to conceptual thought is extremely thick and of extremely long duration. Even Buddha could not teach it directly. As he said,

> Mental grasping is deep and subtle.
> Seeds for it pour forth like a river.
> It is wrong to conceive of a "self,"
> Yet I do not reveal this to infants.

Why is this? The mind of self-grasping is extremely subtle. Since the seeds of mental grasping arise in a continuous stream, if we were to give an ultimate teaching immediately, there is danger that it would be misconceived to be self-existent. Therefore, since we cannot immediately teach completion stage, generation stage is taught first in order to develop completion stage. Different types of deities are explained, their invocation, and so on. Then there is explanation of various symbols, a deity's color, white, for instance, meaning that all phenomena are empty; or statements like, "This deity holding a knife in her right hand symbolizes cutting the entanglement of samsara." "Holding nectar in her left hand symbolizes reaching the security of immortality." "Purification of the fifty-one compositional factors is symbolized by the necklace of fifty-one skulls." In the context of Vajravarahi there are many such explanations. Again, when mindfulness of the deity's own symbolism is taught—"her boar's head is for the sake of destroying dual concepts of clean and dirty"—each color, shape, hand implement, and so on has a conventional meaning and an ultimate meaning. What for? Since beginners cannot enter directly into completion stage practice, they must be guided through symbols, skillful means, and stages of the path. Therefore, in order to explain how the essence of our mind is beyond color and shape, first we teach impermanence; then, bodhichitta meditation and the six paramitas. All of these are principally taught as symbols to point out the true nature of our mind. From the first verse of Vinaya up to the nondual tantra of Kalachakra, all of the teachings of Sutra and Tantra and the many different teachings of the higher tantras are all for the purpose of realizing the essence of our own mind, for the sake of realizing our actual mind.

So it is like space, not existing as color, shape, darkness, light. When we see our elemental mind, our mind at its most fundamental level, it is not helped or harmed by virtue or vice. No one could improve it; no one could harm it. It has never been improved in the past; it will never be improved in the future, either. Nor is there any improving it in the present.

So then, if we seek Buddha, there is no Buddha to be sought anywhere else, there is no buddhahood to be found, other than realizing your own elemental mind. What we call buddha must be spoken of on the basis of our own mind; there is no far-off place we must go to attain buddhahood; because if we realize the true nature of our own mind, it is buddha. As said in *Expressing the Names of Manjushri,*

> Instantly discerning specifics,
> Instantly enlightened.

As for "Instantly discerning specifics," the instant we realize the true nature of our mind we have discerned the specifics of both samsara and nirvana. "Instantly enlightened" means that the instant we realize the true nature of our mind we become a fully enlightened buddha. It is not something far distant. "Instantly discerning specifics, / Instantly enlightened."

Therefore, Buddha is found in our own mind; if we must seek buddhahood elsewhere, it is not to be found. As Milarepa said to Dagpo Rinpoche,

> As for view, I say, Look at mind!
> When we seek a view somewhere else
> It is like someone who is already rich seeking wealth,
> Don't you think, Doctor Teacher?

Such a statement teaches, in succession, view, meditation, and action. Everything happens on the basis of our mind. The result must come on the basis of mind. When examples are given during the Gyelwa Gyatso initiation it is said,

> Look! Look at your mind!
> Elemental mind does not exist!

Saying this, it teaches emptiness. Again, it says,

> In nonexistent elemental mind,
> There are various appearances. What a wonder!

When this is said it shows that although it is empty, luminous mind and emptiness never join nor part.

So first, "Look! Look at your mind!" is said to a beginner. We say, "Look! Look at your mind!" even though the object to be looked at, mind, does not itself exist. Speaking of it as if it did exist and as if we must look at it is done in terms of a beginner's view. In Tantra, when we say, "Elemental mind does not exist at all," this explains the conduct for someone of middling faculties. What sort of view develops at the middling level? The view that "mind is emptiness": it is the explanation of emptiness.

Then, the conduct at the highest level is indicated with "In nonexistent elemental mind, there are various appearances. What a wonder!" This is taking the three kayas on the path. It is the explanation of not abandoning desirable objects but taking them on the path; the explanation of not abandoning delusions but taking them on the path. When we speak of taking such on the path, it is said to be a view that is beyond extremes in which "Mere appearances themselves are included in mind." It is a view that is beyond all extremes. When we speak about "the elemental mind of all sentient beings," the ultimate mode of existence of the mind of all sentient beings is great bliss, EWAM yuganaddha.

In Kalachakra, it is explained as a union of great bliss and great emptiness. There we find,

> The elemental mind of all sentient beings
> Is greatly blissful transcendent wisdom.
> Nonconceptual, inconceivable,
> The essence of luminosity appearing.

It goes on with many instructions introducing the nature of mind. Again, *It is not stained by light or dark, good or bad phenomena.* That is why Buddha says in Sutra,

> If you realize your own mind, it is buddha.
> So, without seeking buddha elsewhere,
> Meditate on this best of perceptions.

Buddha saying, "If you realize your own mind, it is buddha," means that if we can understand our present awareness, we are buddhas. Otherwise, if we must set our own mind aside and seek buddhahood elsewhere, there is none to be found. The resultant fruit does not exist to be sought anywhere else. "Let's leave our mind over here and hope for buddhahood over there"; it won't work. We can realize that we are buddha on the basis of our own mind. As Venerable Milarepa said,

> Buddha is in the palm of your hand.

He is not saying that there is a buddha in our hand. He is saying it because buddhahood is as if right in our hands, because buddhahood is extremely close to us. Whether we recognize it or not is another matter. It is said that we are left behind only by not recognizing it, because, if we recognize it, buddha is always with us. This is saying the same thing:

> If you realize your own mind, it is buddha.
> So, without seeking buddha elsewhere,
> Meditate on this best of perceptions.

9. Samsaric Phenomena Do Not Stain the Essence of the Mind

The brilliant clear essence of the sun
Is not obscured by the darkness of a thousand eons.
Likewise, the clear light essence of one's mind
Cannot be obscured by eons of samsara. [6]

THE SUN IS very clear and luminous. It can dispel all darkness in the world. It is extremely bright and clear. These are qualities of the sun, bright and clear. Its light can illuminate the entire world. The sun can clear darkness but is never stained by darkness itself. No matter how much ash, dust storms, or clouds arise, the sun cannot be stained by dust, clouds, or smoke. That is the quality of the sun. This clear brightness is its original nature, not that it was once dark and then became luminous in dependence upon other conditions: the sun was luminous from the first. Its nature is originally clear. Its nature is originally bright. Even if many eons of dense darkness arrived it could not obscure this essential nature of the sun. Even if the darkest blackness of the longest duration were to come and say, "I'm going to darken and eliminate the light of the sun," it could not sully the clear light of the sun for an instant. In an instant, when the sun rises, it clears all of the world's darkness. It can generate the illumination and brightness of all the light in the world. It is an easy example. The light of the sun, this quality of the sun, cannot be obscured by the darkness of a thousand eons.

Similarly, regarding the clear light essence of our mind, as said in the *Commentary on Valid Cognition (Pramanavarttika)*,

> The nature of the mind is clear light;
> As for stains, they are transitory.

While this commentary is generally from the point of view of the Sau-trantika and Chittamatra systems, yet there is much terminology that is the same as that used in the Essence System[19] of these instructions. It is extremely similar. Thus, the very instant we realize this essence of our mind—this "very instant" meaning "in one moment"—eons of samsara cannot obscure it. The harmful acts amassed over eons of time in beginningless samsara, the karma and delusion accumulated in beginningless samsaric lifetimes, even that can be cleared away in an instant.

In brief, many methods to purify negativity and obscuration are taught: we practice Vajrasattva meditation and recitation, undertake the ritual of the Thirty-five Confessional Buddhas, employ tantric methods such as fire-pujas, also build temples and make representations of enlightened body, speech, and mind. Even though Buddha taught these methods in Sutra and Tantra to purify negativity, we cannot guarantee that they will purify all negativity completely. The best method, the most profound method, to destroy or purify all of the negativity committed under the influence of delusion in beginningless samsara—heinous, inconceivable, limitless karma—is to realize the nature of our mind.

Likewise, the clear light essence of one's mind cannot be obscured by eons of samsara. This means that no matter how many times we have taken birth in the six realms—in hells, as pretas, as animals, as humans, demigods, and devas—through the four types of rebirth[20] or by way of the five paths[21]; and no matter how much harm we have committed in those rebirths, if we realize the clear light essence of our mind for an instant we will be liberated. It can purify all of that negativity. These are called the "instructions by which the great criminal is forcefully enlightened." They are also said to be like "an old woman pointing her finger," and like "a hundred birds chased off by one owl." There are many such appellations.

When someone is introduced very directly to these instructions, even if they are a bad criminal, if they can hold on to the main point, they will be liberated. As it says, the sun *Is not obscured by darkness of a thousand eons. Likewise, the clear light essence of one's mind cannot be obscured by eons of samsara.*

From *Uttaratantra* as well,

Essence engaged by those with the karma,
Like that for the time being, omnipresent,

Forever immutable, of indivisible qualities,
That realized to be the sphere of the ultimate.

Also,

Like a jewel, space, and pure water
Its nature is never deluded.

There are many quotations such as these. Similar to these examples, *The clear light essence of our mind cannot be obscured by eons of samsara.* The meaning of this in brief is that up to now we have not recognized the clear light essence of our mind. When we say this is the clear light essence of our mind, it has primordially been intrinsic to us. Although it has been forever with us, as said in Shangpa Mahamudra of the Shangpa Kagyu,

Because it's too easy, we don't believe it.
Because it's too close, we don't recognize it.

As said, we don't believe it because it is too easy. Analogies for mind's nature of clear light are not confusing or extremely difficult to understand. Since it exists in our own mind, if we take interest and meditate with the help of a good lama's instructions, it is easy. That is why it says, "Because it's too easy, we don't believe it." On the other hand, because it is so close, because it's our own mind and belongs to us, we don't recognize it. We can see a far distant tree yet we can't see our eyebrows, which are so close. It is similar here.

Having set forth the nature of space as an example, what is being said here, in brief, is that although we have this clear light essence mind we do not recognize it. If this can be realized, how should we realize it? When we say "realize" it, we are not talking about something that can be realized by just anyone who does meditation. What is the situation? From beginningless samsara up to the present we have had this clear light essence in our mind but we have taken little interest in it. We have fallen under the influence of delusions such as attachment and aversion. Controlled by them, because of the strength and force of delusion, we can't see the clear light essence of our mind even though it is there. It is obscured. Instead of taking little interest, if we really do this profound practice that we have met because of karma and prayer, by the power of the instructions on the clear light nature of the mind that we receive from a qualified lama and the activation of our previous merit, through being introduced to practice of clear light essence mind without mistake or deception just as taught in valid holy Dharma, then even all of the negativity and obscuration accumulated over thousands of eons is purified in an instant.

It doesn't take many words to explain it simply: *Likewise, the clear light essence of one's mind cannot be obscured by eons of samsara.* It depends on whether we recognize it or not, whether we are obscured or not. It doesn't help that it just exists; what matters is whether we recognize it or not. As for its existence, all sentient beings have it, but we have to know it is there. If we don't recognize it, we remain obscured. As said in the *Mahamudra Prayer,*

> Though beings, by nature, have always been buddha,
> Not realizing it, they wander in endless samsara.
> May we develop irresistible compassion for beings
> Who are experiencing incessant suffering.

What is this nature of beings that has always been buddha? The nature of all sentient beings is clear light mind; there is no joining with or separating from this nature. The clear light nature of mind of people who are unattractive, unlucky, or poor destitute beggars is not of lesser quality than that of others. The clear light nature of mind of people who are rich, resourceful, or impressive leaders is not any better than that of others. The quality of clear light, the essential nature of mind, does not vary depending upon someone's caste, family, or wealth. So what makes the difference? It only depends upon whether we take an interest or not; if we do, we will realize this mind. If we don't have the interest, we will remain obscured.

10. Expanding upon That Meaning

For example, we use the term "empty space"
Yet there is nothing in space to which the term refers.
Likewise, we say, "our own clear-light mind"
Yet there is nothing that is truly a base for the designation. [7]

FOR EXAMPLE, *we use the term "empty space."* Whatever we call space, whether we call it "empty sky," or say that it has a shape, square or round, even or uneven, none of those exist in space. Those expressions do not actually depict space. As cited above,

> "Seeing space" best describes it in words of living beings.
> How do we see space? Think about what those words mean.
> Although the Tathagatas have seen Dharma as it is,
> They cannot find another metaphor better than "seeing space."

There is no better metaphor they could find. Omniscient Longchenpa said, as well,

> Expressing this meaning defeats even the jinas' tongues.

He is saying that if they have to explain the ultimate mode of existence of mind with words, terms, or expressions, even the buddhas' tongues are defeated. Like space, the ultimate nature of the mind does not exist as any shape, round or square; it is inexpressible. *For example, we use the term "empty space." Yet there is nothing in space to which the term refers.* It's not possible to exemplify space with a definition or an expression of some quality or nature. *There is nothing in space to which the term refers.* We cannot see space no matter how hard we try. When we don't check or think about it, we speak about space being blue or "open." However, if we check well with reasoning, investigating more deeply to see just what space is, none of those terms really portray it.

Similarly, although we call it "one's mind of clear light," "essence of the mind," "merely labeled mind," "clear light," "rigpa-awareness," "basis of emanation of samsara and nirvana," "completion stage," and so on, none of these terms can portray or express it. If we say, "one's mind of clear light," for instance, there is no such basis upon which the term can be designated. Even if we say it is "merely labeled mind," there is no shape or essence to be expressed as such. If it had shape or essence, that could be expressed, but since no such thing exists in the mind, no matter how we describe it with examples or metaphors or analogies, that cannot express the actual mode of existence of the mind, mind just as it is. It is said that it cannot be explained. The reason for the need to say this is that most great meditators have a lot of attachment to conventional terms. To counter this, Dzogchen and Mahamudra Dharma language uses many strange expressions such as saying that the "ultimate mode of existence of mind is empty"; saying that it is "unfabricated mind"; saying that it is "mind dropped down to its natural state[22]"; "that which remains when placed," "that which goes when sent." With these, even if we are very attached to them, the words cannot symbolize the mind. They indicate that words have no essence; they are terms that show the essencelessness of terms. They show the unsuitability of the words holding the essence of the mind, which they do not. This is very important.

So, what is necessary? It is said that if we familiarize ourselves through emphasis on practice, we can meditate upon it. We need to accustom ourselves to practice. Without familiarization, just being attached to the words will not help. We cannot be liberated from samsara on the basis of words. We cannot realize the true nature of our mind on the basis of words. As Jetsun Milarepa sang,

> View is empty transcendent deep awareness
> But there is a risk of it becoming only words.
> If we do not ascertain the meaning for certain
> We will not be freed from self-grasping by words.

So there is a danger of losing the view in words, a "verbal view"; a danger that we feel these terms actually portray the deepest mode of existence of the mind. We must ascertain the actual meaning. Ascertaining the "object," the actual meaning, is not something easy. The more we have acted carelessly under the influence of delusion and karma from beginningless samsara up to the present, the more strongly we are controlled by our karmic propensities and imprints. If we have had a habit of drinking alcohol in the past, and someone tells us to stop, it will be difficult to do so. If bad habits that form in early life are difficult to overcome, how much more so are the habits of samsara, which are beginningless! We have taken numberless rebirths since beginningless time. Throughout that time we were always very familiar with delusion, always "meditating" on it. That is why it is difficult to suddenly realize the true nature of our mind; we cannot. However, by meditating and familiarizing ourselves with it, with fortitude and enthusiasm, with the aid of a good lama's instructions, never leaving that state to which we have been introduced, if we can practice on a single cushion with complete renunciation and single-pointed persistence like Jetsun Milarepa or Gyelwa Gotsangpa, it can happen. That is because we have never been apart from our own true nature. If we persevere in examining and familiarizing ourselves, if we apply the methods for recognizing it, it is only natural that we have the ability to realize it. It is the display of our actual nature. It is not something we can't realize. It is something we can realize. Any so-called inability to realize it is because of lack of enthusiasm. Without enthusiasm and perseverance it won't happen. If we have perseverance and prajna-insightful wisdom, the ability to realize it is our actual nature. It is the display of our original mind.

Therefore, without clinging to words and terms like "clear light," with undiminished interest we must practice meditating and familiarizing ourselves with our actual nature. It is taught that we must practice, that practice is necessary. It must be applied, integrated, within our mental continuum, within our being.

Thus, mind's nature has always been like space.
There is no phenomenon that is not included in it.

Thus, mind's nature has always been like space. We have already explained the example extensively above. On the basis of that example, when we depict it we say that this nature of the mind has never existed; is primordially nonexistent. This nature of the mind has primordially been beyond color or shape. This nature of mind is primordially uncharacterized. This nature of mind is primordially the nature of emptiness. This nature of mind is primordially a union of luminosity and emptiness. This nature of mind is primordially free of production, cessation, and abiding. "Primordial," *dö ne*,[23] in this context, is equivalent to *ka dag*[24] in Dzogchen, meaning "primordially pure." It is the same as *ye ne dag pa*,[25] "timelessly pure." The essential meaning of these terms is "not existing as any shape, color, characteristic, etc." and such a mind is said to be the nature of all phenomena.

Mind's nature has always been like space. This example of space is extremely important. There is none better. It is not possible to find a better example than "seeing space." It can't be realized applying other analogies. Space is the best. Mind's nature is primordially like space. There is great meaning in this. If we misunderstand and think that it is not like space but existing with color or form or by way of its own characteristics, then our meditation will be mistaken; it will not lead to good meditation. Why? When we say "primordial," it means that we do not need to rely upon a remedy or antidote. It cannot be destroyed by conditions. Since this facet of ourselves is forever immutable and stainless, it is said to be primordial.

Some think they can have a guru, receive the guru's instructions, then, when they meditate and are introduced to their actual mind, act as if this introduction was not something rare but available in great supply; and then they discard it easily, like throwing it out with the garbage. This is very inappropriate.

Entering the Middle Way states,

> If things possessed characteristics,
> Denying those characteristics could destroy them.
> If emptiness caused things to be destroyed,
> That would be illogical; it is not reality.

If we think that all phenomena are not ultimately empty, then it is a faulty view, contrary to fact. This is similar to the previous. If it were the case that we had to rely upon an antidote in order to deal with phenomena that are not empty and then, by meditating, made all phenomena selfless, then emptiness would be the cause for destroying things. There would be the absurd logical consequence that arya beings' meditative equipoise would cause things to be destroyed; the consequence that, ultimately, production would be impossible; the consequence that conventional phenomena would be able to bear ultimate analysis (which they cannot), and so on. In *Entering the Middle Way*, Chandrakirti presents many such absurd consequences to Bhavaviveka.

This is exactly the same point. Thus, no matter what antidote is relied upon, finally, the ultimate mode of existence of the mind is empty like space.

As it is said,

> Sentient beings are nothing but buddhas;
> However, passing stains obscure them.

Likewise, Buddha teaches that "sentient beings are buddhas," "All beings without exception are precursors of buddhas,"[26] and "the tathagatagarbha pervades all beings." These are all saying the same thing. The nature of our mind is primordially like space. We are primordially buddhas. We are primordially emptied of all faults and endowed with all positive qualities.

In the context of Dzogchen, the meaning of "dharmata samantabhadra," "the reality of samantabhadra, the always good," is that there is no need to abandon "objects of abandonment" or to train in new positive qualities: we are primordially liberated; this is called samantabhadra. Some misunderstand this, saying that samantabhadra is the original buddha who fell like a stone out of the sky! They do not understand the meaning. What is called samantabhadra is not someone who sits above the crown of our head. It refers to the samantabhadra present in our own mental continuum. *Samantabhadra* in Sanskrit—in Tibetan, *dü kün-tu zang-po,* the "always excellent"—is the mind itself. It is mind itself that is samantabhadra. Mind itself has always been excellent; samantabhadra is our usual state. We have always been freed of faults, we have forever been complete in qualities. This is why we speak of "samantabhadra."

As for the word *kün-tu,* "always," as it is said,

> One who knows that past, present, and future are timeless...

This teaches the nonexistence of the three times. Past does not exist, future does not exist, present does not exist. These three times are just imputed by conceptual mind; in actuality the three times do not exist. Hence, "no-time," or the "timeless," is said to be the supreme of all times, and it is in this connection that the term *kün-tu,* "always," is used. Whether down in samsara or up in fortunate rebirths, the mind remains good. No matter how strong attachment, hatred, and ignorance become, this mind remains good. No matter how much we associate with delusion, this mind remains excellent.

We shouldn't think that this mind becomes bad when it is deluded and becomes good when it is freed from delusion. Since that is not the case, "always" means "uninterrupted" or "without cease." At all times up through the attainment of enlightenment, until all sentient beings attain the state of a buddha, at all times and occasions, no matter what sort of path we take, no matter what sort of path and stages we move through, no matter what sorts of remedies we transcend, no matter what sort of qualified path we practice, this nature of mind remains good; so it is called samantabhadra. It is understood that this mind of samantabhadra is primordially freed of all objects to be abandoned, and primordially perfected in all qualities. We can know this; we need have no doubt about it. So that is what we mean when we say that mind's nature has always been like space. The same is said in *Uttaratantra,*

> Since the buddha wisdom exists in sentient beings,
> Their stainless nature is not different from buddhas.
> Therefore, in order to name the lineage after its fruition,
> It is said that all beings have buddha nature.

And similar again,

> The suchness of the defiled and the stainless are, respectively,
> Qualities of the stainless buddhas and the jinas' deeds.

These all carry the same intent. The nature of the mind is primordially the nature of buddha. In the dohas of Shamar Kachö Wangpo come the words,

> Mere luminous awareness of this present moment
> Is the actual face of conventional phenomena!
> If we understand the very fact that it is unfabricated,
> Ultimate truth is also nothing but that.

If we understand this point, that the nature of mind is a union of clear light and emptiness and that that has forever been the case, then we understand the essential point. He goes on,

> Those who label phenomena name the two truths but
> With vast learning and logic, they still miss the main point.

Those with only scriptural learning can't understand it. No matter how many logical reasons they know, hundreds or thousands, it remains mere verbal expression and they are not up to understanding. Great meditators, however, through meditation, when the true nature of their mind is pointed out to them, can arrive at the precise understanding. Hence, this is the most profound meditation. This is the direct cause that actually liberates us from samsara. Study and contemplation act as indirect causes. Liberation must be attained through the direct cause of meditation; just hearing the teachings will not liberate us.

Mind's nature has always been like space. There is no phenomenon that is not included in it. The implication is that mind is primordially like space, forever beyond shape or color, beyond characteristics. When we are introduced to this space-like true nature of the mind, primordially free of mental fabrication, *there is no phenomenon that is not included within it.* How do we understand this essential nature of all phenomena? This clear light nature of the mind is the essential nature of all phenomena. It is the essential nature of all phenomena, concurrent with all phenomena, the destination of all phenomena, the resultant state of great meditators; this is the final result of meditation. We can also say it is where all phenomena are exhausted, as well as the result of all phenomena. It is the essence of all phenomena, the nature of all phenomena, also the character or definition of all phenomena. It is the ultimate mode of existence or true nature of all phenomena. It is also the path of all phenomena. It is the ultimate truth of all phenomena.

When we understand that it is the essential and ultimate nature of all phenomena, then how must we train in it? How can we realize this space-like primordial nature of our mind? Can we know it through dialectic disputation? Can we know it through meditation? Must we absolutely always be with a lama? How about if we go into a small room, close all the doors and windows and stay in the dark. Will we see it then? Or if we climb a nine-story tower and stay in the cool wind and meditate, will we see it then? In dependence upon what sort of path will we know it? In dependence upon what sort of antidote or condition will we know it? A response to these questions follows next.

11. Showing How to Practice with Body, Speech, and Mind

Giving up all physical activity, the yogi sits relaxed.

HERE IS EXPLAINED the "method of generation," "the method for realization." The method for realizing the ultimate mode of existence of mind is explained. This regards the common method for realization, not the uncommon method for realization. *Giving up all physical activity, the yogi sits relaxed.* The next line continues, *Vocal expression does not exist. Why? It is like empty echoes.*

The method to have this realization, Tilopa says, is *Giving up all physical activity, the yogi sits relaxed.* He is saying that it is not good if we are always in movement, going back and forth from place to place. Giving up all physical activity, however, does not mean stopping all travel in general, not going anywhere. It means giving up mundane activity, worldly work. Mundane conduct of traveling, standing, sitting, and sleeping is one of the main forces obstructing our Dharma practice.

It is not good to always be on the go. We say that the "go-mara" has entered our feet. When the "mara of going" has entered our feet, when mara has seized our feet, we remain constantly traveling, not staying still for even a moment. When the "mara of speech" has entered our tongue we remain speaking and never stop. So he is saying to give up whatever worldly activity traveling, standing, sleeping, and sitting we are involved in; it is not very important.

The yogi sits relaxed. Sitting relaxed does not mean going to sleep! What he means, in short, is that delusion, the root and spread of samsara, trying to control enemies and support friends, is all done on the basis of worldly conduct while traveling, standing, sitting, or lying down because we have not practiced the path of this method of realization. So what does *del wa,*[27] "relaxed," or "at ease," mean? It means that if we sit with the mind relaxed and body at ease, we will develop meditation on the basis of equipoise. There is much said in the subject of concentrated samadhi about how, in general, mental suppleness must be developed in dependence upon physical suppleness. We cannot develop good mental suppleness without good physical suppleness. Bliss of mental suppleness then develops first, followed by bliss of physical suppleness. But in the context of practice of the stages of the path, if we do not develop physical pliancy first, we will not develop mental pliancy. Even in the common explanation, there is the teaching that if the bodily posture is straight and erect, the channels will be straight; if the channels are straight, the winds will run straight; and if the winds run straight, the mind will be straight. Since there is such a strong connection between body and mind, the body's comportment is extremely important. If the body always remains involved in mundane traveling, standing, sitting, and lying down, the mind will lack freedom. So the meaning of *Giving up all physical activity, the yogi sits relaxed* is that we need retreat. We need to be in an isolated retreat-like place where we can be alone. As Jetsun Milarepa sang,

> If I am sick and no one asks how I am,
> If I die and there is no one to grieve,
> If I can die in this retreat,
> This yogi's intentions will all be fulfilled.

We must stay in unfixed abode, in retreat. It is said,

> Without arising of fabricated doubt,
> May flowers of the unfabricated bloom!
> Without mental wavering about retreat,
> May fruit of experienced realization mature!

What this means is that in retreat we can develop and increase experiential realization and develop all supramundane realizations; we should have no doubt about that. If we get sick, we can attain enlightenment on the basis of the sickness. If we get a fever, we can attain enlightenment on the basis of the fever. If we are harmed, on the basis of the harm, without becoming terrified, trampling it, we can be released from it. This is the kind of ability or capacity that we need. This makes us immune from fear.

So saying *Giving up all physical activity, the yogi sits relaxed* means we must stay based in retreat. In the *Thirty-seven Practices of Bodhisattvas* comes the verse,

> Abandoning bad objects, delusion gradually diminishes.
> Without distraction, virtuous practice naturally increases.
> Because awareness is clear, the Dharma is ascertained.
> Staying in isolation is a practice of bodhisattvas.

The "bad objects" in the line "Abandoning bad objects, delusion gradually diminishes" refers to abandoning physical activities, such as running around with intention to control enemies and protect friends, doing business, and so on, that are mundane. These are the "bad objects." When we abandon deluded objects, delusions naturally decrease, are naturally controlled. We cannot immediately purify delusions but they gradually decrease.

"Without distraction, virtuous practice naturally increases." So when we are not involved in mundane activity of meeting friends, subduing enemies, and so on, we do not have all of that distraction. When we are not distracted, our virtuous practice can flourish and grow. It is the only chance for it to grow.

"Because awareness is clear, the Dharma is ascertained." Then awareness becomes clear. When attachment and aversion are both gone, when the basis for developing them is gone, our awareness becomes very clear and lucid. When awareness is clear, and we understand Mahamudra or Dzogchen instructions of a profound, vast, and uncommon nature from a qualified master, we will wish to understand more and more, develop higher and higher realizations. As we practice higher and higher paths, we develop the certainty that we can attain results in reliance on them. "Because awareness is clear, the Dharma is ascertained. Staying in isolation is a practice of bodhisattvas."

Giving up all physical activity, the yogi sits relaxed. "The yogi sits relaxed" is an admonishment to meditate well. Meditating, leaving aside excited, agitating physical activities, like Milarepa, we make a determination or vow as firm as a stake pounded into the ground: "From this time on I will not return to the village! If I go back to the village before attaining special experiential realizations, may all the Dharma protectors take my life!"

Attaining supreme realization, in general, is something that all trainees, all beings, will do. But if we can reach a secure position in our practice, that would be great. It is after reaching such a secure position that we can attain realization. What does it mean to "reach a secure position"? It means that the practice of Mahamudra or Dzogchen we are doing is based on valid sources, has an excellent lineage, and can transform our mind through its qualities. If we arrive at such a practice, we have reached a lofty secure position.[28] From that point, with just a bit more contact with a supreme master, realization is attained; we perfectly realize Mahamudra without mistake. Thus, it is until attaining that secure level of realization that we must "Give up all physical activity, and sit relaxed."

Vocal expression does not exist. Why? It is like empty echoes.

Sometimes people praise us, saying, "You're good!" Sometimes they deprecate us, saying, "You're bad!" We hear a lot of pleasant and unpleasant, good and bad talk, a lot of sounds, don't we? Tilopa is saying we should settle in meditative equipoise on them as being like echoes in the sphere of reality. We should think of all sounds as echoes. They are like echoes because, although they resound, they are empty. "Empty sound" means that although it resounds, its essential nature is empty, like an echo. We call out, "*Wa ye!*" "Hey!" and, although the sound comes back to us, there is no one there. *Vocal expression does not exist. Why? It is like empty echoes.*

Without a thought in mind, look at the moon of Dharma!

This means, Look at the resultant Dharma—"Dharma" here referring to the ultimate nature of phenomena. Tilopa sometimes uses the language of Dzogchen. When we speak of "moon of Dharma," "moon" here refers to the result. It is used as a metaphor for having arrived at the result, for success, or culmination. It is a word for ultimate culmination and quintessential truth.

Without a thought in mind, look at the moon of Dharma! In other words, "Leave aside all mundane activity and moving around. There is no need for a lot of recitation and mantra. It won't be possible with a lot of recitation and mantra." Jetsun Milarepa sang,

> When doing Mahamudra meditation,
> Put no exertion in body or speech.
> There is danger that nonconceptual wisdom will fade away!

Mahamudra meditation will not happen if we engage in a lot of physical activity, such as prostration, a great deal of recitation and mantra repetition, and so on. He is saying that if we engage in these there is danger that our nonconceptual jnana-wisdom will fade away, disappear.

Without a thought in mind, look at the moon of Dharma! When he says, "Without a thought in mind," "not thinking of anything," this does not mean to stop whatever thoughts may arise in our mind. What we attend to is beyond mental activity. This is something very important. In the same way, *giving up all physical activity* does not mean we were doing something but it was not allowed and we must stop it with force. In saying that all vocal expressions are like echoes, again, this is not a perception that is forced. Rather it is a reflection that there must be something that transcends all activity of body, speech, and mind.

In the *Mahamudra Prayer* come the words,

> Perceptions of good and bad released on the spot,
> Bad concepts and delusion purified in the natural sphere,
> Ordinary awareness, free of accepting and rejecting:
> May we realize ultimate truth free from fabrication!

We find the same thing here. Perceptions conceiving of goodness are released on the spot. Although thoughts of badness arise they are naturally purified in the sphere. If we lose thoughts of both good and bad, meaning thoughts of attachment and aversion, when both attachment and aversion are lost, what is left in the wake? Nothing but "ordinary awareness." What is "ordinary awareness"? It is unfabricated awareness. What does that mean? It is said that seeing it is inexpressible, like seeing something you can't recognize, like a mute person's dream, and like a mute person tasting sugarcane for the first time.

In short, perceiving all activity of body, speech, and mind as essenceless, when he says that the yogi gives up all activity and sits relaxed, he means sitting upright with the body relaxed.

Vocal expression does not exist. Why? It is like empty echoes. Any vocal expression that is heard, we must realize that, although it resounds, it is like an echo. Whatever is said about ourselves, good or bad, praise or criticism, they are just terms, not objectively existent. Thinking that sounds are like echoes, settle in meditative equipoise in that state of awareness.

Good qualities as well as bad thoughts will appear in our mind, but do not take interest in them. Knowing that they are without essence, cultivate unfabricated awareness, ordinary awareness. *Looking at the moon of Dharma* refers to looking at or realizing the ultimate Dharma realized in such teachings as Mahamudra and Dzogchen. *Look!* in this context actually means "Settle in meditative equipoise without fabrication!" Tilopa is not talking about looking with your eyes but to remain, without fabrication, in that state without joining or separation. It is beyond objects of thought, beyond expression of conventions, beyond physical action like walking and sitting. *Look at the moon of Dharma!* means, "Look at that which is the essence of all Dharma, beyond objects of physical conduct, verbal expression, and objects of thought!"

Body has no essence, like a plantain tree.

The trunk of the plantain tree is empty inside. There appears to be something there from the outside, but inside it is empty. The body is similarly without essence, like a plantain tree, a banana tree. This does not mean that it previously had an essence but that the essence was annihilated or ceased to exist. It is taught that we can understand this if we investigate with logic. As said in *Guide to the Bodhisattva's Conduct*,

> My teeth, hair, and nails are not me,
> I am not bones or blood,
> I am not mucus or phlegm,
> Nor am I pus or lymph,
> I am not fat or perspiration,
> Neither my lungs nor liver are me,
> Nor any other of my organs.
> I am not excrement or urine,
> I am not flesh or skin,
> I am not heat, nor am I chi,[29]
> My pores are not me, nor, in any way,
> Am I the six consciousnesses.[30]

There are a great many examples illustrating the body's lack of essence in the wisdom chapter of *Guide to the Bodhisattva's Conduct*. Is the body the nose? Is the body the eyes? Is the body the ears? Is the body the bones? Is the body the skin? Is the body the blood? Each of these is considered in succession. As is said in the introspection chapter of *Guide to the Bodhisattva's Conduct*,

Engaging in that which is not harmful
For the sake of others and myself
But like an illusion, without self:
I shall always maintain this attitude.

As we engage in that which is beneficial to others and ourselves, when
we check throughout all the parts of our body for what we call "self," we will
realize that we are mistaken and that it does not exist; that "self" is like an
emanation, like a mirage, like a dream, like a city of the gandharvas. Therefore
it lacks essence. This is also taught in the *Sixty Verses on Reasoning;* and in
the *Seventy Verses on Emptiness* there are many clear examples. As you may
know, these scriptures explain the stages of meditation on emptiness; it is
included in their subject matter. In the *Sixty Verses on Reasoning* it is said,

Not abiding, not observed,
Without root, not remaining.
Strongly arising out of ignorance,
Abandoning beginning, middle, and extremes,
Like a plantain tree it lacks essence.
It is like a city of the gandharvas.
An inexhaustible city of ignorance
Appears, like a mirage, to living beings.

Thus, *the body has no essence, like a plantain tree.* In the same way, in *Entering
the Middle Way,* personal selflessness is taught on the basis of the seven lines
of reasoning presented in the chariot metaphor. These all fit with the teaching
here on the body being without essence like a plantain tree.

And this is not just dialectic verbiage: it has to be on the basis of meditative
experience as well. Madhyamaka, likewise, has to be practiced on the basis
of meditative experience. Mahamudra, Dzogchen, and Madhyamaka are all
distinct, yet their meaning is the same. They are all complementary to each
other. The sevenfold chariot metaphor teaches the same thing.

In *Entering the Middle Way,* it is taught,

Don't perceive mind as nonexistent just because body exists.
Don't perceive body as nonexistent just because mind exists.
That is wisdom. In brief, the buddhas
Deny their similarity, as explained in Abhidharma.

This also teaches reasons for the body's lack of essence. There is no essence in the teeth or any of its parts. In the shravaka teachings on personal self-lessness as well, there is explanation of the body not existing by way of its own characteristics, its emptiness of being self-sufficient and substantially existent; these are explained at different stages of the path; but they all point to the body's lack of essential identity. *The body has no essence, like a plantain tree.* We use the expression, "the body has no essence," and say that it is like a plantain tree, but in actuality, as you know, we must contemplate the body being beyond both existence and nonexistence. This is also very important. We do not think that the body first had some essence, but that was annihilated and it came to lack essence, taking some sort of "isolate"[31] of that idea and contemplating it. If we examine the idea of lack of essence well, we will find that it is actually beyond both existence and nonexistence of essence. Generally speaking, when we negate the existence of essence, conventional wisdom would expect that to leave no other option but absence of essence; negating existence leaves nonexistence. But this is the kind of explanation given to someone learning the path. When we really get into meditation there is no explanation like that to be given. If we did, the fruit could not be attained. Saying it exists is reification by thought, and saying it does not exist is reification by thought. In fact it is not existent or nonexistent. Existence is an imputed phenomenon; nonexistence is an imputed phenomenon. Existence and nonexistence are actually relative concepts but neither existence or nonexistence are truly established.

Therefore, we speak of nonexistence of essence because we have clung to the existence of essence up to now. Because of this problem, as a means to stop our clinging, there is no choice but to say that it does not exist. Otherwise, it would not be said. In fact, if we were to say that nonexistence of essence is the final ultimate truth that would not be correct. It must transcend both existence and nonexistence. As Aryadeva says in his *Four Hundred Verses on the Middle Way,*

> First stop the nonmeritorious.
> In the middle stop the "self."
> Finally stop all four views.
> One who knows this is wise.

As a means to stop the nonmeritorious, we have teachings on karma, the natural law of cause and effect, the existence of past and future lives, reincarnation. It is taught that we must abandon harmful actions and accomplish virtue; that we must progress through the paths and stages; that we must practice the precepts of refuge and so on. In these teachings Lord Buddha spoke of the body as being existent, the person as being existent, the aggregates as being existent, that everyone has accumulated karma, that everyone must experience the results of their actions. All of these were taught as a means to first stop the nonmeritorious.

In the second stage when faculties and discriminating wisdom have reached a rather high level, as a means to stop "self" at this intermediate stage, all phenomena are taught to be selfless. All phenomena do not inherently exist. Living beings are empty of existing by way of self. Other phenomena are likewise empty of existing by way of self. Now the first-stage thought of the self being existent is negated. Saying that all phenomena are selfless, having negated self, we have arrived at selflessness. The reasoning behind the sixteen emptinesses has proved or established emptiness for us. At this level we have reached a "somewhat supreme" level of faculties and wisdom. However, this is only meditation on the ultimate in the context of there being an "extremely final ultimate."[32] According to the sutras which reveal inexhaustible discernment, as in the system of the *Questions of King Dharanishvara Sutra,* this "extremely final ultimate" is explained using the metaphor of gradually cleansing a jewel of stains. What is presented as the extremely final ultimate? It is the definitive ultimate meditation, the ultimate object of meditation. At that point it is as Aryadeva says, "Finally stop all four views." It is release from all views, practice free from all views. It is beyond all views, a cessation of views. At this point we must understand that it is beyond all of the four views of existence, nonexistence, both, and neither. As Protector Nagarjuna says in his expression of homage at the beginning of *Root Wisdom (Mulamadhyamakakarika),*

> That which arises in interdependence
> Is without production or cessation,
> Is not annihilated or permanent,
> Does not come or go,
> Is not plural or singular.
> To those highest of speakers who teach
> Pacification of the twenty-four fabrications,
> The fully enlightened buddhas, I prostrate.

Pacification of fabrication means that all fabrications of existence and nonexistence are pacified. "Highest of speakers" means the supreme of speakers, principally those who give the teachings on emptiness. Lord Buddha gave many teachings and Nagarjuna refers to him as the highest of speakers. What does highest mean? It means being beyond the four extremes and all fabrication.

In this context objects and essential nature are not conventionally existent so it is said that they are without essence. We settle in equipoise free from fabrication of extremes. Fabrication of extremes means fabrications of all extremes—of existence, nonexistence, both, and neither—not only the extreme of existence. If we were to think that "nonexistence" was unfabricated and contemplated that, it would be incorrect. Projection, or fabrication, is something that binds us. It has many levels of grossness and subtlety. But whether it is a gross or subtle bondage, it still binds us. As Milarepa sang, if we are chained from attaining enlightenment, it makes no difference if the chains are made of iron or gold. What golden chains was he referring to? He was referring to clinging to the concept of emptiness. If we remain fixated on the thought, "Emptiness and this whole incredible sphere of awareness is so amazing!" we become bound by golden chains. We are tightly bound. It is not fun. Being bound in chains of iron is not pleasant, but neither would we think, "Ah! How nice that I'm bound in these golden chains!" Just as there is no difference between chains of iron and chains of gold, the main reason for our being obscured from the attainment of enlightenment is our fabrications of existence and nonexistence, both just the same. As Sakya Pandita said,

> If any view remains in unfabricated mind
> That view is one with fabrication.

There is no view left over in a mind free of fabrication; what this actually refers to is conceptual clinging to the unfabricated state. Clinging to the unfabricated is again a fabrication. It is like medicine that has turned into poison.

Mind, like being in space, is beyond objects of thought.

As Tilopa says below,

> If mind is without fixed reference point, that is Mahamudra.
> Meditating and familiarizing with that, enlightenment is attained.

He says that mind without fixed reference point is Mahamudra. Since *mind, like being in space, is beyond objects of thought,* it must be without reference point. What does that mean? In general, "reference point"[33] means that we can say "it arrived from here," "it left from here," "it stayed here"—these become reference points. Production, abiding, and cessation are reference points. The mind's ultimate mode of being has no such reference point. This means there is no point of identification, nothing to be identified. What we call the mind is like that, has a nature like that. But if we had to explain, "What we call 'mind' has such and such a nature, this kind of color, this kind of characteristic," there would be nothing to say. We can say, "that which is suitable to experience," but just saying that cannot really communicate what it is. Thus, "when there is no reference point," when there is awareness of that ultimate nature of the mind, "that is Mahamudra."

"Meditating and familiarizing with that, enlightenment is attained." What does meditating and familiarizing mean? In continuous close connection with the guru's oral instructions, when Dagpo Rinpoche said to Jetsun Milarepa, "However many experiences I have, I have familiarized myself with each one of them," Milarepa replied, "Oh that's nothing! Meditate still more!" Milarepa said this a lot. With this kind of continued meditation and familiarization, eventually we will attain unexcelled enlightenment. The words "meditation" and "familiarization" have vast meaning. "Meditation" is as we talk about all the time: "I've got to meditate." "Familiarization" means being insatiable for meditative experience up until enlightenment. Familiarization is not, once we have attained some realization, saying, "Okay, that's enough!" We must familiarize ourselves over and over with realizations we have attained from now all the way up to enlightenment. Otherwise, there will be many bodhisattvas who cycle again in samsara. Even bodhisattvas who have attained the first bhumi or "ground" of arya bodhisattvas, who have pacified all fabrication of subject-object duality and attained the final fruit of direct realization of emptiness, even they are not guaranteed to be free from taking rebirth in samsara; it can happen, it is said. We must therefore have the remedy for that. Having developed such samadhi, at the first realization of vajra-like samadhi, there can still be extremely subtle obscuration remaining, like a subtle stain that is still left after washing. Until we destroy such remaining obscuration we must be inseparable from the antidote. If we are not able to do that there is danger of falling again.

Thus, bodhichitta, such "enlightenment-mind," is free from all fabricated extremes. It is like being in the middle of space, beyond thought. What does the "middle of space" mean? It means the expanse of space; not calculating different directions of east, south, west, and north. He is saying it is like the expanse of space. Vast, measureless, open, free from obstructive contact, nothing to identify, like the inconceivable expanse of space. So, "middle of space" has the sense of "expanse of space."

Sem-nyi, "mind itself"—mind at its most fundamental, "elemental" level—is free from all fabricated extremes. We have attachment and aversion for compounded phenomena. We think of samsara below as something to be abandoned and nirvana above as something to be attained. We have strong feelings about giving up samsara and attaining liberation. The mind has strong clinging toward compounded phenomena. When we are deluded about compounded phenomena, no matter how much contaminated[34] virtue of body, speech, and mind we create, there is no way to realize Mahamudra. Contaminated virtue will not help to realize Mahamudra. Effortful virtue, no matter how much we perform it, will not help. No amount of contaminated virtue will help. So we must create uncontaminated virtue. What is uncontaminated virtue? If we can reach confident realization of our own true nature free of all fabrication, not clinging to, not conceiving of any extreme, we are introduced to Mahamudra, it is said. This is very profound. If we are attached to compounded roots of virtue we cannot realize Mahamudra. Attachment to compounded roots of virtue is a deluded fault, not a method to be released from deception. This is because all compounded phenomena have production and cessation. Once something has production and cessation it is samsara and therefore a cause of deception and will not allow us to realize Mahamudra. Therefore, what do we need? *Mind, like being in the middle of space, is beyond objects of thought.* Detached from compounded phenomena and uncompounded phenomena alike, transcending both, if our meditation becomes the expanse of ultimate suchness, then we realize Mahamudra.

Without discarding or placing, relax and settle within that state. [8]

When we say, "within that state," what state do we mean? Not a state of "mind." It means a state that is not attached to any compounded or uncompounded phenomena. If we relax and settle within that ultimate state without fabrication, we can realize Mahamudra. Thus, *Meditating and familiarizing with that, enlightenment is attained.*

12. Summary of the Previous Points

**If mind is without fixed reference point, that is Mahamudra.
Meditating and familiarizing with that, unexcelled enlightenment
is attained. [9]**

MIND IS FREE from all fabricated extremes. It doesn't come from anywhere, doesn't stay anywhere, doesn't go anywhere. There is no fixed
point where it arises, abides, or goes. We investigate the mind in this way,
especially in Mahamudra; where the mind arises, abides, and goes is investigated a great deal. Yet when this is investigated, no reliable point of reference
is found. There is no such secure, fixed point of reference to be found. What
is this "fixed point" that is missing? It is our dualistic concepts projecting existence, nonexistence, good, bad, subject, and object. Arising, abiding, going,
and so on are also all part of the web of conceptuality. They are fabricated by
thought, by concept. They are bound by concept. No sort of conceptuality
can represent Mahamudra.

What is the gist of this? Mahamudra cannot be realized through fabricated or intellectually contrived meditation. It cannot be realized through a
meditation with signs. A contrived meditation with signs, with intellectual
grasping and clinging, cannot realize it. As said in *Uttaratantra,*

> Since ultimate reality is profound
> It is not an object of mundane meditation.

That is what is being said here. As said in the *Mahamudra Prayer,*

> Without the effort of any assertion to make,
> Nor rejection of any object to deny,

May we ascertain perfect ultimate truth:
Unfabricated dharmata[35] that is beyond intellect!

No assertion we make can convey it. Again, there is no fixed reference point in the mind. Since there is no fixed point of reference it cannot be demonstrated. If, on the other hand, we must refute something and say, "It is not this!" that is difficult. There is "no rejection of any object to deny." Why can't we say it exists? Why can't we demonstrate its existence? Why can't we prove it does not exist? Because it is beyond intellect, it is said. Primordial ultimate reality is beyond intellect. In his *Hitting the Essence in Three Words* commentary, Dza Paltrul Rinpoche says,

Primordial dharmata beyond intellect:
This is the unmistaken way that the base exists;
The way that one abides on the path;
And the way that one abides in the fruit.

This being unmistaken, there is no fixed point of reference. Since it is beyond intellect, there is no fixed point of reference. If it was not beyond intellect, there would be a fixed point of reference, it would exist in the mind, it would be wrapped in the web of conceptuality, caught in the net of the intellectually contrived—in these there are fixed and determined points of reference: this is good, this is bad; this is subject, this is object; this is to be abandoned, this is to be adopted. All of this "perception through signs," or conceptuality, functions. But it is not the ultimate. As said in *Entering the Middle Way,*

Ordinary beings are bound by concepts;
The yogi, without concepts, is free.

Why are ordinary beings called by that term? Because they are bound in a web of conceptuality. When someone is caught in a web of thought they are called an ordinary being. It is also called the period of deception. Who is the yogi who abides in a nonconceptual state? One who rightly abides without projections, in peace, with all fabrication of subject-object duality extinct; that is a yogi. When they see the true nature of their mind, all yogis are liberated.

Therefore, when the ultimate nature of things is explained in a rigorous, exacting way, when the mode of being of all phenomena is explained without mistake; when it is done in conjunction with a holy guru's oral instructions and one's devotion and determination is like a stake one keeps driving into the ground deeper and deeper; relying on the guru and Three Jewels from one's heart, chest, and lungs, with faith, aspiration, and devotion and good understanding, if we meditate upon that basis, as it is said,

Thought turns back, whatever the case.

Thought turning back means thought coming to an end, being finished, reaching a point of exhaustion. What is the reason that thought can be released in ultimate reality? As it is said,

The wise say this is the fruit of investigation.

The result of correctly and perfectly investigating is being able to arrive at the sphere of ultimate reality beyond thought. This is said by all of the wise.

In general, taking the words literally, the view as explained in *Entering the Middle Way* is solely that of dependent origination. However, when it is applied in the context of Mahamudra and maha ati Dzogchen instruction, it becomes even more profound. When it is applied on the basis of actuality, what we mean by "entering the Middle Way" is not just talk. Yet these days there is a Dharma of dialectics. People suddenly sit for examination on the Middle Way. Someone stands up and presents to them a related argument and they contemplate the points and answer. If we really contemplate it, it becomes an understanding of the ultimate. Therefore, it is to such a point of absence of fixed reference that the investigation will arrive; it is not enough, however, just to be able to say, "There are no fixed reference points in the mind." To realize the absence of reference points in the mind, it takes first developing wisdom through hearing the reasons, then developing the wisdom of contemplation by thinking about those reasons that mind lacks fixed reference points. Then, once we have good understanding from that, it is finally through meditation that we must be liberated. With a holy guru's oral instructions, staying in retreat in an isolated place, discarding all mundane traveling and residing, and even thinking about them; then, not being attached to any object whatsoever, making the deer on the mountain our only companions, meditating in a cave in a deserted empty area, our meditative experience will flourish and increase. Then powerful realizations will occur. When that happens we are certain to fulfill the purpose of meditation, we can be liberated by meditation. When we thus realize the absence of fixed reference in mind we are walking in the footsteps of all the great mahasiddhas. When we realize this true nature of our mind without fixed reference points we become capable of demonstrating all sorts of miraculous emanations: flying through the sky, moving through water like a fish, turning dry boulders into dust. We will be capable of miracles out of all proportion. The reason that Jetsun Milarepa could stand inside a yak's horn without himself becoming any smaller or the yak's horn becoming any bigger was because of the mind being without fixed reference points; otherwise, how could we believe such a thing to be possible? But when we arrive at that ultimate understanding, even if it sounds unbelievable, the perfectly valid reasons are obvious to us; it is the nature of things. Jetsun Milarepa said,

> I have never created a miracle; all sentient beings do it. I point out to them how things actually exist. All sentient beings demonstrate miracles. When they make things that do not exist come into being and things that exist disappear, it is all of them doing it, not me!

This is a genuine pure sense of self. That is what it is like, this absence of fixed reference in the mind.

In summary, meditation on the basis of conceptual grasping at compounded Dharma, practice of virtue on the basis of conceptual grasping at compounded Dharma, gathering accumulations on the basis of conceptual grasping at compounded Dharma, and so on, will not help. Mahamudra cannot be realized upon that basis. This sort of thing must be abandoned. If we become attached to fabricated Dharma it does not benefit anyone.

What do we need in order to realize Mahamudra? We need to have previous good karma awakening; have aspiration and devotion genuinely seeing the guru as a fully enlightened buddha from the depths of our heart and bones; and, with such aspiration and devotion, strongly and continuously persevere throughout the day and night. If we can succeed at inducing in our meditation good ascertainment of the actual elemental nature of our own mind, then we have been able to realize Mahamudra. But creating contaminated virtue will not help.

Saying that it is for the sake of realizing Mahamudra, we do prostrations and go through austerities, but no matter how much contaminated virtue we create, it is an indirect cause for realization but cannot be a direct cause. The direct cause is having the guru's instructions appear to our mind and meditating with strong, consistent, "driving-the-stake"-like determination from the depths of our heart and bones. If, in dependence upon this, we arrive at mind free of all point of reference, that is Mahamudra. As said in the *Mahamudra Prayer,*

> This freedom from mental activity is Mahamudra,
> Great Madhyamaka,[36] the Middle Way path, free from extremes,
> And Dzogchen, the Great Perfection, as well, it is said.
> By knowing one, may we attain confident knowledge of them all!

Regarding freedom from mental activity, if our mind is active with speculation—"Is what I'm experiencing Mahamudra or not?" "Is this Dzogchen or not?" "Is this realization or not?" "Is this the true nature, the 'ultimate mode of existence' of my mind, or not?"—once we attend to such mental activity, a point of reference, a fixed point, has been determined. "This freedom from mental activity is Mahamudra." That is why Mahasiddha Tilopa says, *If mind is without fixed reference point, that is Mahamudra.* But just recognizing this Mahamudra without reference point will not help: *Meditating and familiarizing with that, unexcelled enlightenment is attained.*

He says, "meditating" and "familiarizing." When we speak of meditation, there is a meditator. As it is said,

> One who is not being the "meditator" is a meditator!
> The meditator becomes open expanse!

Once we reach secure realization of our ultimate nature, we might speak of doing meditation, but at that point even our mundane activities become meditation, so no great effort is needed. It is an activity that is accomplished very easily and naturally. That is true of any activity. Through familiarization with painting one becomes a skilled painter. It is the same with construction work. If we are very accustomed to making flower arrangements, we can do it easily and naturally. Likewise, when we reach secure knowledge of the ultimate, whatever practice we have becomes meditation. So that is regarding meditation. But even such supreme realization, attainment of such secure knowledge, itself is not enough. We need to keep on familiarizing ourselves with it all the way up to attainment of the precious state of unexcelled perfect complete enlightenment. How do we familiarize ourselves? Repeatedly and continually attending to the meaning, never parting from being based in its meaning. Even if we can attain secure realization of the ultimate truth of all phenomena in meditative equipoise, there is danger of it slackening during various activities between sessions of meditation, the periods of "subsequent attainment" as they are called. During all activities between sessions—talking to people, eating meals, and so on—it is important not to completely forget the meaning understood during meditative equipoise.

We can contemplate what it would be like after mixing meditative equipoise and subsequent attainment together completely, but that does not actually happen except at full enlightenment. While equipoise and subsequent attainment are separate, we must not part from the understanding developed during equipoise when we are involved in activities between sessions of meditation. If we do not part from the perspective of meditative equipoise during mundane activities between sessions of meditation, after some time, we can mix equipoise and subsequent attainment, making them simultaneous and nondual. Therefore, until equipoise and subsequent attainment are mixed, we must keep familiarizing ourselves. Mixing here means repeatedly deepening our understanding. Thinking that we have already attained a supreme realization so everything is fine and complete will not help. *Meditating and familiarizing with that, unexcelled enlightenment is attained.* Mahasiddha Tilopa is saying we will attain unexcelled enlightenment.

13. This Essential Meaning Cannot Be Seen Through View, Meditation, and Action That Make Assertions

Practitioners of Mantra, and of the Paramitas,
Vinaya Sutra, the Pitakas, and so on,
Will not see clear light Mahamudra
By way of the tenets of each of their scriptures.
Because of their assertions, clear light is obscured, not seen. [10]

THIS HAS FIVE lines. Generally speaking, Lord Buddha gave common and uncommon teachings and there have been many incredibly wise and accomplished masters of those teachings who have appeared in India and Tibet. Some of them were of the highest faculties, some had the common ability to manifest signs, some were cared for by their yidam deity, some had no impediment to their knowledge of all of the five fields of knowledge, and so on. There are many differences in the way they reached definite realization through their investigation and practice and they composed commentaries on how to develop their knowledge. So we have both the teachings given by Lord Buddha and the commentaries composed by the masters who followed him. Likewise, we speak of Buddha's Sutra and Tantra teachings.

Practitioners of Mantra and the Paramitas. "Practitioners of Mantra" refers to Vajrayana, the resultant vehicle, and "Paramitas" refers to the Paramitayana, the Vehicle of the Perfections, the causal vehicle. They are called the *di tegpa*[37] and the *dir tegpa*,[38] the vehicle "by which" we go and the vehicle "to which" we go. The vehicle by which we go is the causal Paramitayana. Because of that it is called the vehicle of the perfections. The vehicle to which we go means the resultant vehicle. Thus, there is no teaching of Lord Buddha that is not included in this twofold division of Sutra and Tantra.

Tantra, Secret Mantra, as you know, includes both the old and new lineages, the Nyingma and Sarma. There are new systems and many old systems. There is much to say about the subject. Most of it comes in stories. In any case, there are these two, the old and the new tantras. Another twofold division is that of Mahayana and Hinayana, these various presentations of the teachings given by Lord Buddha. The later scholars who followed him wrote commentaries that can all be included in four schools of tenet systems.

Generally speaking, there is no difference between Vajrayana and Paramitayana. Every teaching that Buddha gave was for the sake of attaining release on the path to liberation and omniscience. No teaching was given for any other purpose. But because of the variation in the aptitudes and faculties of beings, Lord Buddha taught two vehicles, the causal and resultant. He taught the causal Paramita Vehicle to those who were of slightly lesser faculties, and to all of those with extremely sharp faculties he taught Vajrayana.

Regarding distinctions between the two, it is said,

> Though for the same purpose, being unobscured,
> Rich in skillful means, and without difficulty,
> For those with the sharpest faculties,
> The Mantra Vehicle is particularly exalted.

"Though for the same purpose" is a reference to the Mantra and Paramita vehicles both being for the same purpose. To give one example, regarding bodhichitta, there is a twofold explanation of conventional bodhichitta and ultimate bodhichitta. Both are explained in the context of Sutra as well as in Tantra. There can be no practice of Vajrayana without reliance upon conventional bodhichitta. There can be no practice of highest yoga tantra without reliance upon ultimate bodhichitta. Within Tantra there are also many upper and lower classifications such as kriya tantra, charya tantra, yoga tantra, maha anuttara yoga tantra, as well as differences in the way of accomplishing their practices—relying on the deity as a friend, relying on the deity as a king, relying on the deity as a subject, and so on. Thus, in the case of Tantra as well, Buddha gave higher and lower levels of teachings depending upon the level of capability of his listeners. In the general explanation of Tantra there is taught a union of conventional bodhichitta practice with ultimate bodhichitta practice that is a view that is beyond all views, of the mind's ultimate mode of existence free from fabrication. This is the common tantric explanation. As long as an instruction is Mahayana it will have an explanation of such a pure practice and view.

When we say Mahayana, it includes both the causal and resultant vehicles, the Tantrayana and Sutrayana. Therefore, for Tantrayana we definitely need both conventional and ultimate bodhichitta; they are indispensable. In nondual highest yoga tantra of Kalachakra, for instance, they are explained in nondual father-mother Kalachakra, which principally reveals the suchness of inconceivable jnana-wisdom. In Sutra teachings Buddha was generally speaking to all of many levels of capacity simultaneously, and so made it easily understandable, teaching only personal selflessness, for example. When this terminology is raised to a higher level, the words *rang ngo,* "one's own face," or "one's own essential being," are used. Again, speaking mainly in terms of the lower classes of Tantra, their special methods improve somewhat on this view of a personal selflessness. When practice of the path becomes a bit more profound, the words *sem-kyi ngo-wo,*[39] "mind's essential nature," are used. The word *tong-nyi*[40]—"emptiness, shunyata"—is used. When emptiness is taken to an even more profound level, many other terms are used: *sem-kyi ne-lug,*[41] "mind's ultimate nature" or "ultimate mode of existence"; *de-ko-na-nyi,*[42] "suchness"; *de-wa chen-po,*[43] *mahasukha,* the "great bliss" spoken of in Tantra. These are terms of increasing profundity for those of increasingly greater faculties of understanding. The words change a great deal but the ultimate meaning intended is the same, not different. It is this true nature, this ultimate mode of being of the mind that must be recognized in Tantra, and it is this ultimate mode of being of the mind that must be recognized in Sutra. The ultimate nature to be realized in the common vehicles is not different; it is the same reality. Yet when this same reality is explained to those of greater or lesser faculties, Buddha explained it in many different stages of methods or skillful means.

In *Tantra of the Two Examinations* come the words,

> First is taught Vaibhashika,
> After that Sautrantika,
> Then Yogachara,
> After that Madhyamaka.
> Once all tantric stages are understood,
> The vajra master teaches Hevajra.
> There is no doubt about this practice.

Therefore, from the beginning teachings of Vaibhashika to the advanced teaching of Hevajra, why is Buddha teaching? He teaches everything as a staircase leading to realization of suchness, our actual nature, the way things are.

At this point Mahasiddha Tilopa speaks of the Vajrayana, which includes the old and new schools; likewise Sutrayana, including the Paramitayana and all the three pitakas: Vinaya, Sutra, and Abhidharma. Each of these has their scriptures and tenet systems.

By way of the tenets of each of their scriptures, they will not see clear light Mahamudra. Therefore, to realize Mahamudra, just studying Tantra, studying Tantra on the basis of ignorance grasping at inherently existent marks and signs; and study of Vinaya, Sutra, and Abhidharma done on the same basis, no matter how much study and practice of the tenets of these various scriptures we do in such a conceptual way, we cannot realize Mahamudra. Why is that? The term "tenet system" here describes a situation in which someone thinks from the point of view of their own system and fabricates some kind of measure that can bear scrutiny. It is said, in general, that this can facilitate seeing the clear light of Mahamudra. But Tilopa, here saying, "They will not see it," means that it will not be a cause for direct realization. We have to make a distinction here. Otherwise, we might go too far and say that Vinaya, Sutra, Abhidharma, Paramita, Vajrayana, the entire causal and resultant vehicles cannot help to realize Mahamudra. Tilopa saying, "They will not see Mahamudra," means that this kind of study and practice cannot act as the direct cause for realizing Mahamudra.

In short, whether it is teachings, commentaries, or tantra of the old and new systems, none of these can internalize the ultimate. That is because their tenets are intellectually contrived. Tenet systems here involve intellectual grasping. So much disputation is done by the Vaibashikas, Sautrantikas, and Chittamatrins! Within Chittamatra there is also a division into "true aspectarian" Chittamatrins, and "false aspectarian" Chittamatrins. And there is a threefold division of true aspectarian Chittamatrins: the "half-egg" branch, the "equal number of consciousnesses" branch, and the "variety nondual" branch. There are two types of false aspectarian Chittamatrins: those "with stains" and those "without stains." Then within Madhyamikas, there are Yogachara Madhyamikas and Madhyamikas who accept what is renowned in the world. At the root, there is the twofold division of Svatantrika Madhyamaka and Prasangika Madhyamaka. Moving on from there, there are proponents of self-emptiness, and proponents of other-emptiness. Each of these has its own tenets and investigates with logic. Then they fabricate a concept.

What is seen as faulty is rejected. That which has qualities is adopted. Adopting and rejecting, they speak of view and practice and proceed on that basis, talking about views and tenet systems. Such conceptual fabricated mind, intellectually contrived tenets, whether of Vinaya, Sutra, Tantrayana, or Paramitayana, cannot realize clear light Mahamudra. They can indirectly help to realize clear light Mahamudra but they cannot directly help to realize clear light Mahamudra. They cannot be a direct cause for realizing clear light Mahamudra. The reason they cannot engage the object directly is because of being attached to tenets. "I'm a Vaibhashika." "I'm someone with Sautrantika tenets." "I'm a proponent of Chittamatra." "I teach Madhyamaka." Each is attached to their own view and practice. When attachment is present it is a cause for samsara. When we speak on the basis of reality, whatever has attachment is a cause for samsara, not liberation from samsara. Mahamudra, in particular, must be realized in reliance upon skillful means and oral instructions, and we cannot realize it with a lot of conceptual fabrication. Again, as Jetsun Milarepa sang,

> When doing Mahamudra meditation,
> Put no exertion in body or speech.
> There is danger of nonconceptual wisdom fading away!

As he says, there is danger of nonconceptual wisdom fading away. Therefore, it only creates the cause for continued samsara, not liberation from samsara. Thus it does not become an aid to Mahamudra realization.

There is still one more thing we must understand about this. If we can practice without grasping and clinging to the respective views and practices of Vinaya, Sutrayana, Mantrayana, Paramitayana, it can liberate us with realization of Mahamudra. What is it that is rejected here? While explaining the respective view, they cite scriptures. In dependence upon that view tenets are created. It is a conceptually fabricated view. On the basis of this view, determinations are made and boundaries are accepted. These are what we call "tenets"—the parameters of our assertions. It is when we are attached to tenets, whether of Vinaya, Vaibhashika, Sautrantika, Mahayana, Sutrayana, Tantrayana, that they cannot become an aid to realizing Mahamudra. The *Guhyagarbha Tantra* speaks of those who are

> Unrealized and misconceiving.

Lack of realization is a fault. Having set forth a tenet, not understanding it, not realizing it, is a problem. If we have partial understanding of a tenet, that leads to misconceptions. Doubt can also arise. As said,

> Partial understanding does not realize the principal nature;
> There will be doubt about the nature of the ultimate.

We will continue to have much doubt about the mode of existence of ultimate truth. For instance, having set forth an example, if we study it only from the perspective of Vinaya, Sutra, and Abhidharma we cannot directly realize the ultimate nature of the mind. Therefore Sakya masters maintain that we cannot become a buddha through the Sutra path alone and definitely must train in the path of Tantra. They assert that we will not become enlightened by the Sutra path alone, that addition of the Tantra path is necessary. In reliance upon the Sutra path alone without Tantra it won't happen. In *Ascertaining the Three Vows,* it is said as well,

> Without relying upon the ripening, liberating Great Secret [Mantra Vehicle],
> We will not attain. This was said by Buddha.

"Ripening, liberating" refers to the ripening initiation, liberating commentary, and supporting transmission. Without relying upon these, without practicing in connection with the guru's instructions, on the basis of the view and practice of Sutra alone, on the basis of conceptual mind's limited view and practice, we cannot attain complete enlightenment. Therefore there is debate over whether or not it is possible to attain enlightenment through the Sutra path alone; for the most part it is asserted that it is not possible. It takes an extremely long time so we cannot say that it is absolutely impossible. But relative to what is possible in Tantra, the swiftness of the practice, we can say that it is not possible to become enlightened through the Sutra path alone. In the *Jewel Ornament of Liberation,* also, references to "severance of the lineage" do not mean that there is no possibility of attaining enlightenment, but that because it takes such a long time in samsara it is said that the lineage for enlightenment is severed. The meaning is the same.

Thus, based in partial realization, not realizing the principal point, one has doubt about the ultimate. This is said in the *Guhyagarbha Tantra.* The meaning of this is that on the basis of conceptual tenets, view and practice, the parameters of asserted tenet systems, we will continue to have doubt about the ultimate; it will not cut through our mind's reification of phenomena. On the basis of this kind of thinking, attached to our own tenet system, mistakenly not understanding our own essential nature, we cannot realize Mahamudra. It is possible that these kinds of common tenet systems can help diminish the number of the six realms' beings slightly and gradually lighten their manifest suffering, but Tilopa is saying that they are not at all helpful for realizing Mahamudra.

Therefore, we should not be attached to our own tenet system; with such attachment we cannot realize Mahamudra. In Mahamudra here we must use nonconceptual jnana-wisdom only; we cannot use conceptual mind. Mahamudra is not found with conceptual mind. That is why it is taught not to conceptually grasp at tenets, view, or practice. That is why it is taught not to grasp at limited assertions. For the same reason [Nagarjuna] said,

> Since I make no assertions
> I am only faultless.

This is not because of having already made a philosophical assertion or accepted a position and then having taken it back; that would be persisting in stupidity. Rather, it is because no agent, action, or object of asserting a philosophical position actually exists. That is why Nagarjuna says, "Since I make no assertions I am only faultless."

They *will not see clear light Mahamudra by way of the tenets of each of their scriptures.* What does this mean? With tenets we make assertions and claim certain positions. We focus on what we or someone else says and we develop attachment and grasping on that basis. In any case, when we claim a position from the perspective of a tenet system, clear light is obscured. Clear light cannot be seen; it is obscured. Clear light has not ceased to exist. Clear light is in our mind, our mind has clear light. Mind's nature is clear light. Clear light mind is primordial, has always existed. But we don't see it; it stays obscured.

Uttaratantra says,

> Like a buddha inside a wilted lotus, honey of the bees,
> The kernel in a husk, gold in silt,
> A treasure under the ground, the sprout in a seed,
> A buddha statue wrapped up in rags,
> A prince inside his mother's womb,

Or a jewel form in the earth,
Temporarily obscured by stains of delusions,
The buddha nature exists in sentient beings.

Buddha taught this on the basis of nine stains, nine similes, and nine meanings. The nine similes with their meanings all show that sentient beings are buddhas but are obscured by adventitious stains. Each example shows how, by applying an antidote, what must be abandoned is annihilated and a pure result is obtained. There is an extensive explanation of each one.

Thus, if we are attached to tenet systems we will not realize Mahamudra. We will not be able to understand the suchness of all phenomena. That is why when there are assertions, clear light is not seen.

Any assertion obscures, not just those of Vinaya, Sutra, and Paramita. Once we make an assertion we remain obscured. Mahamudra is beyond assertions. It would have to be beyond assertions, wouldn't it? As said,

Free from concepts, great bliss experience never interrupted,
Not grasping things as real, clear light free from obscuring veils,
Beyond intellect, thus nonconceptual, existing spontaneously,
May we have uninterrupted effortless realized experience!

For uninterrupted meditative experience, bliss, clarity, and nonconceptuality are indispensable. To develop bliss, clarity, and nonconceptuality, what is essential is (1) to abandon conceptual grasping, (2) to abandon reifying grasping, and (3) to transcend intellect.

Abandoning conceptual grasping means to abandon grasping tenets. "Incessant great bliss, without grasping." We must abandon conceptually grasping at tenets, views, and practices.

"Not grasping things as real, clear light is free from obscuring veils." Particularly when we are based in samadhi and inner practice with bliss, clarity, and nonconceptuality, we must not reify things or grasp them as real.

"Beyond intellect, thus nonconceptual, existing spontaneously." Since it is beyond intellect it is nonconceptual. "Beyond intellect, thus nonconceptual, existing spontaneously."

In Dzogchen it is explained in four: (1) direct perception of dharmata, (2) experience increasing, (3) awareness culminating, and (4) exhaustion of phenomena beyond intellect.

Seeing ultimate reality directly, our view becomes exalted. When we see dharmata directly, when we see the pure emptiness that is the unmistaken true nature or ultimate mode of existence of all phenomena, it is an exalted view.

As for "awareness culminating," in Dzogchen *rigpa,* "awareness," refers to or is equivalent to what in Mahamudra is called the "unfabricated essential nature of the mind." When this awareness culminates, meditation becomes profound. When the view is excellent, dharmata is seen directly. When meditation is excellent, awareness culminates. When the light of experience increases fully, meditation becomes excellent. Excellent view, meditation, and conduct.

"Exhaustion of phenomena beyond intellect." When the first three occur—dharmata is realized directly, experience increases, and awareness culminates—then phenomena are exhausted, transcending intellect. In the context of Mahamudra, this is the same as seeing the ultimate nature of the mind. In Dzogchen, what is called "phenomena being exhausted, transcending intellect" in Mahamudra is equivalent to seeing the suchness of the mind without mistake.

What is it that presently obscures this? Grasping conception. It is said,

> Without realizing absence of signs of true existence
> One will not attain liberation.
> That was why You taught
> The entire Mahayana.

Without realizing absence of signs of true existence we will not attain liberation. Here we are talking about a fully qualified liberation. In the *Precious Garland of the Middle Way,* the subjective mind realizing the view of emptiness without mistake is the root of the path to realizing fully qualified liberation. It won't help if it is not free from all assertions; it must be.

It is said in the wisdom chapter of the *Guide to the Bodhisattva's Conduct,*

> When things and nonthings
> Do not exist before the mind
> Then, since there is no other aspect,
> All is pacified in emptiness.

And the same thing is said in *Entering the Middle Way,*

> At peace, the jinas' dharmakaya results
> From burning the dry kindling of all objects of knowledge.

At that time there is no more production or cessation.
The kayas manifest with the ending of mundane mind.

When we arrive at the ultimate import it must be beyond fabrication, beyond objectification, beyond a focusing of mental attention, beyond bondage to false projections of true existence. If it is not beyond fabrication of objects we will not see how things actually are.

To realize Mahamudra we really need to have accumulated vast meritorious energy at some time in the past. That karma needs to be awakened in this life through intense and persistent aspiration and devotion to the holy guru as well as timely reliance upon the holy guru. This is what is necessary for Mahamudra realization. Any proliferation and collection of thought, even the slightest concept, will obscure it, and then it will not be possible to attain the result. In the explanation of path-knowledge in the study of the perfections, there is mention of "subtle attachment to the jinas and so forth." Even the slightest clinging to the final resultant state of Buddha's inconceivable secrets of body, speech, mind, qualities, and activities is still subtle attachment and an obstruction on the path, a fault on the path. Once we are a proponent of tenets, we develop some kind of attachment to our own system, our own path, our own guru, our own instructions, our own meditative experiences, our own realizations. All of these are attachments. If we meditate like that it obscures us. If we meditate like that it is not beneficial. Even if we get a glimpse of clear light there is a danger that it again will become obscured; one can be obscured from seeing clear light for the first time or from being able to see it again. That is why the most profound words in Mahamudra are always "unfabricated," "left natural," and "naturalness." There are many prayer requests made, such as, "May all be unfabricated!" "May all be left natural!" "May all be natural!" "May everything happen on the basis of true nature!" Also, "May all be carefree!" "May all be easy-going and lighthearted!" "May rigpa-awareness hit the mark!" There are many stages of how to make such requests. When we make requests and aspiration in this manner, attachment will naturally fade away. Once attachment is gone, there is no way that we will not see clear light mind. What or who is it that obscures clear light mind? It is attachment that obscures it; therefore, if we wish to see clear light, we need to be free of attachment. If we are free from attachment we can see clear light. In short, the meaning of these words is that if we are attached to our own tenets, view, and practice we will not realize Mahamudra. If we are detached, it helps us to realize Mahamudra. It cannot help us realize Mahamudra if we have attachment. Having realized suchness, the actual mode of being of all phenomena, in order to integrate it, we cannot have grasping attachment for tenets.

Mahasiddha Tilopa says,

Conceptual vows degenerate from the meaning of samaya.

Here, regardless of the words, it all comes down to stopping clinging and grasping. Stopping clinging and grasping implies that clinging and grasping are faulty. Once we develop a grasping concept it acts as a substitute for actual reality, and we are prevented from approaching reality any closer. We become more distant from it. In Omniscient Longchen Rabjampa's *Treasury of the Supreme Vehicle,* he says,

> Some, these days, proud of being ati yogis,
> Claim their mass of concepts is bodhichitta.
> In an expanse of darkness, those deluded ones
> Are, by nature, far from the meaning of Dzogchen.

These deluded ones claim that their discursive thought, their proliferation of thought, all of their concepts are an aid to bodhichitta. Proud of Dzogchen atiyoga practice, they cling to deluded concepts that they say are helpful for bodhichitta. He says they are far from the meaning of Dzogchen. This is similar here. As soon as a grasping concept is present, we are far from the meaning of Mahamudra.

Conceptual vows degenerate from the meaning of samaya. In the general view we must gather an accumulation of merit. We make prostrations before a basis for accumulation of merit, arrange an image of Buddha, an image of the yidam. We make mandala offerings and walk circumambulation routes and practice generosity; there are so many practices according to the general vehicles of the teachings that we must do. Protector Nagarjuna makes the prayer,

> Through this virtue may all beings
> By completing accumulations of merit and wisdom
> Attain the two holy forms
> That arise from merit and wisdom.

To summarize this, from accumulation of merit "with object" the two form bodies are attained. In dependence upon our accumulation of wisdom "without object," dharmakaya, the truth body, is attained. Nagarjuna clearly teaches that the two accumulations of merit and wisdom must precede attainment of the three final resultant kayas. So these are indispensable, according to Tantra as well as Sutra.

So, what is the problem that arises from this? When we practice on the basis of this general view, gathering the accumulation of merit, we say that in dependence upon these accumulations we will become enlightened, right? This becomes an idea that we will attain the state of a buddha if we gather the accumulations. We become very hopeful. We hope to attain the state of a buddha. We hope for the perfect "ultimate," the perfect result. Practice done on the basis of such hope, this kind of aspiring mental engagement, does not engage the essential meaning of Mahamudra and cannot help us to realize it, no matter what we say.

In Sutra there are vows to protect. In Vinaya there are lay vows, novice monk's vows, bhikshu full monk's vows, and so on, each with their respective precepts and vows to protect. In the bodhisattva collection of teachings, also, there are limitless, infinite precepts. In the Bodhisattva Manibhadra chapter of Sutra where they are explained extensively, there are so many bodhisattva vows to protect. In the case of Tantra, there are the root vows, and keeping tantric samaya is greatly emphasized as a very important principle. Samaya also has different levels of profundity in the various levels of Tantra; there are millions in highest yoga tantra. Particularly in the areas of receiving empowerment, repeating mantra, the mandala, and so on, there are profound samayas to protect, respective to practicing the two stages of highest yoga tantra.

In short, there are conceptual vows to protect in Vinaya, Sutra, and Abhidharma and samayas to protect in Tantra, which are alike in that, if we guard our vows and samayas with conceptual grasping, we degenerate from the meaning of Mahamudra. If we ask, do protecting samaya in Tantra and guarding vows in Sutra, in general, act as a cause for attaining supreme liberation, the answer is yes, they do.

14. NOW, BY BEING FREE OF MENTAL ACTIVITY, WE CAN REALIZE REALITY AND TRANSCEND SAMSARA AND NIRVANA

No activity in the mind, free of all desire,

THIS IS THE dharmachakra, the "round of teachings," on being Free of Mental Activity.[44] The dharmachakra Free of Mental Activity is expressed in the dohas. Venerable Marpa of Lhodrag had two gurus, Jina Maitripa and Naropa, and it was primarily from his guru Jina Maitripa that he received the dharmachakra Free of Mental Activity; so this is in lineage from Jina Maitripa to Marpa of Lhodrag.

So what is the dharmachakra Free of Mental Activity? What is Mahamudra practice? It is because Mahamudra practice is the dharmachakra Free of Mental Activity that during the period of it being an ear-whispered lineage it was not set down in writing and was specially passed on orally only to disciples of the highest faculties, wisdom, and good fortune. It was felt that there was a danger that the essential meaning would have been lost if it had been written down. It was suspected that the blessings would be lost. That would seem to be why the essential meaning was passed down only from ear to ear through oral and nonverbal instructions to those of the very highest faculties and was kept sealed under the strictest secrecy. If this essence of practice Free of Mental Activity involves conceptual grasping guarding samaya of Tantra or guarding Vinaya and/or Sutra Mahayana vows, it is said that we degenerate from the essential meaning. We're talking about the essential meaning of Mahamudra. Where is this essential meaning? It is explained in the meaning of "mental nonaction." The essential meaning is taught in the dharmachakra Free of Mental Activity. "No Mental Activity" is the same as the essence-meaning. Briefly speaking, "mind" here refers to conceptual mind, so "mental nonaction" means not paying attention to objects of thought. Simply put, it means not being or becoming an object of thought; not being the focal object of conceptual mind. When something is conceived or grasped, that constitutes "mental activity." Whatever is free of conceptual grasping and apprehension is "nonaction" of the mind, Free of Mental Activity.

No activity in the mind, free of all desire. What is the actual reality of the mind? In general in the world we speak of accomplishing virtue, giving up bad conduct, gathering the accumulation of merit, and so on, but in the context of Mahamudra, these are all to be abandoned. When practicing Mahamudra, since these all involve conceptual grasping they are unnecessary. So, what does this mean?

The more we realize ultimate truth of Mahamudra, the more regard we have for the conventional truth of cause and effect. That is because it is the play of the reality of interdependence. The more we ascertain the meaning of Mahamudra, the more we naturally consider acting in accordance with conventional cause and effect to be an extremely important principle. It does not have to be conceptual, thinking, "Now, I must consider karmic cause and effect." That is not necessary because, in order to use our remedy, there is no benefit in guarding vows with conceptual grasping, creating roots of virtue with conceptual clinging, creating contaminated roots of virtue. If accumulations of merit are gathered with conceptual grasping, some say it will enlighten you—I don't know, but it certainly will not help to realize Mahamudra's meaning Free of Mental Activity. Gathering the accumulation of merit must proceed in conjunction with accumulation of wisdom, otherwise the activity renowned as "gathering merit" in the worldly perspective that is accompanied by conceptual grasping prevents us from practicing the "remedy" in this context, "No Mental Activity."

No activity in the mind, free of all desire. "Free of all desire" means freedom from all desire and grasping. Here, the Tibetan word used for "desire," *zhay dö,*[45] uses these two syllables rather than the usual *dö pa.* The meaning is different, with *zhay* indicating gross grasping, and *dö* indicating subtle grasping. So *zhay* refers to grasping that is extremely gross. Where is such gross grasping? It is the common conceptual grasping we have for things that exist in the world. *Dö* refers to the conceptual grasping we have for virtuous acts that are the cause of liberation and enlightenment. It is a little subtler. Gross conceptual grasping, referred to by *zhay,* is understood to be for worldly objects. Conceptual grasping of the accumulation of merit that acts as the cause for liberation and enlightenment is indicated by *dö.*

So this means being completely free of desire. When we speak of not remaining in the "extreme of freedom from desire," this means a solitary peace, an extreme of nirvana. The "nonabiding nirvana" of full enlightenment does not abide in extremes of samsara or nirvana. What does that mean if we are not abiding in extremes of either samsara or nirvana? It means we have complete equanimity toward all phenomena, that we experience the "many" in "one taste." All phenomena are realized to be equal. When all phenomena are realized to be of one taste it is said that we do not abide in extremes. If we do not abide in extremes of samsara or nirvana, we realize all phenomena to be equal, of one taste. When we realize Mahamudra's "equal taste" of all phenomena, Mahamudra's "single-pointed equanimity," we see all of the teachings without exception. When we arrive at Mahamudra's essential meaning, mind Free of Mental Activity, all desire is naturally pacified, naturally disappears.

An example is given:

Naturally arisen, naturally extinguished, like designs on water,

No matter how much thought goes through our mind we do not need to rid ourselves of it with antidotes. For example, winds on the surface of the ocean will occasionally make different designs; depending on the wind's movements, different designs will emerge in the water, but they disappear even as they arise. The earlier designs keep coming and their later moments keep disappearing, but no design remains. This word translated as "design," *patra,* is Sanskrit. It means design, picture, or drawing, like "drawings on water." Where do these drawings that naturally arise and naturally disappear come from? From where do they arise? They arise from the water. Where do they vanish? They naturally disappear in the water. They are one with the waves, aren't they? Where do those waves come from? From the expanse of the ocean. When they dissolve they also dissolve into the expanse of the ocean. While they exist they are also never separate from the ocean. The waves are the ocean itself, never separate from it. The energetic display or play of the ocean ends up in the waves. All of our good and bad thoughts and perceptions in the nature of the six consciousnesses are like waves. Where do these waves of thoughts come from? They come in dependence upon the deepest nature of our mind, which is Free of Mental Activity. They arise in dependence upon the Mahamudra that is our true nature, the Dzogchen, the Great Perfection that is our true nature. They arise in dependence upon the sphere of reality's actual mode of existence. Therefore, whatever thoughts arise, when we cling to them tightly without recognizing their true nature, we grasp as true the duality of both subject and object and are deceived as to the nature of reflexive awareness. We conceive of objects that are awareness's own reflection to have their own independent objective status and are deceived. We mistake reflexive awareness for self; then duality has begun. If we examine this with logic, if we know how to investigate with logic, thoughts are supportive of dharmakaya equality; thus we must realize that all the thoughts that arise in our mind accompany and support dharmakaya. We need to be able to realize that all thought in our mind arises and is extinguished of its own accord.

Naturally arisen, naturally extinguished, like designs on water. For the yogi who can realize that thoughts are like this, all thought is the manifold display of dharmata, ultimate reality. All thought is the movement of dharmata, is connected with dharmata. The more the wind fans a fire, the stronger the fire becomes until it can burn a whole forest. Similarly, if the yogi develops stable ascertainment that whatever thoughts arise—"arising and subsiding of their own accord, like patterns on water"—arise from and dissolve into the expanse of dharmata, the more thoughts arise, the more they support the yogi's realization of dharmata reality. They are the moving display of dharmata. They give access to dharmata. They boost realization of dharmata. Such a yogi needs to have thoughts!

Thoughts are the magical manifestation of mind. When we recognize that thoughts are the miraculous display of mind, thought becomes supportive of dharmata realization, becomes supportive of virtuous practice. When wind blows on the ocean, designs appear, but they also continually disappear just as soon. Similarly, whatever thoughts arise from the depths, previous thoughts disappear as soon as later thoughts arise. Otherwise, if all thought remained present it would prevent later thoughts from arising, wouldn't it? But that is not the case; as a later thought arises, the previous thought ceases. The root is one's own mind, nothing else. We do not move from that state. We meditate in equipoise on that very realization.

In dependence upon that,

If we do not leave the meaning of nonabiding and nonobservation,

What sort of meaning is it that we remain with here? That of *nonabiding, nonobservation.* This means no object "abiding" and no subjective mind "observing." Where is this object that does not abide? Where is it, what is it?

It doesn't exist. Where is form? Form is not found. Where is sound? Sound does not abide anywhere. Where are scents? Scents do not abide anywhere. Where is taste? Taste does not abide anywhere. Where is tactile sensation? Tactile sensation does not abide anywhere. Where are mental phenomena? They do not abide anywhere. Form, sound, smell, taste, touch, all phenomena, do not abide anywhere. If they existed, mind would have to see them. What mind sees them? When we check for the observing mind, it is not found. Past thoughts have already ceased. Future thoughts are yet to arise. We say that we see the present instant of awareness, but that is just an indication, an imputation by thought; even that moment does not exist. Where is the moment? It is just a figure of speech because when we examine it with more and more subtlety, it is the same as past moments that have already disappeared and future moments that have not yet arisen. The present also does not exist as "a moment" of time. Therefore, if we never leave aside the understanding of this meaning of "no object and no observing mind"; if we reach secure realization of such a meaning, the way things actually are; if we do not leave this state of our ultimate nature, that is called samaya. We should examine the meaning of this word. It is called our samaya, keeping our commitment, if we never move out of awareness of this meaning of "no object, no observer." In the context of Tantra this is said to be the best samaya.

In the general tantric context, in the Kunrik ritual[46] many samaya commitments are explained:

> Do not eat things like meat.
> Actions that harm sentient beings
> Are deeds that should never be done.
> Never abandon the Three Rare Jewels,
> Nor ever give up bodhichitta,
> The essence mantra, the mudra,
> The deity, or the guru.
> Never commit harmful deeds
> Nor ever transgress the guru's teachings.

Likewise, in the context of the Chakrasamvara tantras, Mahamaya, and the *Four Seats,* relying on these deities, each has methods to accomplish the four enlightening activities and methods to accomplish samaya in reliance upon that. However, when giving teaching on the essential meaning here, since it is a combination of the views of Sutra and Tantra, the way of explaining samaya is a more profound one.

There is a metaphor about a "hundred rivers meeting under one bridge." Say there are a hundred rivers that must all go below a bridge. Similarly, many principal and retinue deities are to be generated, there are many generation mantras to be said, practices for accomplishment and great accomplishment to be done. Each deity has many commitments to keep in connection with all of these, but just like a hundred rivers that must all pass under a single bridge, they are all subsumed solely under the essential meaning of "No Mental Activity." Because of that, Mahamudra view is, again, said to be a combination of Sutra and Tantra. In this context it is in accord with *Uttaratantra*.

In what sutras did Buddha explain this? There are twenty-one sutras of definitive meaning. There are the two *Mahaparinirvana Sutras,* the longer and shorter; *The Great Drum Sutra, The Great Cloud Sutra, The Samadhiraja Sutra,* and so on. All of these are sutras that teach the ultimate essence-meaning of No Mental Activity. In particular, the best and most profound source for the teaching on No Mental Activity is found in the highest yoga tantra of nondual father-mother Kalachakra. It is mainly in the jnana chapter of Kalachakra, the chapter on wisdom of deep awareness. It is the same in the *Tantra of the Two Examinations:* the speaker "I," the phenomenon "I," the conscious listener "I," the "I" established by the Teacher of the World, the mundane "I," the transcendent "I," the innate-born "I"—all of these terms come in the teachings on the essence-meaning of No Mental Activity.

If we do not part from the meaning of nonabiding and nonobservation, that is samaya. No object, no subjective mind. Because of this Jetsun Milarepa said,

> My Guru Marpa of Lhodrag says that appearances are not objectively established, that all appearances are nothing but mind. He says that the illuminating mind does not exist; that mind is nothing but emptiness. With even the illuminating mind not truly existent, he pointed out mind's emptiness to me. He pointed out to me the emptiness of emptiness as well: that emptiness is empty of being a solely vacuous nihilistic emptiness; he pointed out spontaneity to me.

Milarepa said that he was naturally liberated from the base by recognizing the quality of spontaneity.

"Appearances are mind. Mind is empty. Emptiness is spontaneous. Spontaneity is naturally liberated." He teaches on the basis of these four "pointing-out" instructions. This is the very same thing. No object exists, no subject observes. It is said in the *Ornament of Sutra* as well,

> Aware there is nothing but mind,
> Then realizing that mind itself is empty,
> The intelligent, aware of the absence of both,
> Abide in dharmadhatu.

This is really talking about the same thing.

If we do not depart from the meaning of nonabiding and nonobservation, the root verse continues,

We don't transgress samaya and are a lamp in the darkness. [11]

He says that this is the samaya. Samaya of what? Of Tantra. It is said to be the best samaya of Tantra. It is the most profound samaya. If we can abide in this meaning of "no object, no observer," we don't need to make any other conscious effort to guard samaya. Jetsun Milarepa expressed this in his *Perfection of Definitive Meaning of the Fivefold [Mahamudra]*:

> Accomplished from all bases, Three Jewels of Refuge,
> Perfected in the state of unfabricated awareness—
> Though we pray to them, it is not necessary!
> How blissful is the yogi, free of mantra repetition!

This is the same thing, again. "Accomplished from all bases, Three Jewels of Refuge." This means that the Buddha Jewel, Dharma Jewel, and Sangha Jewel have primordially been intrinsic to us. It is said that the ultimate Three Jewels is perfectly complete within the state of our unfabricated awareness, complete in the state of the ultimate nature of our mind; its suchness, Free of Mental Activity. The ultimate Three Jewels are not separate from us. That is why we may pray to them but it is not necessary. Generally, for us to claim that we do not need to pray to the Three Jewels of Refuge would be very boastful, wouldn't it. Yet when the essence-meaning teachings on No Mental Activity are given and their ultimate intention is rigorously explained, strictly speaking, that is exactly what Venerable Milarepa saw: that the Three Jewels are complete within the state of our own unfabricated awareness. Without that ascertainment, however, just to say that the Three Jewels are already complete within us and that we don't need to pray to them is incorrect.

We need the deep confidence of realization to be able to say that. Once we have confident realization, stainless understanding, we will be able to have ultimate courage that the Three Jewels are complete within our own unfabricated awareness and that we do not need to pray to them.

"How blissful is the yogi, free of mantra repetition!" He is saying, "I don't need to do recitations or make prayers, don't need to call the guru from afar."

In the context of Tantra there are so many samayas to protect; it is very difficult if we need to guard each and every one. Just think how many deities there are, even in kriya tantra alone! If we have to guard the samaya of each one of them individually it is difficult to keep them all, isn't it? Therefore, the Dharmachakra essence teaching on No Mental Activity is a lamp illuminating the fact that all phenomena are concomitant with dharmakaya equality. These teachings are a repository of all the ultimate teachings; they incorporate all paths; they are the one and only ultimate reality in which all phenomena are finally extinguished. These words come from the *Ten Suchnesses* teachings in the dharmachakra essence teaching on No Mental Activity. If we can really abide by the meaning of such an ultimate meditation, we are keeping the most profound of samayas. *We don't transgress samaya and are a lamp in the darkness.*

Thus, "samaya" is something high. When we speak of not transgressing it, this sets a lower boundary. If we can abide by such a samaya it is said that the samaya does not degenerate or decline. It is said that we do not transgress it. Here Tilopa means that we *cannot* transgress it. It is to this that the word "samaya" applies. In general when we practice a deity we must keep samaya, and it is sometimes possible that the samaya degenerates. For instance, keeping daily recitation and mantra repetition commitments can sometimes be difficult. We forget, don't we? At that point samaya has degenerated a bit. It happens. When the fourteen root downfalls of Tantra are taught, it is rather difficult to keep from transgressing them all. If we can reach the ultimate nature on the basis of the essence teachings on No Mental Activity—no abiding, no observing; arising and subsiding of its own accord like designs on water; free of all desire—if we arrive at this, a realization of the way things are, their ultimate nature, there is no way for samaya to degenerate. At that point, even conduct that is unconscientious cannot harm samaya; mental wandering cannot harm samaya. When we arrive at an understanding of the actual way things are free from fabricated extremes, it is said that we can never transgress our samaya. There is no risk that the transgressions named in Tantra—contradictions, transgressions, degeneration, breakage—will occur. Without such confidence of realization, without having practiced the essence teachings, the dharmachakra of No Mental Activity, even if we think we are keeping samaya, that thought itself is breaking samaya. In which case, just saying "I'm keeping samaya" doesn't help. If we realize how to keep the actual meaning, it is the most profound samaya. Then we are called a lamp in the darkness. Just as holding up a lamp in the darkness illuminates everything, the dharmachakra of No Mental Activity illuminates, makes understandable, the ultimate nature of all phenomena. It is the state, the situation, of the ultimate that is being called a lamp. The darkness referred to is that of conceptual grasping, the desire spoken of above, everything from general craving of samsaric things to the specific subtle grasping of the paths to liberation and omniscience. Darkness in this instance does not mean unknowing or ignorance. *Ma-rig-pa,* "unknowing," is a general term. Here we need a specific understanding of the reference to darkness: conceptual grasping of the attainment of liberation and omniscience, the final unexcelled results; clinging to experiences of bliss, clarity, and nonconceptuality in meditation; any grasping at qualities of the path: that is what is represented by the word "darkness" here. To dispel such darkness we need a lamp. Just as we need to light a lamp to illuminate a dark room, to dispel what is meant by darkness, here we need to internalize the lamp-like ultimate, which is the dharmachakra of Mental Nonactivity. A raised lamp dispelling the darkness is like a lamp of the ultimate that frees us from all desire, with grasping and clinging representing the darkness. Once mental activity occurs, everything has gone dark.

> Free from all desire, if we do not abide in extremes
> We shall see all teachings of the three pitakas. [12]

In general, what we call samsara is grasped as something to be abandoned and nirvana is grasped as something to be attained. Then, in the context of Tantra, there is grasping at deities, grasping at the mantra repetition of deities, grasping at how many mantras we recite.

Similarly there is grasping at lamas, grasping at a lama's instructions, grasping for a lama's blessings. Whether attachment is for deities, gurus, mandalas, whatever, it is not appropriate. What we call attachment and grasping is to be abandoned. "Good" grasping must be abandoned; "bad" grasping must be abandoned. As Jetsun Milarepa sang,

> If entangling binding concepts
> Are gently loosened, we are liberated.

Entangling binding concepts includes all "good" and "bad" concepts. When we say *Free from all desire, if we do not abide in extremes,* this means being free from all attachment and grasping and not abiding in either of the two extremes. What are the two extremes? The extreme of existence and the extreme of nonexistence. Or we can call them the extreme of samsara and the extreme of nirvana. In short, as soon as we have two extremes it is an obstacle.

The root text says, *Free from all desire, if we do not abide in extremes we shall see all teachings of the three pitakas.* The import of this is that we do not need to single-mindedly study all of the three pitakas. As Jetsun Milarepa sang,

Continuously studying all of existence as scripture,
I've never studied one written text.

He says that he studied the whole world as scripture. Even a stone appeared to him as Dharma instructions. If a bird takes off, it is practice. If a fire is lit, it is practice. If there is a waterfall, it is practice. Therefore it is said that appearances are the guru indicating something to us, the guru nonverbally teaching us something. In general it is said that appearances are the nonverbal indications of the guru, and that dharmata reality is the ultimate guru. In saying that appearances are the indicating guru, Milarepa said that everything—childish beings building a house on top of a mountain, trees, rocks, rainbows—all of these are his guru. Each of these has an oral instruction based upon it and an account of its origin. That is why he said that all appearances are his indicating guru, that the whole world and all appearances appear to him in the aspect of the guru, and that he has never studied a printed text. He never experienced the absolute need to memorize a scripture. He never memorized a root text, rocking his body back and forth. Even if we spent our whole lives studying the pitakas, if we can't realize the nature of the ultimate without mistake, it will not help us. It won't help to claim that we are the incarnation of any number of mahasiddhas or great meditators.

What is the principal Dharma knowledge? Being able to correctly apply instructions that are beneficial to our mind. As said in the *Seven Points of Mind Training,*

Hold to the principle of having two witnesses.

Thus we must hold important the idea of being witnessed in all of our actions, which is to say we should mainly proceed on the basis of instructions on the meaning of mind. We need to develop certitude, a definite ascertainment of the meaning of those instructions. If that can happen, *We will see all teachings of the three pitakas.* Even if we spend our whole life studying the pitakas it will not help. There was a geshe who asked Milarepa to give him the general definition of pramana, and the particular definitions of direct perception, inferential cognition, contradictory and related reasons, and reasons that appear but are not ascertained. Milarepa answered,

> I do not know anything about medicine turning to poison
> Or Dharma turning to sin, harming all beings, myself and others!
> But all appearances are decidedly mind and mind is empty clear
> light.
> All of this is not hidden to me,
> There is nothing I must infer through belief!
> If you need contradictory, or appearing but unascertained reasons,
> I have no need to present perfect contradictory reasons,
> Because they are what you constantly put forth!
> Since they are contradictory to the holy Dharma Buddha taught,
> They are the perfect contradictory reasons!
> Since all of your behavior contradicts Dharma,
> It is the perfect presentation of contradictory reasons!
> Contradictory reasoning is the measure of your Dharma practice.
> Since it is all connected with delusion, this is the perfect related
> reason.
> As the delusions in your mind get worse and worse
> And your conduct gets rougher and rougher,
> You appear as the facsimile of a Dharma practitioner!
> Both contradictory and related reasons are complete:
> And that is a reason that appears but you don't ascertain it!

That is the situation. Even if we spend our whole life studying the collections of teachings, it doesn't help—when we meet with some mishap it all falls down. If we practice in reliance upon precepts of practice assisted by the holy guru's instructions, and make the "stake-driving-like" repeated, persistent, focused supplication the way Milarepa relied upon his guru Marpa and the way Naropa relied upon Tilopa, there is no question that these instructions are effective; there is no mistake in the instructions. If we practice texts composed by scholars it is possible we can make a mistake or wrong turn on the path. By making stake-driving-like requests just as was done by someone who has already developed final experiential realization of the profound essential points, when the teachings are given there is no mistake. We need have no doubt about the validity of the instructions. There is a saying, "Not drooling over other instructions." When we see an apple we salivate: we need not salivate over other instructions in this way.

In his *Hitting the Essence in Three Words,* Paltrul Rinpoche says,

> The dividing line between stillness and movement has collapsed.

After we have realized this ultimate mode of existence of the mind it is said that the dividing line between abiding and moving mind collapses, disappears. Right now the dividing line between stillness and movement in our mind has not collapsed. There is a dividing line between stillness and movement: first when our mind is abiding, we say it is abiding, and beyond the boundaries of that abiding, there is another separate time when the mind is moving. Then there is another dividing line with what we call *rigpa,* "awareness." When we arrive at the ultimate practice of the instructions of the essence meaning, these three—abiding, moving, and awareness—are all one. Whatever occurs, whether stillness, movement, or awareness, they all occur in the expanse of dharmata. Their emanation is from the expanse of dharmata. And their cessation is in the expanse of dharmata. The dividing lines between these have collapsed, so to speak. While abiding, emanation can occur; while emanating, abiding can occur. Arising does not contradict abiding; abiding does not contradict arising. Whether abiding or arising occurs, it is all the shifting display of dharmata. If this is all described verbally there is no end to it. But the important point is that they all seem to become one. When that happens we will *see Dharma of the three pitakas without exception.*

Otherwise, there is no benefit in debating the point "The subject, sound, is impermanent, because of being a product" until we are white-haired. To attain omniscience we must give rise to experience of profound states. In Kharag Gomchung's doha, he says,

> There is no end or certainty to conventional words
> Better than that, get the Buddha's intention!
> The holy ones of early monasteries and hermitages
> Thought, "Why not stay alone like the rhinoceros horn?"

"There is no end or certainty to conventional words." They are endless. Even if we spend our whole life learning the pitakas there would be still more; there is much remembered even of Lord Buddha's own three periods of teaching.

"Better than that, get the Buddha's intention!" In connection with the holy guru's instructions, inserting the holy guru's instructions into the depths of our heart and bones, vowing to give up everything to stay on a single seat, praying with driving intensity; when we meditate on this basis it is said that we can "get the Buddha's intention."

"The holy ones of previous monasteries and hermitages thought, Why not stay alone like the rhinoceros horn?" To be able to "see all the pitakas without exception" it won't help the book-scholars to carry around many pounds of scriptures on their backs. If we cannot free ourselves from all desire, if we cannot reach the practice that does not abide in the two extremes, even if we spend our whole life studying the scriptures, we will not "see all of the pitakas without exception."

> **If we mount this meaning, we will be liberated from samsara.**
> **Absorbed in it, all harm and obscuration will be burned.**
> **We are said to be a lamp of the teachings.**

This means "mounting" the ultimate nature of our mind, a lamp free of mental action, a lamp in the darkness, free of all desire, not attending to an object or observer that are like designs on water that arise and subside of their own accord. "Mounting the meaning" means arriving at that meaning. It means to be successful in the practice, not just to be doing the practice. If we can arrive at the full measure of that meaning, if we can experience it, we will be freed from the prison of samsara. Not just aspiring to the meaning of Mahamudra, the ultimate nature of our mind, but on the basis of that aspiration, if we can bring the practice to culmination we will be freed from the great prison of samsaric suffering. *Meditative equipoise on the meaning burns up all harm and obscuration.* "Equipoise" means settling in this meaning or experiencing it. If we absorb ourselves in it or experience it, if we mentally see or experience suchness, or we can say, if we attain stability in it; in fact, the words "attain stability" are good. If we attain such stability, all harm and obscuration will be burned up, consumed. There is no need for accumulating billions of Vajrasattva mantras or using different methods for clearing misfortune. If we have absorbed ourselves in that meaning, it is the panacea, the medicine that heals hundreds of illnesses.

Sometimes Mahamudra is referred to as *kar-po chig-thub,* the "sole able white one." The "sole able white one" is refuted by the Sakyas. They say, "This talk of yours about a 'sole white one that can accomplish everything' doesn't make any sense. Is there refuge at the beginning or not? Is there dedication at the end or not? If they are present, it is not a 'single' able one; it is two able ones." That is how they refute it. What they are talking about is something quite different, however. There exists a rejection of that criticism. This "sole able white one" is terminology used to describe one who has already arrived at the actual nature of reality, the Freedom from Mental Activity taught in Mahamudra instructions, not from the very beginning recitation of refuge, gathering accumulation of merit, and reading about shunyata; these cannot even reach the "sole able white one." So this objection is indeed a case of not comprehending what the "sole able white one" is referring to. In fact, it is like a sole white medicine, a panacea, a single medicine that heals hundreds of diseases. To burn up all bad karma and obscuration, if we had to purify each one individually relying upon separate deities and antidotes, it would take a very long time, wouldn't it? Without need for that, once we have attained stable experience of the ultimate mode of existence of our mind, all harm and obscuration are burned up in a single instant. All negativity and obscuration is consumed in this way.

We are said to be a lamp of the teachings. We become a lamp of Buddha's teachings. In this context "Buddha's teachings" is not referring to Buddha's teachings in general. It is said in the *Ten Suchnesses* that the teachings on No Mental Activity are the essence of Buddha's teachings. So we become a lamp of the essence of Buddha's teachings. Generally there can be many different lamps illuminating Buddha's teachings. Even someone who meditates on impermanence purely is a lamp of the teachings. Anyone who practices refuge purely is a lamp of the teachings. Someone who practices conventional bodhichitta is also a lamp of the teachings.

However, here, "lamp of the teachings" refers to someone who is free of all desire, beyond all extremes, not engaged in mental activity, not grasping at the existence of objects or subjective observing mind; Mahasiddha Tilopa is saying that the yogi who is in equipoise in this state is a lamp of the teachings.

15. Urging of Compassion for Beings Who Have Not Realized It Thus

Silly beings, uninterested in this meaning,

THERE ARE SOME who do not have much faith in the dharmachakra of No Mental Activity, the essence-meaning of mahamudra. Here, Mahasiddha Tilopa does not mean all sentient beings in general but rather some who cling to tenet systems—those with attachment to their own system. There are quite a few such intellectual logicians. Such intransigent stubborn "silly ones" who lack the eye of wisdom

Are always carried away by the river of samsara and finished.

They never get free of the huge ocean of samsara and will experience inconceivable suffering in worse realms of existence. In his *Treasury of Knowledge,* Jamgön Lodrö Taye says,

> Most Tibetan teachers say this is Chittamatra,
> Holding Asanga and his great brother[47] to be somehow inferior.
> The scriptural systems of the two path-blazers are
> The only sun and moon adorning the sky of Buddha's teachings
> So it is correct to give up bias repeating the echoes
> Of constellations of secondary texts, and to practice as they did.

"Most Tibetan teachers say this is Chittamatra": Some Tibetan teachers say that the practice of Madhyamaka Other-Emptiness expounded by the Sakya Gorampa Sonam Senge[48] is of Chittamatrin view and no higher than that, and they swear that is the case throughout both India and Tibet.

"Holding Asanga and his great brother to be somehow inferior": They view Asanga as vastly different from the other great path-blazer, Nagarjuna.

"The scriptural systems of these two path-blazers are the sun and moon adorning the sky of Buddha's teachings": But there is no place to go in the sky of Buddha's teachings except to the scriptural traditions of the two ornaments of Buddha's teachings, Nagarjuna and Asanga. Either we must first take the view of Arya Nagarjuna that principally teaches the profound, or we follow the scriptures of Jina Asanga's lineage of vast conduct. Those two are the sun and moon adorning the sky of Buddha's teachings.

"So it is correct to give up bias repeating the echoes of constellations of secondary texts, and to practice as they did." He is saying that the stacks of other secondary scriptures, like constellations or echoes, are nothing to be particularly surprised or impressed about. But these are the issues over which some become *uninterested*. Why are they uninterested? It is because they don't understand the mahamudra essence-practice of No Mental Activity. When someone has very little merit, wisdom, or effort, many facilitating factors are missing or extremely rare, and many obstructing and contradictory conditions arise, so they cannot develop aspiration for this path.

In the sixth chapter of *Entering the Middle Way* it is said,

> If when someone, even an ordinary being,
> Hearing about emptiness, feels joy rising within,
> And feels their eyes moisten with tears of joy,
> And gets goose bumps all over their body,
> Such a person has the seed of full enlightenment.
> They are a vessel for the teachings;
> The holy truth should be revealed to them.

If someone, even an ordinary being, must have such predispositions to be taught about emptiness, then to practice Mahamudra, someone must definitely have a huge collection of merit, much perseverance, and a great capacity for wisdom. Otherwise, without accumulated merit, it is doubtful these teachings will just come to them in the course of their life.

Even in the case of shunyata, Chandrakirti says in his *Autocommentary*, and I agree, that some previous masters such as Dignaga and Dharmakirti did not realize it correctly. Just being a master scholar does not help. Even to aspire to understand this meaning we need a great causal collection of merit.

Silly beings uninterested in this meaning are always carried away by the river of samsara and finished. In *Uttaratantra* it is said,

Where is liberation for those averse to Dharma?

It is taught that even the five heinous deeds can be purified. If antidotes are used, the five heinous deeds can be purified. Similarly, even when vows and samayas degenerate, the negativity created can be purified by using various antidotes, extensive and abbreviated. In the Vinaya teachings it is said,

With concealment, a "defeat" may not be restored in this life.
Without concealment, it is purified by revealing it.

Thus, even "defeats" of pratimoksha vows can be purified by expressing them. In the *Bodhisattva Pitaka,* also, there are many faults to be avoided but, for the most part, they can all be purified with antidotes if they occur, and there are many methods taught for that. So it is said that liberation exists for all of these. But where is liberation for someone who hates Dharma? In this context *Uttaratantra* says that this applies principally to the essence meaning. It is such a profound instruction on the essential meaning that is inconceivable, free of mental activity and all desire, by which enlightenment may be attained in this very life, in this very body. If someone is not interested in such an essence of Buddha's teachings or disbelieves them, there is no liberation for them, it is said. "Where is liberation for those averse to Dharma?" They *are always carried away by the river of samsara and finished.* The huge river of samsara is always running. We're talking about samsara of the six realms' beings, of course. They are always carried off in the river of samsara by karma and delusion. They are carried off without choice. And the worst thing is that we are talking about a very long period of time, not just for a couple of years.

How pitiful, silly beings suffering unbearably in the worse realms.

In lower realms, inconceivable suffering of the hell, preta, and animal realms is unlimited, severe and compulsory, incessant, and experienced for a very long time. *How pitiful, silly beings suffering unbearably in the worse realms.* Those silly beings experiencing such unbearable suffering are foolish, aren't they? They are indeed foolish. Being uninterested in the excellent teachings of mahamudra, No Mental Activity, if they develop distorted false views about these teachings, that is really foolish, isn't it? It is the most foolish of foolish things you could do. The instructions say they are pitiful. Such beings are an object of compassion, a source of compassion.

In the *Mahamudra Prayer* it is said,

> Though beings by nature have always been buddha,
> Not realizing it, they wander in endless samsara.

This is expressing the same thing. Regarding the nature of beings, if we look at the ultimate nature of beings' minds, all sentient beings have always been buddhas, not "sentient beings."[49] But since they do not recognize the fact that they are buddhas, because of not realizing it, for no reason, they enter into the vast ocean of samsaric suffering. The *Prayer* goes on:

> May we develop irresistible compassion for beings
> Who are experiencing incessant suffering.

As we feel compassion for them, they become a source of compassion.

If we are unable to bear it, want liberation, rely upon a skillful guru,

When there is such suffering it is not at all bearable. The suffering is immeasurable, extreme. Do we wish to be free of such unbearable suffering? Yes we do. Of course, all sentient beings want happiness and don't want suffering. But just crying out, "I need to escape!" "I want freedom!" won't help at all. What do we need to attain liberation? First of all we need a precious human rebirth. Otherwise, there is no possibility of ascending directly from lower realms to liberation. We need to have first escaped the lower realms of existence and attained a good human rebirth, but not just any: one with the freedom and opportunity to practice Dharma. We must meet a qualified holy guru. Then we must practice the good instructions we receive from the guru. In this context what we mean by a skillful guru, a master guru, is not someone who can recite the three pitakas unhindered. It means someone who has freed their own mind, cutting through the whole tangle of doubt by realizing the profound mahamudra teaching of No Mental Activity through the wisdoms of hearing, contemplation, and meditation; one who is capable of compassionately ripening the minds of others. Someone who has freed their own mind through realization and ripens the minds of others through compassion is said to be "auspicious in body and realized in mind." Only such a qualified lama is considered a *skillful* or masterful guru in this context; without such qualities, even if they can recite the entire scriptures backward and forward, they are not said to be skillful. Such a lama who is auspicious in body and realized in mind, whose own mind is liberated through realization and who ripens the minds of others through compassion, this is the *skillful guru*. We must rely upon the blessings of such a skillful guru. Once we have such a lama,

And their blessings enter our heart, our mind will be liberated. [13]

If such a lama's blessing enters our mind we can realize Mahamudra. Liberation must occur through blessing; what we call "blessing" is something essential. As said in the *Prayer,*

> Since esteem and devotion are the "head" of meditation,
> Bless us with the great meditators'
> Unfeigned faith, always supplicating
> The guru who reveals the instructions!

What is referred to here as "esteem and devotion" is something very important. In Jigten Sumgön's *Drigung Doha of Fivefold [Mahamudra Practice]*[50] come the words,

> If the sun of aspiration and devotion does not shine
> On the snow mountain of the guru's four kayas,
> The river of blessings will not flow down.
> Therefore, emphasize the attitudes of aspiration and devotion.

Thus, he gives great emphasis to aspiration and devotion. Lord Buddha himself also said,

> You must have a virtuous spiritual guide! You must venerate him
> or her! You must have faith in him or her!

We need faith. In *Uttaratantra* also, it is said,

> The ultimate truth of self-risen ones
> Is something realized through faith itself.

Thus, self-risen shravakas and pratyekabuddhas also absolutely need faith in order to realize the final ultimate mode of existence of phenomena.

There is a bit of difference between *de pa,*[51] "faith," and *mö gü,*[52] "esteem and devotion." Faith tends to refer simply to belief. Esteem and devotion, on the other hand, at its best, is having decided that the guru is definitely a buddha, feeling that whatever happens to us, good or bad, is the guru's compassion, and that the guru knows everything that happens. If we are able to understand what the guru does and validly uphold what the guru teaches, that is esteem and devotion. Such esteem and devotion as Naropa had for Tilopa, without fluctuation, is a prime example. It is more profound than faith. If we have a skillful guru and have esteem and devotion for them, blessings enter our heart. When Tilopa said, "I, Tilopa, have nothing to teach! If we see ourselves we are liberated!" and slapped Naropa with his shoe and Naropa fell down, it is said that, at that moment, all of the cessations and realizations in Tilopa's mind were imprinted in Naropa's mind, like a *tsa-tsa*[53] printed from a mold. Such a thing happens primarily through blessings.

Blessings do not come through just asking for hand-blessing, and the lama just placing their hand on our head. The lama must be qualified and the disciple must be a qualified vessel with the good fortune and karma for the realization to be awakened. It won't happen without all the causes being present. When we fling a flower during a tantric ritual it is said that we have the fortune to realize the deity upon which the flower falls. The flower falls upon this deity because we have the good karma for it from previous lifetimes, not just because we recite BEDZA MAHA SUKHA. We must have the good fortune and karma for it. The fortune and good karma must also be connected; in the ritual a prayer is made to that effect: May the flower strike that deity for which the disciple has the fortune and good karma! People definitely need such fortune and good karma for a yidam deity.

Therefore, this is what is meant by blessings entering our heart; otherwise just touching foreheads will not help. Neither would it help to just hold a "dharani-thread-vajra"[54] to our heart. Nor can blessing enter our heart just by taking a blessing pill of some kind. What is the best blessing? It is based upon one whose own mind is liberated through realization and who liberates the minds of others through compassion, meeting a disciple with an infinite accumulation of merit and powerful perseverance as well as very skillful wisdom. When these two meet together, that is when we can talk about *blessings entering our heart.*

There is the prayer,

> May I never misperceive the liberated life
> Of the glorious guru for even an instant.
> With esteem and devotion for all the guru does,
> May the guru's blessing enter my mind.

Here, again, the guru's blessing entering our mind depends upon the previously mentioned conditions being met. We say, "May I never misperceive the liberated life of the glorious guru for even an instant." It is also said,

> Whatever deeds the guru exhibits,
> Always honoring them with wondering aspiration
> And never thinking of them as faulty,
> May I always see the benefit of the guru's deeds.

Whatever good or bad deeds the guru appears to do, it is all necessary for controlling beings. We need to understand that the guru's every deed is essential to subdue beings. Even if they had a fault from their own side it would not make the slightest difference; and while we are training on the path we need to keep the view that everything the guru does is necessary in order to subdue trainees. Even if they killed someone it would be in order to subdue trainees; if they drank beer and liquor it would be in order to subdue trainees; even their laughter is for the sake of subduing trainees: this is the kind of thinking to sustain. When we think along these lines we will never develop mistaken ideas about what the guru does and we will see all they do as excellent.

The guru's blessing enters our heart on the basis of perceiving all they teach as valid. Otherwise, having esteem and devotion for the guru when the guru is nice but disliking the guru when the guru scolds us a bit is called the "devotion of an ordinary being." It won't work. We have good examples to look at, don't we, in how Naropa related to Tilopa, and how Milarepa related to Marpa. It is a good example of an unbroken lineage. Like the beads of a mala, each lineage guru is glorious. They don't hold the lineage of the mere words but the lineage of the meaning, the real lineage. The real lineage depends upon the lineage holder becoming a guru whose "own mind is liberated through realization and who ripens the minds of others through compassion"; it is not very powerful or beneficial to just give a transmission and commentary and consider that the lineage. The actual lineage is on the basis of the process described above. Mahasiddha Tilopa is saying that if blessings enter our heart in this way *our mind will be liberated*. Blessings enter our heart for the reasons stated above. When they enter our heart our mind will be liberated; we will "attain" or "realize" our own mind; we will be able to realize the meaning of Mahamudra, the meaning that can free our mind from the dust of unknowing. He is saying that our mind is liberated from craving and clinging, that we can be liberated from all craving and grasping, gross and subtle.

16. The Essential Meaning of This

Kye ho! These samsaric things are the cause of meaningless
    suffering.
Since fabricated things lack essence, look at the essential meaning!
Beyond all subject-object duality is the king of views.
If we have no distraction, it is the king of meditations.
If we exert no effort, it is the king of action.
If we lack hope and fear, the fruit will manifest. [14]

Kye ho! *These samsaric things are the cause of meaningless suffering. Since fabricated things lack essence, look at the essential meaning!* To comment on the first two lines, when we say *kye ho!* it is a cry of distress arising out of insufferable compassion seeing that the suffering experienced in samsara is so unbearably intense, of such long duration, and so lacking in all meaning. A similar expression in Tibetan is *ah ka ka.* Why do we have compassion? Because *samsaric phenomena are the cause of meaningless suffering.* Samsaric phenomena also include contaminated virtue; it need not necessarily be just attachment, aversion, and ignorance. All contaminated virtue is also samsaric. Any phenomenon that has grasping ignorance is included in samsaric phenomena, and samsaric phenomena are the cause of meaningless suffering.

Since fabricated things lack essence, look at the essential meaning! How many rebirths have we taken in beginningless samsara up to the present? How many lives, how many enemies have we subdued, how many friends have we cultivated? How much have we done out of delusion, out of attachment and aversion? Yet we have never been able to finish it. We continue it even now, but there is never a point at which such work is finished. There is never a point at which worldly samsaric work is finished.

Why are compounded things *essenceless*? Because there is no benefit in them. Controlling enemies and cultivating friends cannot achieve any essential purpose; that is why such work is essenceless. So what has essence? When Mahasiddha Tilopa says to *look at the essential meaning,* he means to look at the actual mode of existence of phenomena, the ultimate nature of things. He is saying, "Look at the essence of your mind! Look at how your mind actually exists!" In other words, "Engage in Mahamudra practice! Engage in Dzogchen practice! Engage in Great Madhyamaka practice!" He is saying to investigate the mind. That is what he means by *Look at the essential meaning!* and not at any samsaric contaminated virtue; he is saying that this is of no benefit.

Samsaric phenomena, again, are not just thoughts of attachment, aversion, and ignorance, but all contaminated virtue also. Any virtue that is not connected with practice of the union of luminosity and emptiness, luminosity-emptiness yuganaddha—for instance virtue that goes to an extreme of emptiness devoid of compassion, and vice versa, compassion without emptiness—all such practices are included in samsaric phenomena, phenomena that perform a samsaric function.

Since fabricated things lack essence, look at the essential meaning! What is this essential meaning to look at? He says that the *king of views* is *beyond all subject-object duality.* So it must transcend duality. If it transcends duality it is the king of views. That is the essential meaning that Tilopa tells us to look at. If we practice that suchness, that meaning itself, if we experience it, the essential meaning of mahamudra No Mental Activity, if we practice the ultimate mode of existence of our own mind free of all grasping and clinging, it is beyond external objects and beyond inner grasping mind; we call it nonmanifest, unobserved. These are the same. Since no object whatsoever exists, apprehended objects are noninherently existent. Since no mind perceives or observes, apprehending mind is noninherently existent. Correctly immersing ourselves in actual suchness *beyond all subject-object duality,* he says, is the *king of views.* Out of many views or perspectives, it is the king, the pinnacle of all views; he says that this is transcendent conduct, practice that transcends subject-object duality. If we arrive at the ultimate mode of existence released from subject-object duality, this is the king of views.

If we have no distraction, it is the king of meditations. So the king of views was explained as nonduality. If we can attend correctly to that view realizing suchness free from duality, *without distraction,* that is the *king of meditations. If there is no distraction, it is the king of meditations.*

We need undistracted conduct. In the short *Vajradhara Lineage Prayer*[55] it is said, "Since nondistraction is actual meditation." We need conduct that is undistracted. We need to be undistracted, to maintain undistracted mindfulness. *If we have no distraction, it is the king of meditations.* Such a king of views is beyond all subject-object duality. If we can apply ourselves to this ultimate view of the actual nature of our mind beyond duality, correctly and without distraction, it is the king of meditations.

Holding "with mode of apprehension mindful, free of distraction" does not mean just remaining in that view. Being undistracted means to continue to induce the experience. We are introduced to the view at some point, and having been introduced to it we need to explore it continuously, repeatedly, and develop deep conviction in it. That is what is meant by being undistracted.

In Sutra, after having realized truth of dharmata directly on the path of seeing of the first-stage bodhisattva, one must then proceed to meditate on the second stage and so on. One must proceed through all nine stages of the path of meditation. Thus, in Sutra contexts as well, it does not help just to recognize the king of views realizing without mistake the suchness that is the ultimate mode of existence of phenomena. One must continue to meditate on it without distraction again and again, with the aid of much scriptural citation, reasoning, and oral instructions. That being the case, in general consideration of the two types of meditation, the solitary meditator's placement meditation and the great pandit scholar's analytical meditation, this is done primarily on the basis of the former, the *kusali,* or solitary meditator's, placement meditation. In kusali placement meditation we make the stake-driving-like supplication to the guru, set aside all analysis of scripture and reasoning, and meditate with faith and conviction in exactly what the guru has instructed. That is the king of meditations free of distraction.

If we exert no effort it is the king of action. Ja-tsol, "effort," is short for activity and effortful accomplishment or effortful action. It refers to prostrations and other virtues that are contaminated due to conceptual effort grasping at inherent existence. Having hope for results, hope for return, hope for maturation, hope for attainment of good qualities, hope for elimination of bad faults, hope for attainment of all good meditative experience and all good realizations, hope for elimination of all bad thoughts and delusions: these are said to be "effortful action," connected with action and effort. Here, Tilopa teaches us that we need a view and meditation that are free of such effortful action. He is teaching us that if we act and exert ourselves on the basis of a pure view and meditation that is free of such conceptual effortful action, that is *the king of action.*

We need to be like a bird flying through space. When a bird is soaring through the sky it is completely free of anxiety and terror. It is said that we need to be like a fish gliding through the water or a bird flying through the sky, without stress or fear. In this way effortful action is transcended; in the language of Dzogchen, we have "awareness beyond intellect" and many terms similar to Mahamudra—"free of effort," "absence of effortful action." In Dzogchen comes the term "awareness gone to the limit," or "culmination of awareness." Tilopa is saying that when awareness reaches such culmination, it is the king of action.

If we lack hope and fear, the fruit will manifest. We must be free of hope and fear in all of these. Who has hope and fear? In all three of these—the king of views that is beyond duality, the ability to cultivate the king of meditations without distraction, and the king of actions transcending all effortful action (intellect not clinging to anything, no object observed)—we must be free of hope and fear. No hope of attaining good view, meditation, and action; no fear of losing good view, meditation, and action. Without hopes and fears we don't have anxiety and paranoia, do we? Tilopa teaches us here to be without hope and fear like a lion going wherever it wants, like a fish gliding through water, like a bird soaring through space.

If we lack hope and fear the fruit will manifest. Venerable Milarepa sang,

> I, Milarepa, am not afraid of ghosts!
> If Milarepa was frightened by ghosts,
> "Realizing ultimate truth" would not mean much!

And,

> Having realized elemental mind, ghosts do not scare me.
> If ghosts scared me after realizing elemental mind,
> Staying on high boulders would have little meaning.

He is not talking about just sitting up on high rocks, of course, but the work he was doing there, manifesting all resultant realization, transcending all views, all meditation, and action.

Twelvefold "nailing"[56] is taught: three nails of view, three nails of meditation, three nails of action, and three nails of result. In the Yolmo Gangra doha[57] on the nails of view, meditation, and action, Milarepa sings,

Among the three nails, it is oneself who is nailed,
The nail itself is dharmata emptiness,
And the one doing the nailing is the holy guru.

When we practice on the basis of the twelvefold nailing—three nails of the view of dharmata reality, three nails of meditation, three nails of action, and three nails of result—the most excellent nail is dharmata emptiness. The nailer is the precious guru. The one nailed is ourselves. The result of having been thus nailed, Milarepa says, is absence of fear. He lost himself. When we are free of hope and fear in this way, the result manifests.

Beyond observed objects, mind's nature is luminous.
With no path to travel, keeping to the buddha path,
Accustomed to no object of meditation,
One attains unexcelled enlightenment! [15]

Beyond observed objects, mind's nature is luminous. Here, "observed" in general means clung to as inherently existent—not simply observed, as the word implies, but rather clinging to the object as inherently existent. When objects are grasped to inherently exist, there is attachment to them. When we transcend clinging to inherent existence, it is said that we are "beyond observed objects." What is not clung to as inherently existent? In the context of Secret Mantra it is meditation on the deity, recitation of the mantra, focusing on the mandala, generation of the five manifest enlightenments, the many meditations on the deity mandala and celestial mansion; all of these should not be grasped as inherently existent. This does not mean just clinging to the inherent existence of external objects of form, sound, scent, taste, and touch, but to the internally generated deity, recited mantra, supporting residence and so on; these are the meditations indicated here, that are "not observed," not clung to as inherently existent. In this way we "go beyond" observed objects, we "escape from the midst of objects," we "transcend observed objects," we are "without observed objects." When we say "transcend," it means we have gone beyond them. Then we are perfected; the paramita is attained.

There is nothing to engage within observed objects. We must transcend them. If we transcend all such clinging to objects it is unsuitable for us to then remain always meditating on the deity and reciting mantra as we did before. It is the same even for emptiness meditation. If we grasp emptiness meditation as inherently existent, it is attachment. Grasping emptiness as inherently existent, grasping impermanence as inherently existent, grasping selflessness as inherently existent, grasping the sixteen emptinesses as inherently existent, grasping the inconceivable secrets of Buddha's body, speech, mind, qualities, and activities as inherently existent, we become attached to all of these objects. Therefore, to be free from all extremes, we must transcend conceptual clinging not only to the extreme modes of existence of gross objects but even to such subtle objects as these.

That is how we *transcend observed objects.* Mahasiddha Tilopa says that if we transcend observed objects, *the mind's nature is luminous.* What is meant by "mind's nature" here? It should be understood to mean "objectless." He is saying that because there is no object observed, the nature of the mind is illumined, is clarified. When we speak of "objectless view," "objectless meditation," "objectless practice," "objectless deity meditation," "objectless mantra recitation," "objectless emptiness meditation," "objectless bodhichitta meditation," "objectless love," "objectless compassion," "objectless samadhi," and so on, all of these refer to this "objectless" nature of the mind. When the meaning of being "objectless" becomes clear, that is the nature of our mind. In this context it is not correct to think that "nature" is equivalent to "ultimate mode of existence"; here, *nature of the mind* means "beyond observed objects" or being "objectless." In *Discriminating Dharmata* (*Dharmadhar-matavibhanga*) four applications are taught:

1. application to observation;
2. application to nonobservation;
3. application to not observing objects; and
4. application to observing nonobservation.

This context calls for the second application, application to nonobservation. If the nature of the mind—described as the mode of existence of the ultimate nonobservation, the ultimate suchness of nonobservation, or the mode of existence of the suchness of nonobservation—manifests, if it becomes clear, that is the luminosity Tilopa speaks of here. The Tibetan *sel*[58] here does not mean "clear," as in normal usage when we say that something is clear. Rather it refers to the clear nature that is experienced when the perfect state of awareness manifests and is perfectly and definitely experienced.

So what is the nature of the mind? The nature of the mind is "nonobservation." We arrive at nonobservation when we transcend all observed objects. First there is observation. Observing objects, we become bound by good instructions. Then we arrive at nonobservation when understanding of nonobservation's view, meditation, and action is induced. It is like what Shantideva speaks of,

> When neither existence nor nonexistence
> Remain before the mind,
> Without any other aspect,
> There is complete peace of nonobservation.

Thus when we say that *the nature of the mind is luminous,* it means that the nature of the mind is "nonobservation." When this is clarified at the basic level we transcend objects and the nature of mind appears.

At the path level he says, *With no path to travel, keeping to the buddha path.* At the basic level we need to visualize or get a picture of what is being said. At the basic level we need the ultimate mode of existence of the mind pointed out to us. At the basic level we need to reach secure realization of the ultimate. When we reach that, there is *no path to travel* and we *keep to the buddha path.* If we can clearly experience the meaning of nonobservation, then there is no path to travel. Tilopa is saying that there is no need for the five Hinayana or Mahayana paths, no need for a path to travel, that there is no path to travel. However, in saying that there is no path, he is saying that all paths to be traveled are transcended, not that there is no path at all to be traveled in general. In saying that there is no path to be traveled, he is saying that we go beyond paths to be traveled, that we transcend paths to be traveled. We have to make this distinction between the general and specific meaning because otherwise we deny the existence of all spiritual development. When we say there is no path to be traveled, on what basis do we say that? The basis is "nonobservation." Once we have secure realization of it, the person with such realization is said to be beyond paths to be traveled. Venerable Milarepa sang,

> No meditator, nothing to be meditated upon,
> No place to go, no path at all,
> No resultant kaya-bodies, no jnana-wisdoms
> Therefore there is no nirvana.

What is all of this negation about? It is not a general denial of the existence of all of these things. It must be applied to a specific meaning as opposed to a general statement. To whom does no path appear? In whose perspective does no resultant state exist? For someone who has already attained secure realization of the state of nonobservation, who has transcended all grasping at the inherent existence of phenomena, who has understood the suchness that is the ultimate mode of existence, who has fully understood the meaning of nonobservation: for such a person there exists no basis, path, or fruit to be attained. This distinction must be made because if it is asserted to be a general statement about existence and nonexistence, there could be no explanation of a view to be understood. In the context of Madhyamaka in particular this is an important point to refute. That being the case, it is an important principle in Madhyamaka that there are three types of occasions: times when we are not checking or investigating at all, times when we are lightly investigating, and times when we are intensely investigating. None of the assertions in the system of Madhyamaka about transcending viewed objects, transcending fabricated objects, or transcending objects grasped as inherently existent are blanket statements refuting existence in general.[59] And out of those of supreme, middling, and least faculties who have developed the view in their mind, it is those of supreme faculties who transcend observed objects, who securely realize nonobservation. It is such a person who has no need of basis, path, or resultant state. This kind of description of stages is necessary because if we were to say that there is no view, meditation, and action for all practitioners of Mahamudra, that would be extending the pervasion too far.

With no path to travel, keeping to the buddha path. Therefore there is no path of small, middling, or great vehicles. There is no need for the five paths, the ten grounds, and so on. Milarepa sang,

> Mahamudra cuts through all with one path.
> The ignorant are deceived counting paths.

He says that there is one path to take in Mahamudra. Again, he is speaking about those of highest faculties. It does not apply to those who progress by stages, only those who attain all at once. Since he is speaking of the practice of those of highest wisdom and faculties, he says that there is one path to take. Having realized the sole ultimate mode of existence of phenomena, one has already understood all phenomena; there is no need to consider the five paths and ten stages. That is why he speaks of the ignorant being deceived by numerous paths and stages.

So this is the context in which it is said that there are no paths to count, no paths such as those of the Hinayana to travel, only the path to buddhahood. Keeping to that, we can reach the valid path to enlightenment, we can reach a secure realization of the buddha path.

When we say "buddha," most of us feel that it must be someone with a crown protrusion and lotus markings on their feet, but that is not the case. If we manifest the ultimate mode of our mind, that is buddha. When the ultimate nature of our mind is not manifest, we are a sentient being, a limited, suffering being. By reaching a secure realization of the ultimate mode of existence of our mind, when we are introduced to our actual mind, we are buddha. While not introduced to our actual mind we are a sentient being. Apart from this distinction, it is not absolutely necessary for us to always think of someone with a crown protrusion and lotus feet when we speak of buddha.

About someone like Venerable Milarepa it is said,

Because he attained buddhahood in a single lifetime
Just hearing his name draws forth the liberating path.

His is an example of buddhahood being attained in one body in a single lifetime.

Accustomed to no object of meditation, one attains unexcelled enlightenment! Tilopa is saying that since there is no meditation, there is no object of meditation. There is no phenomenon of "meditation." Teaching something like Mahamudra meditation, if we had to explain, "The phenomenon of meditation is like this, the object of meditation is like this, Mahamudra is like this, Dzogchen is like this, Madhyamaka is like this," there is no explanation we could give. It is something that is beyond all extremes. Within the sphere of all fabrication of subject and object being totally pacified, there is no object to be meditated upon.

Therefore, when we accustom ourselves to just that absence of meditation or object of meditation, there is no meditation. When we are in "nonmeditation," since there is no meditation, there can be no object of meditation. If there is meditation, there will be an object of meditation. What we call meditation is just imputed by thought and exists only within interdependence, so we can understand that in actuality meditation does not exist. Therefore, when we analyze with logic it is emptiness; there is no meditation. This is not an assertion or tenet but the ultimate to which all those of highest wisdom and faculties are introduced, the ultimate that they stably realize by meditating with driving intensity on the guru's oral instructions, when their karma of vast Dharma training from previous lives is awakened. When someone like that is introduced to the deepest mode of existence of their mind they can realize what is meant by "nonmeditation." Without going through every line of reasoning individually, this is why pure awareness does not engage in meditation, why meditation is not necessary. It does not need to be based in scripture and logic. In general we do need scripture and logic but we do not need to rely upon them for the singular, decisive, self-sufficient path of Mahamudra.

Therefore there is *no object of meditation.* If there is no meditation, there can be no object of meditation. Tilopa is saying that if we can *accustom* ourselves repeatedly *to the absence of* meditation and *an object of meditation* we can *attain unexcelled enlightenment.* What does this mean? He is saying that if we cling to the existence of the "three spheres" of meditation—meditator, meditation, and object of meditation—that is not meditation. The state of unexcelled enlightenment is not attained through it. That is why we must go beyond all objects of meditation. Therefore, when the three sets of four applications of mahamudra are taught, when "single-pointedness," "freedom from fabrication," and "single taste" reach culmination, it is called the "kingdom of dharmakaya without meditation." The state of buddha is referred to as being "without meditation"; it is not the "kingdom of dharmakaya with meditation." Venerable Milarepa also spoke of the "kingdom of dharmakaya being without meditation" because "meditation and objects of meditation are destroyed."

A previous Drugpa Kagyu lama said that he was going to do the three-year, three-month retreat. He went to a cave, but after he had been there only a day he came out. When he was asked why he had not stayed in retreat for the allotted time he replied,

> I had planned to stay for three years and three months but after
> a little meditation I realized that "three years" is just a word,
> imputed by concept. It was pointed out to me that the "medita-
> tion" I was going to do for three years was also just a convention
> and that actually there is nothing to meditate upon, no medita-
> tion to do at all! So I came out!

That is the kind of understanding that we have when we realize through familiarity what "no object of meditation" means. As Venerable Milarepa said, "because meditation and object of meditation are destroyed," there is no phenomenon upon which to meditate, no "mind of a meditator." For this reason, when we realize the emptiness of the three spheres of meditation—agent, action, and object of meditation—we say that there is "no object of meditation."

This is also the meaning of the term "great meditation of nonmeditation." If we get used to it we will attain unexcelled enlightenment. If we can induce definite understanding of the objectless, absence of self-nature, no meditator, no meditation, no object of meditation, we will attain buddhahood, the ultimate bliss of unexcelled enlightenment.

So at the basic level it is beyond observed objects, at the path level it is beyond any path to travel, and at the resultant level, without object of meditation, enlightenment is attained. Thus the meaning is applied at base, path, and resultant levels.

17. HOW TO PRACTICE THIS

Kye ma! Worldly things cannot be well checked
Or analyzed, like illusions or dreams.
Dreams and illusions do not exist in actuality,
So, disillusioned, give up worldly activity.
Sever attachment and aversion to entourage and land.
Staying alone in the forest, meditate in retreat.
Abide in the state of nonmeditation.

WHEN WE SAY *Kye ma!* it is a sign of distress. When we have already manifested actual Mahamudra it is natural to have compassion for sentient beings who have not. Generally, when the practice of combined emptiness and compassion is taught, compassion is developed in dependence on emptiness and emptiness is generated in dependence upon compassion; the two are deeply related. Development of compassion in dependence upon emptiness is especially emphasized. Once we have understood the view of emptiness, we will naturally develop compassion.

Emptiness is the ultimate mode of existence of all phenomena. Once we have realized it, we have realized our own ultimate nature and we will feel sad for all sentient beings who have not realized it and who do not take an interest in emptiness, the true nature of their mind, or Mahamudra practice. They are completely mistaken about the true nature of things; their attitude is completely opposite to the actual way things exist. Therefore, when we meditate on compassion for them, pure compassion arises. When we say, "Too bad, he has a headache!" it is not completely pure compassion unless we have this kind of awareness. It is an ordinary kind of compassion, like when we say, "He is broke. I need to give him some money." Ordinary compassion is compassion that wishes to dispel only temporary suffering; there is no particular connection between it and emptiness. There is also the risk that it is conceived as truly existent.

As said in the *Commentary on Valid Cognition,* in the chapter proving Buddha's validity,

> Since love and the like do not contradict ignorance
> They do not destroy tremendous faults.
> That which is the root of all faults
> Is the view of the disintegrating collection as a self.

Now we know that love is not contradictory to wisdom realizing emptiness. In this context, by developing compassion in dependence upon wisdom realizing emptiness, compassion and emptiness become a unified pair. Thus, having perfectly realized our own Mahamudra nature, we feel compassion for all sentient beings who have not realized it.

When we generate the mandala in Heruka ritual we say,

> For samsaric beings who have not realized truth of Dharma,
> Having manifested dharmata-reality myself,
> I shall enable them to realize profound suchness.

All sentient beings are buddha but, not realizing the truth of Dharma, they remain circling through samsara. This time, when we put forth the effort to understand the meaning of profound emptiness taught in Heruka tantra, through the power of that we will become able to bring all sentient beings into that understanding. Thinking this, we generate bodhichitta before going on to generate the mandala. When we contemplate the procedure in the tantra itself, it also begins with the *Kye ma!* exclamation. This is not just a poetic device.

Worldly things cannot be well checked. In general when we say "the world" or "the universe," it is something incredible, inconceivable, infinite, something beyond intellect. However, in this context the reference is to samsaric work. Samsaric work is for the sake of many things: subduing enemies, cultivating friends, name and fame, material gain, power, impressing others. When condensed, samsaric activity can all be included in attachment, aversion, and ignorance. What are samsaric phenomena? Without choice, being continuously driven and controlled day and night by attachment, aversion, and ignorance to subdue enemies, cultivate friends, and so on, always tormented by delusion, sources of suffering and their results, experiencing immeasurable suffering of the three realms. When we speak of checking and investigating them well, can we do that? Tilopa says *worldly things cannot be well checked,* that they are *like a dream or illusion.* He says that they cannot be investigated, that there is no investigating all those samsaric phenomena. That is because, when we check, they are not to be found. The more we check them the more we can see that these worldly phenomena are insubstantial; they are void; they are vain and lacking any essence. In Madhyamaka, because of the fact that they cannot be investigated, it is said that conventional phenomena "cannot bear" investigation by logic. It is also said that there is no need to investigate conventional phenomena with logic. If conventional phenomena are subjected to logical analysis the investigated phenomena are not found, so it is said that they cannot bear logical analysis, that they cannot be investigated with logic.

It is said,

> What you assert, the reality of impermanent phenomena,
> I do not accept even conventionally.
> But because they produce results, although they don't exist,
> I assert that which is accepted in the world: that they do exist.

The acceptance of phenomena as they appear to others, as in Madhyamaka philosophy, is equally applicable here. When we speak of conventional phenomena accepted in the world, such as that Lord Buddha and the bodhisattvas emanated in this world, that they exhibited deeds such as the twelve major deeds, miracles, and inconceivable activities; all of this is accepted by others. The world accepts the existence of these. When these are subjected to ultimate logical analysis, however, and their deepest mode of existence is explained precisely, no deed in the world exists to be investigated.

Again, as said in *Entering the Middle Way,*

> If, when explaining just this suchness
> Other texts are refuted, there is no fault.

When ultimate truth is explained in a precise, strict manner, that Dharma will in no way accord with worldly Dharma. When ultimate truth is the primary topic and it is strictly presented, it will never agree with the worldly view. The worldly view is just mistaken about conventional phenomena. To the world, all conventional phenomena are true, inherently existent, existing by way of their own characteristics or definitions. When their ultimate nature is precisely and strictly explained, they cannot be investigated, their entities do not exist. Their causes are unobserved, their results are unobserved, and their entities are unobserved; therefore, conventional phenomena cannot be analyzed. When the root of the mind is investigated, all phenomena of the world cannot be analyzed, so it comes down to the same meaning. This is because the whole world is emanated by the mind. All activity is the miraculous emanation of the mind. That is why the more we investigate the mind in Mahamudra practice, the more we can see the essencelessness of samsaric phenomena. For example, if we try to take mind out of the equation and ask, "Is a cup truly existent as it appears to that perspective that feels it is externally objectively established?" the answer must be no, the cup is not truly existent. Examination of externals alone is not valid and does not serve a valid purpose; we cannot progress on the path in that manner.

Now there is a general difference in explanation between these instructions and Madhyamaka. In Madhyamaka a lot of time is spent thinking and investigating all phenomena with logic, instead of first seeking out elemental mind and then explaining that all phenomena lack inherent existence. In this context the yogi first investigates and settles the nature of elemental mind. From the very first there is explanation of

The yogi who has severed reification from the mind.

For the yogi who has already severed reification from the mind, all appearances of samsara and nirvana that arise are miraculous emanations of the mind, the display of the mind itself, so they need not be investigated; they all lack inherent existence, are not established by way of their own character, have no entity, no cause, no result. In this way reification in the mind is stopped from the beginning. By investigating the root of the mind we can understand that all phenomena lack inherent existence. In Madhyamaka it is more a case of applying emptiness to each specific phenomenon in turn. When a trainee's faculties are at the very highest level it will be explained from the beginning that objects are not inherently existent and that therefore the grasping mind is also not inherently existent; and then, since both subject and object are noninherently existent, the yogi abides in the sphere of reality, dharmadhatu. In Madhyamaka the paths are explained one by one like this. Mahamudra is *chig chöd*, "simultaneous" or "of a single stroke," which is why it provides instructions given from the very beginning by which even a serious criminal could be forcefully enlightened. All of this involves introduction to our own illumination, the luminosity of our own mind: looking at our own mind from the very beginning, investigating and determining the nature of our own mind, eliminating reification from our mind.

When the teacher who gives us the instructions to look at our actual mind, to investigate our mind, says, "Look at the essence of your mind!" the teacher has the disciple investigate the comings and goings of their own mind, and through that investigation, when the disciple sees their mind's essence, they recognize that all the various appearances of samsara and nirvana are its own display, that all the various appearances of samsara and nirvana are miraculous emanations of mind. When we recognize that the various appearances of samsara and nirvana are mental imputations and the reflexive display of mind, that is the point at which we understand the reason it is said all phenomena of samsara and nirvana cannot be investigated, cannot be conceived. So the mode of procedure in Madhyamaka is a bit different. In this case when we say phenomena cannot be investigated we do not mean that they cannot be investigated by logic. Rather, reification is first removed from the mind. Having already thoroughly investigated the mind, we can then understand that the various appearances of samsara and nirvana are the miraculous emanations of mind. That is the mode of procedure that must be followed here. When that is understood, then no matter how much we attempt to analyze the mode of appearance of worldly phenomena and worldly phenomena themselves, we cannot investigate them, we find nothing to think of. Why not? Because they are like dreams and illusions. One hundred and twelve similes are given in Sutra to illustrate the illusory nature of all phenomena. For instance, in the initiation ritual of Gyalwa Gyatso, the parallel is used of the reflection of Vajradhara in a clear mirror. Examining the reflected image, we see it does not arise from anywhere and does not abide anywhere around the mirror, in front, in back, and so on. Then it goes on with the example of the Sanskrit alphabet or other sounds being proclaimed in the proximity of a rock wall and an echo being heard. Examining the echo, we see sound has indeed been sent outward, but there is no one really calling back. There is extensive use of such figures illustrating that phenomena appear yet are empty, lacking inherent existence. Again, all of this proceeds on the basis explained above.[60]

In short, appearances are like illusion, like dream, like a city of the gandharvas and so on. Many of these examples are mentioned in Nagarjuna's *Sixty Verses on Reasoning*. Like dreams, like a city of gandharvas, conventional phenomena are false, hollow, lacking an essence. Another verse speaks of the lack of inherent existence in all production and abiding:

> A city of confusion and inexhaustible beings
> Appear like a mirage.

Beings appear like a mirage, an illusion, a dream, a city of the gandharvas. We usually say, "All phenomena are not truly existent; for example, your dream," putting forth dream as an example of phenomena not being truly existent. In the present context, however, for the yogi who has already stopped reification in the mind it is not absolutely necessary to present the example of dream. Daytime appearances can exemplify illusion just as well as dreams. Daytime appearances are "the dream" in fact; there is no dreamlike quality to be sought somewhere else. While training on the path, however, the example of dream or something similar is needed. Whether or not we use all eight illusion-like examples, the example of dream is indispensable.

Why the figure of dreams and illusions? To illustrate something that does not actually exist, that is not real. It is said, *Dreams and illusions do not exist in actuality*. Dreams and illusions are similar. Having said that, dream and illusion are put forth as examples, but if we think about it, in actuality, this means that dreams and illusions themselves do not exist. If we were to think otherwise, that dream and illusion are examples but they somehow exist, that would be mistaken. This is not saying that dreams and illusions exist. Just as dreams and illusions are essenceless, all worldly phenomena are essenceless. The meaning here, again, is that dream and illusion are put forth as analogies but when we investigate the reality of the situation, dreams and illusions also are not real. Fire arises from two sticks rubbing together, then that fire consumes the two sticks. Having consumed the two sticks, the fire finally goes out naturally; no fire remains afterward. Similarly, having decided that purportedly self-defining characteristics are noninherently existent, the characteristics of the example must also disappear. That is why it is said, *Dreams and illusions do not exist in actuality*.

What does it mean that dreams and illusions do not exist in actuality? It means they do not ultimately exist, that they have no intrinsic identity; that they do not exist in the sphere of reality, dharmadhatu. That goes for both the meaning and the examples. Just as dreams and illusions do not exist in actuality, all worldly phenomena have no intrinsic identity, do not exist in dharmadhatu, do not ultimately exist; that is what "not existing in actuality" means. And this does not mean that only dreams and illusions do not exist in actuality; all phenomena in the world are not intrinsically existent, not existent in the sphere of reality, not ultimately existent.

Tilopa says, *So be disillusioned and give up worldly activity.* He says that we should therefore be disillusioned with all samsaric activity. Why be disillusioned, or saddened? Because of seeing the essenceless, useless nature of samsaric activity. Saddened by it, we should give it up. In the Gyalwa Gyatso ritual come the words,

> I am disillusioned with samsaric things,
> I abandon all worldly activity;
> So, Protector, please allow me to enter
> The holy supreme city of great liberation.

We ask, "Please place us in the supreme city of great liberation." Actually the deity Gyalwa Gyatso does not "place" us anywhere; we have to go ourselves. But, to be able to go we request blessings of body, speech, and mind. It is not as if we can happily place all responsibility upon Gyalwa Gyatso and ask the deity to take us. We have to primarily do it ourselves but we request blessings for our body, speech, and mind from all of the lineage gurus, yidam deities, and other holy beings for the ability to do it. Practice of Mahamudra must be attained through the power of blessings. This is very important for us in addition to having highest faculties, the deepest of wisdom. On the basis of highest faculties and wisdom, the indispensable special quality we need in complement to that is what is called the "power of the blessings"; this is very important. The power of the blessings of the root guru are received if someone has deep confidence realizing that the guru is actual Buddha, that the yidam is actual Buddha; then blessings of body, speech, and mind of the root guru and yidam deity are received. By power of the blessings, previous good karma is awakened to realize Mahamudra. Simultaneously awakened is the omnipresent family line of dharmata. The naturally abiding lineage is awakened; at this point the introduction occurs. Therefore, it is very important to receive blessings in order to proceed. Without them, no matter how much we apply ourselves to the scripture and reasoning of Mahamudra, shaking our head and body, it won't help. The fact that Mahamudra is attained through the power of blessings is extremely important. It is because of that that our Practice Lineage principally depends upon aspiration and devotion. The Practice Lineage principally rests upon the faith of aspiration and devotion. Without faith we will not receive blessings. For blessings to enter us faith is the first essential.

Therefore, when we speak of becoming disillusioned, we ourselves must feel this, thinking, "It lacks any essence!" When we examine worldly activity with logic, it is not found. When reification has already been cut off and we have already been introduced to the actual mode of existence of our mind, all that is seen "out there" is the miraculous manifestation of the mind. It is of no benefit, without essence, like a sand castle. We are vastly disillusioned with samsaric phenomena. It doesn't help to become disillusioned only after we have a terrible headache or are struck by some serious disease that is difficult to remedy. Disillusionment, in any case, is something we need from this very moment onward. If we can develop this disillusionment, train in this essential point when we are healthy in body and mind, that is the best disillusionment.

By saying *Give up worldly activity,* Tilopa means discard all worldly activity. What is worldly activity? All that pertains to this life—name, gain, authority, impressing others, and so on, including all contaminated virtue. Any activity that is contaminated by ignorance and delusion is worldly activity. Contaminated virtue means if, for instance, we are giving something to someone but we are looking to see if anyone else is watching us or not. Then, if we think someone is watching, giving a large amount of donation, whereas if we think no one is watching, striding away without giving anything. There is no benefit in this kind of conduct, but it happens. Likewise, when we are doing recitation or other practice like meditation, if it is done for recognition and reputation, hope for return or karmic maturation, in short, with a mind of ego-grasping, even if it is virtue it is included in worldly activity. So Tilopa instructs us to give up all such activity, to discard it.

Furthermore, he says, *Sever attachment and aversion to entourage and land.* Entourage means parents, relatives, friends. Land means place. Continually thinking, "This place is so nice," if we become attached to a place, this is attachment to land. He tells us we must sever all association with delusion: attachment, aversion, ignorance, pride, jealousy. Milarepa said to Dagpo Rinpoche,

Son, you have resolved samsara.

Milarepa said this to Dagpo Rinpoche when Dagpo Rinpoche had reached confident realization of his ultimate nature, unmistaken realization of the oral instructions of Mahamudra. "Son, you have resolved samsara." For a yogi who has severed mental reification it makes no difference whether they are staying alone or among many people. For a yogi who has severed mental reification it makes no difference if they spend all day meditating or sleeping. If we can reach such a state, everything is fine. Until we attain it we must strive by all means to cut off all delusions.

Once we have cut all delusion toward entourage and land, then where should we go? Tilopa says, *Staying alone in the forest, meditate in retreat.* "Alone," he says. No friends or relatives with you at all. An isolated place where there are usually no travelers and no bothersome noise at night. We go to be alone like Milarepa, in isolated forests, mountain retreats, at the foot of dried-up trees; any place where there are no conditions for attachment, aversion, and the other delusions to arise. As mentioned in the *Thirty-seven Practices of Bodhisattvas,*

By abandoning bad places, delusion will gradually diminish.

We need to stay in a place where delusion can gradually diminish. That is the purpose of staying alone. *Meditate staying in forests and retreats.* Retreat does not necessarily mean someplace with nice meadows with streams and lots of wildflowers and fruit growing. Take Venerable Milarepa, for example: he stayed in so many retreats, including six outer dzongs, or "forts," six inner dzongs, six secret dzongs, another twenty-two dzongs, and eight caves—four major caves where he was widely renowned to have stayed, and four major caves where he stayed but it was not widely known. These were all places of rock, dry caves, ugly places where we wouldn't be able to spend even an hour! Retreats do not always have panoramic views, beautiful waterfalls, fruit, and a short commute to town! Retreat should be done in a place where no one could even conceive of staying! That is the kind of place where Venerable Milarepa stayed. Places where foxes, deer, and goats might go but where human beings would not consider it. That is what we mean by "retreat." It should also involve being itinerant, without staying in a fixed abode.

So we are *Staying alone in the forest, meditating in retreat.* What should we meditate on? Tilopa says, *Abide in the state of nonmeditation.* This has a whole commentary of its own. When we say "meditate" here, it does not mean meditating with our legs crossed. It doesn't mean having something to meditate on, a deity, mantra, mandala, or celestial mansion. How should we meditate? He says, *Abide in the state of nonmeditation.* He is telling us to abide in Mahamudra realization of the way things actually are, transcending all meditation and objects of meditation. We must *abide in a state of non-meditation,* that is, abide without moving from the state of nonmeditation. Nonmeditation does not mean that we are not meditating on something that we could be meditating upon. What is referred to as Mahamudra is beyond meditation and objects of meditation. How so? To transcend meditation and objects of meditation we absorb ourselves in the unfabricated ultimate nature of mind, empty of identity, illuminating in nature, which shows itself in various aspects and which has the three kayas complete within it. We poise ourselves within the unfabricated, we relax in the state of the unfabricated, we settle in the state of the unfabricated. When we speak of "poising" or "placing" our mind, there is nothing to place anywhere; we simply relax within that state. There are not a lot of words used to describe it. After a while the sound of words could distract us.

In any case, Tilopa says don't move from the state of nonmeditation. As it is said,

As the essence of thought is said to be dharmakaya
Not "being" anything but appearing as anything,
Pray bless the great yogi who sees its unceasing display
To realize the inseparability of samsara and nirvana.

These are the best words to describe it: "Not being anything but appearing as anything." When meditating on Mahamudra, a variegated display appears to the awareness of the meditator: good things, bad things, various appearances of samsara and nirvana. Whatever varied appearances of samsara or nirvana arise, it is fine; we do not accept or reject them. If a good thought arises do not think, "that's good," and put hope and effort into it. Bad, deluded thoughts like anger will also arise. Don't think, "Oh, now that's a bad thought!" examining it and suppressing it. Do not approve or reject any thought. Settle right in the unfabricated state. It is said that if a thought arises we should just recognize it. Why have we circled around in samsara up to now? We circle because of not recognizing, not identifying, thought; just giving thought free rein without paying any attention to it, allowing thought to wander as it will. We have spoiled our thought, allowed bad habits to develop. When our thoughts are spoiled out of control, allowed to go down a path of bad conditioning, they drag us along; we are then controlled by our thoughts. Gross thought just takes us wherever it wants to go and we run after it. We just follow blindly as if thought is our clear-sighted guide and we have to go wherever it leads. In that way we are led under the tyranny of thought.

Counter to this, when thought arises, identify it. Once we have identified that a thought has arisen, do not then examine it to see if it is good or bad. Even if some excellent quality has appeared, do not rejoice in it. If a negative thought appears, do not stop it and feel bad about it. Whatever quality of thought appears, just look at the entity of its appearance and it will disappear after having merely appeared, like a design that has been drawn in water. We must proceed on the basis of this essential point; make it a precept.

When beginners are given instructions on mind they are first taught to examine why certain thoughts arise when they do. For example, if Bodhgaya appears in their meditation for a moment, they are told to investigate whether Bodhgaya had come to them or their mind had gone to Bodhgaya. A beginner is not instructed in the process of first noting thought's arising, looking at its entity, and then noting its disappearance; there is no discussion of whether thought naturally disappears or not. There is instruction to look at the essence or entity of thought once it has just arisen, but not yet any instruction about thought's disappearance. Later on, when they meditate on Mahamudra instructions, when they realize that the natural arising of thought does not harm the "abiding" of the mind, and that the "abiding" of mind does not harm the arising of thought; when they realize that the singular nature of Mahamudra encompasses all of thought's movement and proliferation, and encompasses all three stages of meditation—abiding, movement, and awareness—at that point, the arising of thought and its identification become simultaneous for them. It is after we have reached secure realization of the ultimate that the dissolution of thought becomes simultaneous with its arising, that there occurs what is called simultaneous arising and release of thought.

This is extremely important. It is similar to the teaching of Dzogchen. This is the basis of nonmeditation. Whatever quality of thought arises, not judging whether it is good or bad, just identify its arising. It is taught that once it has been identified, thought is egocentric yet devoid of essence. There is nowhere from which thought first arose, no place where thought remains at present, and nowhere to which thought disappears. When we investigate the arising, abiding, and disappearance of thought, thought is not found. When we don't find thought we may wonder, "Is this the thought that could control me, that had me under its control?" Then we realize, "I have freely allowed thought to control me!" Then after some time no matter how many thoughts arise to the yogi they are all successively released as soon as they appear. That is what is called "simultaneous arising and release." At that point the more thoughts arise to the yogi, the more they complement the ultimate reality of the mind; they are that reality's ever-changing display. Until we recognize that fact, the more thoughts arise, the more they become an obstacle for us, giving rise to hope and fear as we examine and cling to them. Once thought has manifested as an obstacle it becomes an obstruction on the yogi's path. Previous good experience that may have occurred will be lost and future good realizations will be obstructed. Therefore, while we must identify thoughts, thought urges us on to dharmata reality; it is the display of dharmata. When we understand that thought is the play of dharmata we know that the more we understand reality, the more we understand that thought is its play. That is when it is said that "thought is siddhi," that thoughts themselves are spiritual attainments. The meaning of this is that through conviction in dharmata reality and understanding of its fundamental importance, thought is transformed into siddhi and thought becomes of assistance to the yogi. Thought becomes the shifting manifestation of the yogi's own ultimate reality. The more thoughts arise, the more they boost the yogi's practice, the more they further and heighten meditation practice.

It is these kinds of stages of profound methods that are taught in Mahamudra. This is why Tilopa speaks of *abiding in the state of nonmeditation*. There is no meditation to be done. No deity to meditate on. No mantra to recite. No mandala to meditate on. These are all said to be imputed by concept. Dharma practice that clings to inherent existence will not do. Again, as Venerable Milarepa sang,

> When meditating on Mahamudra
> Do not exert your body or speech.
> There is risk that nonconceptual wisdom will disappear.

This means for us to remain unmoving in a state of nonmeditation. Here the word "abiding" is understood to mean abiding in the state of nonmeditation. The words "abide in the state of nonmeditation" are used but in actuality there is no abiding or place to abide; we must connect the expression with the meaning of what is actually being expressed. Abiding in the state of nonmeditation means not moving out of the state of nonmeditation. It is said that, not moving away from nonmeditation, we relax and settle in nonmeditation. Otherwise, even if we speak of "abiding" in nonmeditation, there is no abiding or place of abiding. All clinging to objects of samsara and nirvana can be naturally released, like ice melting into water. When water becomes ice it doesn't change its nature; in fact, there is no essential difference between ice and water. Nevertheless, in dependence upon certain conditions, ice melts into water.

Similarly, the ultimate nature of our mind does not move outside or away from Mahamudra nature or essence. But not recognizing Mahamudra nature for what it is, we mistake Mahamudra for "I," for self. We "muddy up" Mahamudra. Out of delusion we "soil" Mahamudra and mistake it for "I" and self. Like water that has become ice, our Mahamudra is in bondage. When we now rely on the guru's instructions with esteem and devotion, with deep gratitude for their presence and instructions, perceiving them as an actual buddha and making repeated requests; and when our previous good karma ripens, it is on this basis that recognition may occur. When this happens, it is not as if we have found some new thought or experience. We are simply recognizing our ultimate nature that we did not see before for what it is. When we recognize it, the ice melts into water again. Other than that, there is no new realization or new quality that is attained. As taught in *Uttaratantra,*

> There is nothing about this to clarify,
> Not the slightest thing to present.
> Perfectly look at the perfect itself.
> If we see the perfect we are freed.

There is no fault to be dispelled or clarified, no quality to be newly established. By looking without fabrication at perfect ultimate truth itself, when we settle in equipoise within that state we are freed.

As for the benefits, it is said,

> If we attain nonattainment we attain Mahamudra.

In our Mahamudra preliminaries, as well, come the words,

> Observing no agent, action, or object of attainment,
> Abandonment and attainment nondual, base and result inseparable,
> In a nature of all things lacking true reality,
> May I manifest resultant Mahamudra!

When we speak of no object, action, or agent of attainment, we are speaking about the resultant state. "Attaining nonattainment" means that there is nothing to be newly attained. If we obtain an unattainable result, that is something good, isn't it. If we speak of attaining some fruit we immediately think that by studying and practicing there is some concrete result "up there" to be obtained. It is not like that. Saying that we attain nonattainment implies that up to now we have not recognized the resultant state that has been within us from the first in a causal mode. When we recognize it we will see what we already have, not something that we have newly obtained. When we understand the meaning of this we understand "attaining nonattainment." The words "if we attain nonattainment" mean just that: there is nothing attained, not that there is some unobtainable thing that exists out there which we must obtain. We are manifesting something that we already have. As Venerable Milarepa said to Dagpo Rinpoche,

> As for view, I say, look at mind!
> When we seek a view somewhere else . . .

"As for view, I say, look at mind!" This is the same as saying, "As for the result, I say, look at mind!" Resultant Mahamudra, the ultimate result, is present in our mind, not something we newly attain. Therefore "nonattainment" in the phrase "if we attain nonattainment" means that there is nothing outside that we need to newly obtain, nothing for us to obtain from outside in reliance upon remedies and other conditions. It is said,

> Nothing to attain in dependence upon antidotes,
> Nothing to attain in dependence upon conditions,
> Nothing to attain in dependence upon paths . . .

Since there is absolutely nothing to be newly attained, it is called "nonattainment." What does this mean? It means that resultant Mahamudra does not depend upon remedies, conditions, or paths, but is intrinsic to us. This intrinsic quality is our true nature or ultimate mode of existence—its capacity and reality. We say that we "attain" this result in dependence upon its being pointed out to us, but because there is nothing for us to newly obtain in dependence upon remedies, conditions, or paths, it is called "nonattainment."

So if we say, "May I attain nonattainment," what are we saying? We are saying, "May it be pointed out to me," "May I recognize it," "May I reach secure realization of it." Again, this resultant state, our ultimate mode of existence, is referred to by the word "moon," as in "the resultant moon," or "May I reach secure realization of the resultant moon." All of these are prayers to manifest the resultant state. But they are just words that we have to use because there is nothing in addition that we need to obtain. "Attainment" is just a necessary word for us to use. When we say, "If we attain nonattainment we attain Mahamudra," it means we will attain the essential meaning of Mahamudra, dharmadhatu, the sphere of reality.

A tree grows with trunk, branches, and foliage;
If its single root is cut, the hundreds of thousands of branches
     will dry up.

For example, to dry up a huge tree that has vast branches, leaves, flowers, sap, and fruits, all these do not need to be cut one by one. If the root can be cut where it goes up, the hundreds and thousands of branches, leaves, sap, flowers, fruits, and so on will all dry up. They will naturally dry up; nothing further need be done.

Likewise, if the root of mind is cut, the foliage of samsara will
     dry up. [16]

Similarly, if the root of mind is cut, the foliage of samsara will dry up. What does it mean, to "cut the root of mind"? It means being introduced to the ultimate mode of existence of mind. When we speak of investigating and cutting the root of mind, or manifesting mind's suchness—actually the Tibetan *tsä dar chä*,[61] "investigate and cut the root," says it best—we are talking about severing mental reification, or cutting reification in the mind. Reification is not about looking outward and cutting external things. If the yogi is able to cut internal mental reification, the whole collection of samsaric thought—all that foliage—will dry up. *The foliage of samsara will dry up.* Similarly, in the *Sukhavati Prayer* by the Fifth Karmapa Dezhin Shegpa come the words,

Samsara's suchness is nirvana.
Concepts' suchness is jnana wisdom.

May I have the wisdom to realize dharmata reality
That transcends both singularity and plurality.

Samsara is something to be abandoned. Yet when the yogi stops mental reification he has been introduced to the ultimate nature of samsara, its suchness. Not thinking of samsara as something to be abandoned, when the yogi examines samsara's mode of existence he will realize that samsara's nature is suchness, emptiness. Therefore, there is no need for a separate nirvana as a goal to be attained. If we can realize the suchness of samsara, that itself is nirvana. "Samsara's suchness is nirvana" means just that; it is of no use setting the suchness of samsara aside and hoping to obtain nirvana somewhere else.

"Concepts' suchness is jnana wisdom." So who apprehends samsara? What sustains it? If samsara has no inherent existence, if samsara does not exist by nature, then who apprehends and sustains it? Samsara is sustained by concepts under the control of karma and delusion. When we speak of concepts, here, that which is fully imputed or fantasized, this refers to the root of samsara, the six klesha-delusions. When our main mind and fifty-one mental factors—five omnipresent ones, and so forth—are influenced by delusion and karma, this is all included in conceptual imputation. There are many levels of grossness and subtlety within the category of conceptual thought as well. Therefore, since it is concept that apprehends and sustains what we call "samsara," it is concept that owns and claims samsara, that thinks, "It is mine." Therefore when the yogi who severs reification in the mind investigates thought, the yogi realizes that suchness is the nature of thought. When the yogi realizes suchness is the nature of thought, the yogi can realize that thought's nature is the five jnana-wisdoms: mirrorlike wisdom, equalizing wisdom, discriminating wisdom, accomplishing wisdom, and dharmadhatu wisdom.

"May I have the wisdom to realize dharmata reality that transcends both singularity and plurality." Neither singularity nor plurality exists in the nature of anything. The Fifth Karmapa is saying, "When I arrive at my true nature, which transcends singularity and plurality, may I have the wisdom to realize dharmata, ultimate reality." "Realization of dharmata" is the phrase we use, but it is mere imputation. Dharmata wisdom is realized when the root of mind is cut. Expressing the same idea,

Clear light nature is unobserved, like space.
Yet transcendent wisdoms' unceasing display

Expands in mandalas knowing all of existence.
Homage to unfathomable clear light of the heart!

In short, if we can finely investigate and cut the root of mind, all samsaric and nirvanic concepts can be pacified and extinguished.

These lines in Aryadeva's *Four Hundred Verses on the Middle Way* also express it:

> The view of one
> Is the view of all.
> The emptiness of one
> Is the emptiness of all.
> Who sees the suchness of one thing
> Sees the suchness of all things.

If we can realize without mistake the nature of one phenomenon, then induced by that, we can comprehend the nature of all phenomena. Similarly, therefore, if we can cut mental reification, if we can finely investigate and cut the root of mind, if our ultimate mode of existence can be effectively pointed out to us, then induced by that, with the three kayas appearing in the varied display of its luminous nature, we can realize the emptiness of all phenomena.

That being the case, there is extensive explanation of the "imputed three kayas" and that which is imputed, the "actual three kayas." Having the three kayas complete within us is on the following basis:

> Essence is empty (dharmakaya),
> Nature is luminous (sambhogakaya),
> Appearance is in various aspects (nirmanakayas).

In Dzogchen terms it is,

> Basis, birthless dharmakaya;
> Radiance, ceaseless sambhogakaya;
> Display, varied appearing nirmanakayas.

These two presentations are the same. There is some difference in the wording but they both indicate the three kayas complete within us.

When we arrive at this point we say,

> I go for refuge in the channels, winds, and drops.
> I go for refuge in bliss, clarity, and nonconceptuality.
> I go for refuge in essence, nature, and compassion.

These are included in having the three kayas complete within us. Similarly, in chöd practice there is a confession in which we say,

> Before the Mother Machig nirmanakaya I reveal and confess:
> That not having realized mind's mode of existence is buddha,
> I have engaged in worldly activity under the influence of fleeting delusions.

The three kayas are all included within that as well. In taking appearances onto the path in chöd, there is also prostration to the hell beings, pretas, and animals; prostration to attachment, aversion, and ignorance; and prostration to conceptual thought. All of these also principally point to the presence of the three kayas in sentient beings.

If we have already cut mental reification of mind's true nature, if we have been able to cut the sole root of the mind, the deep implications of all phenomena can be released. If a murderer can stab someone at a secret meridian point, for instance, they are instantly killed. Similarly, if we can thoroughly investigate and cut the root of mind, the whole play of samsaric and nirvanic phenomena will appear to us. *Likewise, if the root of mind is cut, the foliage of samsara will dry up.*

> For example, darkness accumulated over a thousand eons,
> That whole mass of darkness, is dispelled by a single lamp.
> Likewise, our own clear-light mind instantly dispels
> Ignorance, harm, and obscuration amassed over eons. [17]

The analogy is very dark blackness. Darkness gathered over thousands of eons means extreme darkness. Even *darkness accumulated over many thousands of eons, that whole mass of darkness, is dispelled by a single lamp.* Even though it is just one small lamp it can clear all the darkness, full darkness accumulated over many thousands of eons. When we light a lamp it can clear all of the darkness.

Similarly, we have inconceivable negativity that we have accumulated in beginningless lives in samsara up to the present. And you know we have experienced inconceivable suffering in worse realms of existence as a result. Even though we are so obscured by ignorance, we now have a fully qualified guru. Through focused practice, without wavering or doubt about these Mahamudra instructions, and making the "stake-driving-like" appeals with aspiration and devotion, when we experience a moment of clear light dawning in our mind, that instant of clear light mind dispels the "ignorance, harm, and obscuration amassed over eons." It can dispel all of the ignorance, negativity, and obscuration amassed over many thousands of eons. It can even purify the inconceivable, limitless negative karma we have accumulated in beginningless samsara. It can purify even karma of the five boundless, or heinous, crimes. There is no negativity accumulated in the mind that it cannot purify. Therefore, this is the supreme of hundreds of methods and thousands of antidotes. It is the most fundamental method for purifying negativity and obscuration.

18. How It Transcends Intellect

Kye ho! Intellectual Dharma does not see what transcends
    intellect.
Fabricated Dharma does not realize what "nonactivity" means.
If you wish to attain "transcendence of intellect" and "nonactivity,"
Cut the root of your mind and leave awareness naked.
Immerse conceptual thoughts in that bright stainless water.
Do not approve or reject appearances; leave them as they are.
Not abandoning or adopting, all of existence is liberated in
    Mahamudra.
In birthless alaya—"foundation of all"—imprints, harm, and
    obscuration are abandoned.
Don't be proud and calculating; settle in the essence of
    birthlessness.
Since appearances are reflexive, we run out of mental creations.

Kye ho! Intellectual Dharma does not see what transcends intellect. By
"intellectual Dharma," Tilopa refers to Hinayana Dharma—not to
Mahayana, but to the teachings of the Hinayana shravaka and pratyeka-
buddha vehicles. He refers to these as "intellectual Dharma." In this context
he does not just mean Dharma that is grasped by intellect; we should understand it to mean Hinayana Dharma. He is saying that Hinayana Dharma is
intellectually contrived Dharma. In dependence upon intellectual Dharma,
through the Hinayana path itself, the meaning of Mahamudra that transcends intellect cannot be realized. That is because the view, meditation, and
action are all conceptually calculated and considered. Once view, meditation, and action are intellectually contrived, the meaning that transcends
intellect cannot be realized. For instance, no matter how much a Hinayanist
studies selflessness of the person, they cannot train in that which transcends

intellect; they have conceptual grasping of a selflessness of persons. They cling to the idea of partless particles of matter and partless moments of consciousness. In that way they have tremendous grasping for personal selflessness. That is why Hinayana Dharma cannot realize the meaning of that which transcends intellect, cannot realize clear-light mind of Mahamudra, mind's original fundamental nature.

Fabricated dharma means effortful Dharma. For example, we meditate but do so with effortful striving. We do some practice but it is effortful practice. We create virtue but it becomes contaminated virtue. In any case, this refers to all calculated or intellectually contrived Dharma, with grasping and clinging to signs of intrinsic identity, of self. All Dharma with subtle self-grasping ignorance is fabricated Dharma, compounded Dharma, contaminated Dharma. If we grasp at such contaminated, compounded virtue, the benefit of the virtue will be used up. There is certainly some benefit but it is lost in an instant.

So Tilopa says that because it is fabricated Dharma it *cannot realize the meaning of nonactivity*. This means that it cannot realize the meaning of Mahamudra. Mahamudra is given many different names. That which "transcends intellect" is Mahamudra. Likewise, "nonactivity" is Mahamudra. There is no kriya tantra in Mahamudra, no "action tantra"; that is because it is "nonactivity." Mahamudra is intrinsic to our mind; it does not need to be accomplished through new compounded roots of virtue. That is why it is called "nonactivity."

If you wish to attain "transcendence of intellect" and "nonactivity": Why must we speak of transcendence of intellect? Because intellect refers to being caught inside a fence of our own dualistic intellectual grasping. Transcendence of intellect, Mahamudra practice, is beyond intellect, outside the fence of concepts. Someone who wants to stay inside the fence of concepts cannot understand "transcendence of intellect." Likewise someone who remains performing contaminated virtue cannot realize the meaning of the "uncontaminated," "nonactivity" Mahamudra. If we really wish to practice and attain realization of Mahamudra, "transcendence of intellect," "nonactivity," we say that we want to "eat and drink Mahamudra."

If we want to eat and drink Mahamudra practice, we must *cut the root of our mind and leave awareness naked.* By not moving from the state of our own elemental mind, we cut the root of our mind. This means that we must cut the root of mind without moving from the state of our elemental mind, our most fundamental mind. If we had to move from the state of our elemental mind to cut the root of our mind, it would be a mundane Dharma. We must cut the root of mind without moving from elemental mind, not moving out of the state of our true Mahamudra nature.

When we speak of cutting the root of mind, what is it that is cut? There is no cutting but of our own mental reification. We must check over and over, how is our mind? In general, even after having attained realization of Mahamudra we must still emphasize awareness of mind. Until attaining the supreme fruit of unexcelled perfect, ultimate, nonabiding nirvana, even after realizing Mahamudra, if we become unable to thoroughly investigate and cut mental reification, there is a danger that our nonconceptual wisdom could again become obscured. This is because our predisposition for reification, for projection of inherent existence, has developed over an extremely long period of time and is extremely subtle and difficult to identify. Because of negative predispositions being extremely powerful and deep, sometimes even if realization of Mahamudra has dawned because there was some karma for it, there is the risk that it can again become obscured. That being the case, we must still cut the root of mind, cut mental reification.

Once we have cut the root of mind, then what must happen? Once we have an unmoving realization of our elemental mind, we must *leave awareness naked*. What awareness are we speaking of? Our own unfabricated true nature of Mahamudra that was pointed out to us. As you know, in Dzogchen, mind and awareness are explained as two different things. The awareness we are speaking of here is identical to the awareness of Dzogchen's twofold division. Beyond the six consciousnesses,[62] the presence of an instant of one's own reflexive transcendent wisdom is referred to as "awareness." Not obscured or covered over by the six consciousnesses, beyond that obscuring stain, there is a jnana of discrimination, our own reflexive transcendent wisdom. That is what is called *rigpa*, awareness. This is the type of awareness referred to as "looking inward" in the precept,

> Looking outward, samsara,
> Looking inward, nirvana.

Saying "leave awareness naked" is the same as saying "Don't do much conceptual analysis." That *rigpa*, that awareness, has never been stained by defilement, has never been stained by conceptual consciousness. For example, we don't see the sun when clouds cover it. The sun is not visible to us, but the clouds don't really affect the sun's own heat and light; the clouds cannot cover that or change the sun in any way. Likewise, our own individual rigpa, deep awareness that transcends the six consciousnesses, cannot be obscured no matter how much we are controlled by concept and delusion.

Therefore, without many hopes for the good and fears of the bad, settle without fabrication in equipoise on this very present moment of awareness. "Leave awareness naked!" means "Leave awareness in its own natural state," "Leave it bare," "Leave it unfabricated." Don't analyze thoughts, don't hope for good and dread the bad. Whatever the quality of the present moment of awareness, without fabrication, settle in equipoise upon it. Gently relax in the present moment of awareness without doing anything to fix or adjust it; freely settle.[63] Milarepa sang,

> By freely settling, true nature is seen.

"Freely settling" means settling without fabrication. When we set a cup down on a table we freely set it down. There is no apprehension or concern, no shifting it back and forth. Gently relaxing and completely settling is "freely settling." This all relates to "leaving awareness naked." To say "leave" or "settle" here means to recognize naked awareness, to be introduced to naked awareness. He is saying that we need to experience naked awareness.

Immerse conceptual thoughts in that bright stainless water. Tilopa refers to the cessation of conceptual thought as thought being immersed in bright stainless water. Concepts are like muddy water. Rigpa-awareness by comparison is pure shining water. Since bright shining awareness is obscured by conceptual stains, the muddy water of concepts is immersed in radiance. The muddy water of concepts includes conceptual grasping of form, sound, scent, taste, touch, and so on, all grasping of the six consciousnesses. That is the stained water that is immersed in clear water. The whole collection of concepts must be allowed to cease. The whole collection of concepts naturally disappears, is naturally extinguished.

Do not approve or reject appearances; leave them as they are. There is no approval or rejection of appearances to be done. It is as if we do not need to see, to manipulate, appearances of form, sound, scent, taste, and touch. In any case we do not need to grasp and approve or reject them. As Tilopa said to Naropa,

> Son, appearances do not bind us, grasping does!
> Sever grasping, Naropa!

Appearances do not bind us. It makes no difference what appears. Appearances are good. What is it at present that obscures us? Grasping. What does this mean? We are not satisfied with mere appearances but are obscured by our instinctual grasping or belief that that which we impute to exist in appearances is actually there deep within them. Otherwise, appearances themselves do not hinder yogis in the slightest. Mahasiddha Nyemo,[64] in his doha *Victory Banner of Siddhi,* said,

> Leave wealth and such. For the renounced yogi
> Wealth is like it would be for wild deer in an empty valley:
> If it's there, that's fine; if it's not, that's fine.
> This inner freedom from grasping is so delightful!

If there is no grasping in the mind of a yogi who has abandoned the collecting and hoarding of money and other wealth, that is perfect. If there is no grasping in the mind, even with hundreds of thousands of dollars, hundreds of thousands of gold coins, hundreds of thousands of houses, it makes no difference. "Wealth is like it would be for wild deer in an empty valley." When deer arrive in an empty valley there is no worry at all. Farmers, on the other hand, will have many things to worry about, worrying that deer may eat their crops, worrying, "Here come deer! They're going to eat my crops!" "Here come water buffalo!" "Now, cows are coming! My corn harvest is all going to be eaten!" If deer arrive in an empty valley and there is no place or foliage for them, nothing need be rejected. When there are no deer that is not a problem, either. "If it's there, that's fine; if it's not, that's fine." It's fine whether there is wealth or not. This is contentment, of prime importance.

"This inner freedom from grasping is so delightful!" If we can sever all conceptual grasping, the wealth and property we have will not harm us at all. Even without much wealth to enjoy, it can become a whirling firebrand[65] that entices us, and we can become attached to it even though it is not there. We consider something precious and become attached to it, bound to it. The enticing firebrand becomes something very powerful and we become very weak. We follow wherever the firebrand leads. That is why "the inner freedom from grasping is so delightful." That is why we must not approve or reject appearances. Appearances do not need to be stopped. In the context of Madhyamaka it is said to be a fault if we intentionally stop appearances; that it is unsuitable to stop appearances. Leaving awareness as it is, natural, means that whatever appearance presents, we leave it just as it is. If beauty appears, leave it as beauty. When the unlovely appears, also leave it as beauty. If we think something is beautiful and volunteer for it, grasping develops. If we think to get rid of something because it is not beautiful, again grasping has developed. If we think a sound is very pleasant and seek it out, this is grasping. If we think a sound is ugly and unpleasant, that is also grasping. Therefore, *do not approve or reject appearances; leave them as they are.*

Not abandoning or adopting, all of existence is liberated in Mahamudra. There is no abandoning of anything as bad or negative, no adopting of anything as good or virtuous. If we can realize our ultimate nature without adopting and abandoning, all of the phenomena included in samsara and nirvana can be liberated in the single essence of Mahamudra. Like the example of a hundred rivers all flowing under one bridge, all appearing, existing phenomena from Buddha above to hell below are liberated in the single essence of Mahamudra clear light. Realization comes in the nature of the single clear light Mahamudra. That is why it is said that having realized one phenomenon, all phenomena of samsara and nirvana can be known, can appear in unceasing varied display; we can see it all as the essence of its unceasing varied display. Once we have realized our single Mahamudra mode of existence, even without being taught, we can understand all fields of knowledge in the world such as science. Because such vast knowledge is realized without adopting or abandoning, it is said that all existence is liberated in the seal of Mahamudra.

Yet some scholars tease our Kagyu tradition. They say,

> This meaning of what is called Mahamudra—what sort of realization is it? By realizing Mahamudra, all the various appearances of samsara and nirvana are understood to be the display or play of the single elemental mind. When the yogi is liberated through that correct realization of the ultimate, all phenomena are revealed to naturally arisen wisdom! Without training gradually in any of the phenomena of samsara and nirvana, by opening the treasury of knowledge, they suddenly know everything they didn't know before! Everything is naturally known without study! No need for beginning training; all who were stupid become wise! All those without wisdom come to have sharp wisdom and can see all phenomena of samsara and nirvana like a *kyurura* fruit in the palm of their hand! Yet, according to your Kagyu tradition when you realize Mahamudra, the guru seems to be stupid, someone who doesn't know how to eat, drink, or speak!

The reason they say this is that we ourselves do say similar things: "Oh, he's a mahasiddha! He knows nothing of worldly things! He does practice and knows nothing else!" That is why they tease that they become stupid. Yet, there is no disputing it; it is actually similar to the truth. They are interpreting it differently, of course. The situation is actually different, but when they put it that way, it does sound a bit strange.

In birthless alaya—"foundation of all"—imprints, harm, and obscuration are abandoned. What is alaya, the foundation of all? In this case we do not understand it as alaya-vijnana, foundation consciousness. Here we understand it to mean birthlessness. "Birthlessness" here means birthless elemental mind, the birthless true nature of the mind. It is the basis of appearance of all phenomena of samsara and nirvana. It is the basis from which all phenomena of samsara and nirvana are produced. Again, as said in the *Treasury of Dohas*,

> Elemental mind is the seed of all,
> Emanating samsara and nirvana.
> Homage to wish-fulfilling jewellike mind
> Which grants bestowal of all desired fruits!

Mind is like the wish-fulfilling jewel. The alaya-basis of all is the basis from which all phenomena of samsara and nirvana are born. Birthlessness refers to birthless elemental mind. When birthless elemental mind becomes fully expansive, the illumination naturally extinguishes all imprints of negativity and obscuration. No need to accumulate recitation of Vajrasattva mantras or do fire-pujas specifically for the purpose of purifying harm and obscuration! Once we know the birthless ultimate nature of the mind, that purifies negativity and obscuration.

In the *Sutra of the Ten Grounds,* Buddha taught ten "equalities," among which, if we can realize the equality of birthlessness, we can naturally realize the other nine. Nagarjuna, at the beginning of his *Root Wisdom,* also principally presents the equality of birthlessness:

> Not from self, not from other,
> Not from both, not causeless,
> Nothing whatsoever
> Is ever born.

Thus, not born from self, not born from other, not born from both or neither, on the basis of the reasoning refuting birth from the four extremes, we realize the emptiness of all phenomena. In the present context as well, birthlessness is very important. When the alaya clear light elemental mind that is the basis of all is realized and becomes fully expansive, there is no need to teach antidotes to destroy all of the deluded imprints, negativity, and obscuration accumulated over beginningless samsaric lifetimes. Negativity and obscuration are abandoned just by the mere manifestation of that birthless alaya, our ultimate nature, like ice melting into water or snow falling on hot rocks. When snow falls on hot rocks it melts at the very instant of contact. Similarly, when the yogi has realized birthless alaya there is no need to intentionally abandon all negativity and obscuration; it will naturally be extinguished.

Don't be proud and calculating; settle in the essence of birthlessness. In this case, pride or haughtiness refers to self-grasping ignorance. The mara of pride is the self-grasping ignorance that thinks, "I." Whatever Dharma practice is done with such pride-of-self remains contaminated; it will not reach uncontaminated paths. Paths free of ignorance are uncontaminated paths. Contamination and contaminated paths mean the presence of this pride-of-self. This is what we must strive to free ourselves of: self-grasping ignorance, pride of self.

Being "calculating" primarily refers to hoping for results—thinking, "If I create such karma now, I will receive such and such results." Such hope for results is being calculating. So, without the ignorance and pride hoping for particular results from Mahamudra practice, not hoping for any response, not hoping for maturation or results, *settle in the essence of birthlessness.* This ultimate nature of our mind has forever been birthless; it did not become birthless in dependence upon remedies and paths. Tilopa is saying to settle without contrivance in the birthlessness that is the primordial birthlessness of our own ultimate nature. "Settling in the essence" means settling in our ultimate mode of existence, settling in the natural state, settling without fabrication; not some other "essence" that exists which we must somehow place ourselves into. "Settling without fabrication" closely describes it.

Since appearances are reflexive, we run out of mental creations, or our mental creations are extinguished. If we can understand that all of the intellectual Dharma that appears to us is Mahamudra, all intellectual Dharma is extinguished in reflexive luminosity. Realizing that all forms, sound, scents, tastes, tactile sensations, and all phenomena of samsara and nirvana are reflexive illumination, reflections of our own mind, clinging concepts are brought to the point of being exhausted, extinguished. That is in regard to appearances being reflexive. What is it that those appearances are appearances of?

Appearances are created by our mind as the display of our ultimate reality, by the force of our predispositions. If we can realize these mentally created phenomena—the display of our own ultimate nature appearing through the force of our predispositions—to be birthless elemental mind, they will all be exhausted, finished. We pray, "May appearances be extinguished." We also use the word in common expressions such as, "Don't worry, it's over, it's finished." The above prayer is still made even after this "extinguishing" has taken place.

All appearances are reflexive appearances and in actuality are not truly existent. It makes no difference how many noninherently existent appearances arise. Whatever good qualities or bad concepts appear, they are mentally created, they are display of mind, they are play of mind. Since they are the display and play of mind, if we can settle in equipoise on their birthlessness they are naturally exhausted. When rain dries up, crops naturally dry up. Likewise, all phenomena are naturally exhausted, like a pond when its source is cut off. Similarly, if we can recognize all mentally created phenomena to be reflexive appearances, not truly existent and appearing through the force of predispositions—if we can realize them to be mentally created, not real or truly existent—then all conceptual clinging is extinguished and our predispositions will be consumed, used up.

19. View, Meditation, Action, and Results

Freed from boundaries and limits is the supreme king of views.

IF WE EXPERIENCE absence of limits and boundaries, it is the supreme king of views. In our Mahamudra ultimate nature there are no boundaries such as between subject and object, no end or limit, no center or outer edges whatsoever. That is why it is called "without limit or boundary"; there is no boundary to meet, no limit to be contacted. "Freed from boundaries and limits is the supreme king of views."

Boundless, deep and vast, is the supreme king of meditations.

Boundless . . . Without distraction. Here "boundless" means endless, without end or limit. "Deep and vast" means inexhaustible. Meditating on this without wandering, watching with undistracted mindfulness, is the king of meditations. "Deep and vast" means perfectly expansive; not narrow but open; carefree; not wandering. As said, "Nondistraction is actual meditation"; if we can abide without wandering, that is the king of meditations.

Cutting extremes, unbiased, is the supreme king of conduct.

If we are free from extremes, beyond approving and negating, that is the king of conduct. Being free of approving and negating, we are unbiased. Cutting extremes means to be free of all extremes—the four extremes and eight extreme projections.[66] Being unbiased means transcending approving and rejecting. If we transcend all approving and rejecting, that is the king of conduct.

Thus, being free of boundaries and limits is the king of views. If all intellectually contrived phenomena are exhausted, if we are able to transcend on the basis of our fundamental true nature, that is the king of views; if we can remain abiding in that without wandering, that is the king of meditations; and if we are free from approving and negating, free from all extremes, that is the king of conduct.

20. THE RESULT ABIDES IN SPONTANEITY WITHOUT NEED FOR HOPE AND FEAR

Without hope, naturally liberated, is the supreme result. [18]

WITHOUT HOPE OR fear, without hoping to attain certain results in the future or fearing that we will not attain such results, if hope and fear are *naturally released,* that *is the supreme result.* Absence of hope and fear means that hope and fear have become the expanse of dharmata, that all hope and fear have become the expanse of Mahamudra's ultimate mode of existence. When this happens, Mahasiddha Tilopa says, it *is the supreme result.*

21. HOW EXPERIENCE ARISES FROM CORRECT PRACTICE

At first, it's like racing mountain rapids.
In the middle, it moves slowly like the River Ganges.
At last, all rivers meet the sea, like the meeting of mother
and child.

To achieve the state of unexcelled perfect enlightenment, beginners must proceed gradually in the Hinayana through view, meditation, and conduct. They do not have the ability to immediately engage in the vast, profound meditation of the Mahayana. Therefore they begin with the Hinayana shravaka Vaibashika, then Sautantrika; then they are taught Mahayana Chittamatra, then Madhyamaka, then the stages of Tantra. After that, they proceed in reliance upon a yidam deity such as Hevajra. In this way they train in stages with all three—view, meditation, and conduct—developing in concert, gradually.

Ascending gradually through the Hinayana, what is the view first taught to a beginner? Karma. In the case of a beginner whose faculties are suited to developing by stages, the view is that of karma. Of course we are talking about strong conceptuality here, good, bad, and so on. Virtue is good; wrongdoing is bad, to be abandoned: this is all gross conceptuality. Tilopa compares the mind at this stage to a racing mountain stream of thoughts. For instance, it is good to gather accumulations; it is bad to harm and promote distorted views of reality. It is a strong view, a gross view with strong conceptuality. That is why Tilopa makes the comparison with the water of a stirred-up, swiftly running mountain stream. This refers to a beginner in Sutrayana practice, Hinayana or Mahayana. What is similar to the water of a fast-moving stream is the flow of thoughts clinging to views such as that gathering accumulations is good and that harm and distorted views are bad. The thoughts are like the water of mountain rapids that flows very strongly and makes a loud roar.

During the *middle* period, when we are freed of such a mode of apprehension, freed of such conceptual grasping, our mode of apprehension *flows more slowly, like the River Ganges.* This is now a reference to tantric practice. When we enter tantric practice it is like the River Ganges, which moves very slowly in its flow. The view conceptually grasping that gathering accumulations and virtue is beneficial, and creating negativity and distorted views is harmful, is pacified. When these concepts are pacified, this middle period of meditation is compared to the leisurely flow of the River Ganges. The River Ganges moves very slowly and does not make loud noise. Similarly, when we enter the tantric path and are freed from these grasping concepts, we can abide in a view which sees no virtue or wrongdoing creating benefit or harm.

At last, all rivers meet the sea, like the meeting of mother and child. So there is this type of view that develops on the tantric path when it is perfected in the expanse of emptiness. It is likened to all rivers flowing into the sea, or like the meeting of mother and child. *At last, all rivers meet the sea, like the meeting of mother and child.* All of the many rivers of the world finally have nowhere to go but into the ocean. Similarly, when all modes of view and apprehension disintegrate, they arrive at the sphere of reality, dharmadhatu, nonabiding nirvana.

At first, good and bad are viewed as existent. In the middle, good and bad are viewed as nonexistent. Finally arriving at that mode of being that is without good and bad, it is like the meeting of mother and child. The beginner's view, that doing good and bad create benefit and harm, is *like the rushing rapids of a mountain stream.* In the middle, the tantric view of no good or bad really creating benefit and harm, is *like the leisurely flow of the Ganges.* At last, when the rivers meet the ocean, with good and bad not existing except as mere concepts, all phenomena being equal, of a single taste in the expanse of dharmata, Mahasiddha Tilopa says that it is *like the meeting of mother and child.* This is Mahamudra's "nonmeditation," the nonmeditation kingdom of dharmakaya. In the Sutra context it is referred to as the equality of all phenomena. Here we have arrived at that equality. Svatantrika Madhyamaka speaks of a "basis of appearances," a union of appearance and emptiness free of fabrication. Prasangika Madhyamaka speaks of emptiness free of fabrication, union, and equality, with these being realized in four stages. When we arrive at this union, this equality, it is finally like the meeting of mother and child. Understand the meaning on the basis of the analogy.

Thus, in Sutra, there are concepts that good and bad exist. In Tantra, the view is that good and bad are not real, the mode of apprehension being like the leisurely flow of the Ganges. Finally, without good and bad, it is like all rivers meeting the ocean.

Venerable Milarepa said,

> First I created bad karma; in the middle I created good. Now, freed of both good and bad karma, the basis of karma is exhausted, so I will not be creating any more in the future!

The first and middle stages Milarepa speaks of are similar to the beginning-stage rushing rapids and the middle-stage leisurely flowing river. Finally the freedom from creating either good or bad karma that he speaks of is like the final stage, in which the rivers meet the sea. Another interpretation is that the beginner's meditative equipoise has stronger conceptuality, like the rushing rapids; then, after they have attained some stability, the meditative equipoise of those of highest faculties is like the slowly flowing Ganges; and finally, free of discarding and remedying, all of samsara and nirvana mixed in one taste, the "path clear light" and "basic clear light" merge inseparably like a river meeting the sea, like the meeting of mother and child. It is those with the very highest of faculties who attain this.

22. How to Dispel Obstacles

If those of little intelligence cannot abide in this state,

THERE ARE SOME of weak intelligence, however, who are not able to understand the meaning of these instructions. If they must understand immediately, they cannot. No matter how much they are skillfully instructed, if they do not have the karma from previous training, they will not be able to realize the essential meaning through their training in this life alone. If someone of weaker intelligence, of less powerful natural or developed wisdom, cannot maintain awareness of this essential meaning that is free of all good and bad, that is the ultimate mode of existence of all phenomena, is there anything that can be done? Yes, there is:

Apply breathing techniques and cast awareness into the essence.

Breathing techniques are dealt with in the Six Yogas of Naropa. The usual instructions are those on vase-breathing, "middle breathing"[67] and numerous other instructions on breathing. Therefore, with multiple breathing techniques and methods of meditation, the subtle winds are the base of the mind, the channels are the base of the winds, and the base and key to the subtle winds is in the eyes, therefore breathing techniques are practiced.[68]

Cast awareness into the essence. Awareness has to be "inserted" into the key point. By means of the subtle winds penetrating the points, when appearances arise to the mind they are cast away as being of no consequence. To start with, awareness itself must be identified; it must be introduced or pointed out. Put another way, it is said that awareness must be seized; we must be able to grab it.

Casting awareness into the essence means that whatever thought arises, it is cast into the essence, rigpa-awareness. If good thoughts arise, we abandon them in essence-awareness; if bad thoughts arise, we abandon them in essence-awareness.

For the time being, various different subjects, mistaken in their conventional conceptual mode of apprehension, appear. Yet they proliferate from within awareness and finally, when they are recognized, they collect back into awareness. Recognizing that their proliferation and withdrawal both happen within the single state of rigpa-awareness is "casting awareness into the essence." When Venerable Milarepa understood this, no matter what apparitions devas and spirits displayed to him, he cast them all into the essence, meditating that they were the display, the miraculous manifestation, of rigpa-awareness. Because of this he could not be harmed. When someone is unable to understand this, they grasp all inner subjectivity and external objects as being different; and grasping subjects and objects as separate enables terrifying hallucinations to occur. To pacify all terrors, when we understand that all conceptual hallucinations arise within the single dharmata awareness, they become less important. Waves arise from the ocean and dissolve back into the ocean, but the waves and the ocean are not really separate. Similarly, when thought first emerges, it emerges as the display of dharmata reality. When we recognize that, when we understand that thought is the manifestation of rigpa-awareness, thought ends within rigpa-awareness. Thought is extinguished within the state of rigpa-awareness. That is the meaning of casting awareness into the essence. "Cast" here does not mean throwing something away. Casting awareness into essence means never leaving the mode of view or the confidence of rigpa-awareness, placing a seal of dharmakaya upon whatever arises in awareness. We need rigpa-awareness's "subjugation," it is said.[69]

Through mode of view, holding the mind, and many branches,

It is said that we must maintain a perspective, a *mode of view,* seeing all phenomena as our Mahamudra awareness, our ultimate mode of existence, our true nature; that we not be controlled by clinging, grasping concepts but be unmoving from a mode of view of all phenomena's selflessness and equality, all phenomena's yuganaddha, all phenomena's freedom from fabrication. We abide by way of this mode of view.

We must also *hold the mind.* Holding the mind means whatever thought we have, we always remain mindful, focused upon it. In general, we can think of mode of view as pertaining to periods of meditative equipoise and holding the mind as pertaining to periods of "subsequent attainment," between sessions of meditation. Regarding this meditative mode of view, the ability to nondually mix periods of being "in meditation" and "out of meditation" does not exist except at the state of full enlightenment. As long as meditative equipoise and subsequent attainment are thus distinct, this *mode of view* refers to *casting awareness into the essence,* in other words, equipoise with all fabricated duality completely pacified. When we arise from equipoise, when we are holding the mind during periods of subsequent attainment, we continue to repeatedly remember the meaning that we understood during our meditation. During meditative equipoise we do not move from our mode of view. Then when we have arisen from equipoise, during periods of subsequent attainment, we repeatedly bring to mind that which we experienced during meditative equipoise, the essential ultimate nature of our being. Whether we are eating, sleeping, moving, or sitting, we must not stir from or give up keeping that awareness in mind during all of our activities. *Branches* refers to methods, skillful means. We use these skillful means until we have realized our Mahamudra ultimate nature.

Persevere until you abide in awareness. [19]

We must persevere in training until we realize the deep awareness of our Mahamudra true nature. *Persevering* means we must rely upon perseverance and effort, persevering by means of various methods, whatever is necessary to sustain our effort, and attain realizations on that basis. Until we have realized Mahamudra awareness, we must strive to abide in it. Whatever thoughts arise, good or bad, in all of our activities, whether eating, sleeping, moving, or sitting, they begin and end within rigpa-awareness. Until we have securely realized that they are produced within rigpa-awareness, we must strive to realize that. As mentioned above, we must persevere until we can bring all activity into the yoga of the clear light of sleep, yoga of moving and sitting, yoga of eating, yoga of dressing.

The essential meaning is that we must put forth effort until all existence appears to us as a pure land. Simply put, until we become aware that all of existence is infinitely pure, is the display of dharmata reality, we must strive in the precept of rigpa-awareness. We must put effort into realizing rigpa-awareness. We must maintain our mode of view in rigpa-awareness. We must hold the mind within rigpa-awareness. We must identify rigpa-awareness. We must look with rigpa-awareness again and again, meditate in rigpa-awareness again and again. We have to be in rigpa-awareness. We must not let ourselves be carried away by our predispositions for ordinary concepts and grasping. No matter how much they occur, we must put forth effort and, by relying on strong antidotes, not let ourselves be hindered by ordinary grasping conceptions until we realize our Mahamudra deep awareness.

23. Revealing the Path to That

By having karmamudra, bliss-void wisdom will dawn.
Blessings of method and wisdom join in union.
Elements slowly falling, spinning, drawn back upward,
Are brought into the places and made to pervade the body.
Without attachment to it, bliss-void deep awareness dawns. [20]

THIS EXPLANATION is in terms of the liberating path, completion stage. In general we speak of two paths: the method path and the liberating path. Here Mahasiddha Tilopa is talking about the liberating path. It is practiced on the basis of the discipline of nonemission of semen. It is intended mainly for lay practitioners, not the ordained.

There are four types of mudras: karmamudra, dharmamudra, samayamudra, and mahamudra. *Having karmamudra* to heighten realization of essence-meaning is taught in the Six Yogas of Naropa in two types of meditation: in reliance upon inner fire in one's own body; and in reliance upon the method of consort practice. According to glorious Lord Atisha's *Lamp on the Path*, it is not permitted for the ordained to practice with karmamudra. This refers to consort practice, of course; literally, relying upon the method of another's body. First the trainee is taught how to generate deep awareness of great bliss through *tummo*, "inner fire," practice in their own body, by melting of the elements through "short-ah" meditation, blazing, and dripping. Once that is achieved the trainee is taught the method of relying upon another's body, and through auspicious interdependence of body, realizations arise in the mind; this happens in reliance upon *karmamudra* consort practice, literally, the "action seal." "Realization arising in mind through auspicious interdependence of body" means bliss-void deep awareness arising in one's mind through union with the karmamudra consort. Deep awareness, nondual union of *bliss-void jnana-wisdom dawns.* Four unifications are taught in

Tantra: unification of appearance and emptiness, unification of luminosity and emptiness, unification of awareness and emptiness, and unification of bliss and emptiness. In Kalachakra, nondual bliss-void wisdom is taught in two: the Mahamudra EH syllable, and the immutable great bliss WAM syllable. The union of EH and WAM is the union of bliss and emptiness. EWAM unification, the union of bliss and emptiness, arises in dependence upon karmamudra practice.

Karmamudra practice is not ordinary sexual activity. There are many methods one needs to have perfected first, many facilitating conditions that must all be present. The ability to engage in karmamudra practice will be indicated, will be prophesied, by the dakinis and by the guru. The thought, "Oh, now is the time to rely upon karmamudra" also arises in one's own mind. Otherwise, just putting on tantric outfits and "going for it" will not have the slightest benefit. When the time has arrived to rely upon karmamudra, the dakinis will indicate it. Then through consort practice, bliss-void jnana wisdom will arise. This is a profundity of the liberating path.

Blessings of method and wisdom join in union. When the realization of the union of the method of great bliss and the wisdom of emptiness arises in the mind, this is the blessed union. Union here means the union of one's own and another's body. On that basis there are four joys or blisses and four emptinesses that are experienced in succession: joy, supreme joy, special joy, and innate joy. That is on descent of the elements; four more joys are experienced during their ascent. There are four joys going upward and four joys going downward. The four emptinesses that accompany these four joys must be *joined in union* with them respectively at each stage. This is just a brief allusion to the extensive explanation that is required to teach this in all of its detail.

Elements slowly falling, spinning, drawn back upward, are brought into the places and made to pervade the body. Without attachment to it, bliss-void deep awareness dawns. If we do not have attachment as the drops of the body flow down, spin, and are induced to return upward, filling the points of the body and pervading the entire body, by their well penetrating the points of the body, nondual bliss-void wisdom will dawn. This is very profound, the point at which actual wisdom of bliss and emptiness dawns. It is something that is actually very difficult. The falling of the elements is easy but their spinning is difficult. Then spinning becomes easy but drawing the elements upward is difficult. This is what is actually meant by our often-used phrase, "auspiciousness convening in the body, realizations appearing to mind." What sort of auspiciousness must come together in our body? It is when the drops fall, spin, return upward, and are brought to pervade the entire body causing blissful heat to expand. When blissful heat expands, realizations arise in the mind. At this point we must be free of attachment. It is a problem if we fall under the influence of attachment. For example, in *Ascertaining the Three Vows* come the words,

> Even in pratimoksha vows, that to be abandoned
> Is delusion and the "self-characterized"; all the scholars agree.

Shravakas are taught to abandon delusion. In Mahayana as well, transformation of the delusions is taught. In Tantra it is taught to make delusions the path. Although these different methods exist—to abandon delusion, transform delusion, and make delusion the path—in the final analysis all the scholars agree that we must ultimately eliminate the delusions and grasping inherently existent, "self-characterized" phenomena. They must be abandoned. Otherwise, if we fall under the influence of the delusions and grasping inherent existence, any path of abandoning them cannot help us. As drops slowly descend, spin, reverse, and are drawn upward, expanding blissful heat throughout the entire body, as auspiciousness convenes in the body and realization of nondual bliss-void wisdom dawns in the mind, if we fall under the influence of clinging attachment, leave aside dawning of jnana-wisdom, even the slight experience that was first developed will quickly be lost. That is why it is taught, "Arrange it without emission." It is said to surpass even the moral discipline of keeping a bhikshu's vows. The moral discipline of nonemission is the best moral discipline, the supreme, highest of moral disciplines. Thus, this instruction is being taught in terms of the liberating path, the stage of completion, within which it is a method path. The Six Yogas, in general, are method paths, skill in means, yet are mainly taught in the context of completion stage, second of the two tantric stages of generation and completion. Generally speaking, the Six Yogas of Naropa are supporting practices of completion stage Tantra but not the actual completion stage "paths." In the present context, for example, if we have good practice of this it becomes actual, perfect completion stage realization. If we can practice perfect completion stage realizing "auspiciousness convening in the body and realization dawning in the mind," the drops slowly flow downward. In the second stage the drops spin in the path of the vajra. Then they must go through the stages of returning upward, being drawn, and carried. Then, when auspiciousness convenes in the body, bliss pervades the entire body. After some time of accustoming to it, the slow descent, the spinning, the reversal, the drawing, the bringing, can all happen simultaneously. Without need of meditating on the stages, it can all happen at the same time. If we have managed to arrive at such a method of the profound liberating path, certain qualities are attained.

> Long life without white hair, waxing like the moon,
> Luminous complexion with the strength of a lion,
> Common siddhis quickly attained, we mount the supreme. [21]

Here Tilopa speaks of some of the qualities that are attained. If we have been able to have such auspiciousness convene in our body and realization arise in our mind, what sorts of qualities arise? We will have *long life without white hair,* that is, without signs of aging. We will not become old-aged. He says that the complexion of our body will be luminous as the moon, *expanding like the moon.*

Luminous complexion with the strength of a lion: We become very clear and bright; it can even cause those who look at us to experience bliss and joy. And we have strength like a lion; these are all common siddhis. *Common siddhis quickly attained, we mount the supreme.* Such common attainments, long life without aging, light of the body expanding like the moon, one's whole complexion being as bright as the sun, the strength of a lion, these are quickly attained. After this we *mount the supreme.* The supreme fruition is called supreme siddhi. First common siddhis are quickly attained; after that we can "mount the supreme" or delight in the supreme, meaning that the supreme siddhi can engulf us or descend upon us, that we can abide within it.

> May these pith instructions of Mahamudra
> Abide in the hearts of fortunate living beings! [22]

This is a prayer. These are the essential instructions of Mahamudra that Tilopa gave to Naropa on the banks of the Ganges, that river of the East. Generally speaking, there are many different "pith" or "essential" instructions on Mahamudra. Yet it is said that these are the real pith essentials of Mahamudra. They are brief and very profound and, if practiced, can liberate us in this very lifetime without abandoning our present body.

May these pith instructions of Mahamudra abide in the hearts of fortunate living beings! May the practice of Mahamudra remain in the hearts of living beings! The mention of beings with "good fortune" is very important. It is not good if these instructions are revealed to those without the good fortune for it. For example, lion's milk can only be contained in a precious jewel vessel; poured into any other ordinary cup, the cup will break, spilling the milk.

So what sort of person has the good fortune? The kind of person who does not doubt the truth of Mahamudra, who delights in the meaning of Mahamudra; someone who has fervent aspiration and high regard for the guru who teaches Mahamudra; whose aspiration and devotion is not too tight or too loose. Mahasiddha Tilopa prays that the instructions remain in the heart of such a fortunate person. Otherwise, according to Sakya Pandita,

> If the deluded meditate on Mahamudra
> It will cause most to take rebirth as animals,
> Or else to be born in the formless realm.

If the ignorant or deluded without the necessary good fortune meditate on Mahamudra, he says that they will take rebirth as animals. It is said that if someone constantly meditates on nothing at all in total blackness it causes animal rebirth. If someone thinks meditating in a state of nonconceptuality means that they have to stop all thinking, to cut off all their thoughts, they will be born as an animal. There is also a danger that, out of the three realms— the desire, form, and formless realms—such meditation can cause rebirth in the formless realm; in particular, the formless realm's state of "nothing at all." So what Sakya Pandita says is true. Thus Mahasiddha Tilopa prays that, without delusion, the practice may remain in the hearts of those with the supreme good fortune for it.

> This completes the twenty-three vajra verses on Mahamudra taught by the sovereign of Mahamudra siddhas, Tilopa, to the learned and accomplished Kashmiri pandit Naropa on the banks of the River Ganges. Great Naropa then taught it to the Tibetan lotsawa, Great King of Translators Marpa Chökyi Lodrö, who translated it and made it definitive at Naropa's northern abode of Pullahari. ITHI! May all be virtuous! [23]

Pandit Naropa then taught it to the great Tibetan lotsawa, King of Translators Marpa Chökyi Lodrö. Then Marpa Chökyi Lodrö translated it and finished setting it down definitively at Pandit Naropa's abode of Pullahari in the north.

> Seeing the root guru as actual Buddha,
> And correctly striving with faith and conviction
> In the molten essence of the guru's nectar instructions,
> May I realize the indivisibility of my mind and the guru!

Thus, this *Gangama* Mahamudra commentary was taught by the Tenth Sangyes Nyenpa Rinpoche who was born in Bhutan, Paro, Tagtsang. Rinpoche also transcribed the commentary himself from recordings of his teaching.

APPENDIX 1: TILOPA, FROM THE
GOLDEN GARLAND OF THE KAGYU

BY THE THIRD KARMAPA RANGJUNG DORJE[1]

HIS HUMAN LINEAGE

THE LIFE OF the buddha emanation Tilopa is inconceivable and inexpressible, yet, briefly, is taught in four qualities: his human lineage, his being an emanation of Chakrasamvara, his being Chakrasamavara himself, and his being an emanation of all buddhas of the three times. The first part reveals his human lineage, the period from birth up to when he overwhelmed the dakinis and heard Dharma teachings.

He was born in Zahor, East India, in a city called Jnanakor that had many desirable qualities and was a source of much knowledge. His father was Brahmin Clarity, from an exalted family line, and his mother was Brahmini Endowed with Clarity. First they had a daughter named Brahmini Clear Lamp. Seeking to have the son they lacked, they made offerings to all the Brahmins, rishis, and worldly devas. In particular, they made vast offerings to the Three Jewels of Refuge and made prayers. They also prayed to Chakrasamvara and Vajrayogini. As a result, nine months and ten days later they had a son.

At that time, East India was pervaded by light. When the Brahmin name-givers were invited and checked their divinations, some seemed to indicate that he was a deva, some a naga, some a human being, and some indicated that he was a buddha. They didn't know what to say. They knew that he was of a particularly exalted nature but they could not say whether he was a deva, naga, yaksha, or buddha. They would only say that he was a supremely amazing being, and that he should be cared for extremely carefully. They gave him the name Brahmin Clear Light. He was very lovingly cared for with pure foods such as the three white foods and three sweets.

When he was a year old his mother had placed him at the edge of some shade and was speaking pleasantly to him when a frightful shadow that had not been seen before fell upon the boy. When they looked behind it there was an ugly old woman who had the thirty-two marks of an enlightened being. His mother was terrified and told her to get out.

The old woman said, "Even if you care for him with love, there is no place death will not come!"

When they asked what they could do to prevent his death she said,

> Along with nice-sounding baby names,
> If you gave him symbols of holy Dharma, that would be good!

When he was taught Dharma in symbols and language he understood without any impediment.

When he was sixteen he also studied the Vedas and became endowed with many good qualities. Then, the wrathful black dakini that had appeared before came again. She said,

> Write texts and tend buffalo!
> Send Brahmin Clear Light
> To stay in the forest!
> The dakini will make a prophecy!

His parents said, "Every prophecy she made so far has come true! We should follow her prophecy now!"

The next morning he went with his father to drive the buffalo. Then his father returned and went home. His son fed the buffalo then leaned back against a tree and began to write. The ugly hag with the thirty-two enlightened marks appeared again and asked him about himself.

He said, "I am from the city of Zahor. My father is Brahmin Clarity, my mother is Brahmini Endowed with Clarity. My sister is Brahmini Clear Lamp and I am Brahmin Clear Light. These are sal trees. I am making a living herding buffalo. With my writing, I am practicing Dharma."

The woman was enraged. She said, "All of this, your country and so on, is not correct! You're not going to get enlightened studying texts, either! If you're going to attain enlightenment, where is the buddha of suchness of blind self-risen great transcendent wisdom?"

The boy was a bit shocked and asked, "How is that?"

> *E ma!* How could it be?
> Your father is Chakrasamvara and
> Your mother is Vajrayogini.
> I am your sister, Goddess Bestower of Bliss.
> Your country is Oddiyana of the West.
> You, brother, are Panchapana, "Holder of the Five."
> If you want experience, buffalo herder,
> In the Bodhi Tree Forest
> The meaning of the ear-whispered lineage, unwritten,
> With outer, inner, and secret meanings,
> Is possessed by the stainless dakinis!

About her prophecy, she then said,

> Siddha endowed with samaya,
> Accept this prophecy, if you will!

He said, "To go there and know the dakinis, the way will be very difficult. There is no way I could go."

The dakini brought three things: a jewel ladder, a jewel bridge, and a key. She said,

> With my blessing you won't have any problems.
> With the ladder and bridge you will overcome seals and
>   concealment.
> The key will release the chains on the result.
> Now, give up all doubt and go!

He asked his parents' permission. His mother was very unhappy, but his father said, "It will be all right because it will happen just as she said. Go!"

Taking these three auspicious objects with him, he went all the way to the Western country of Oddiyana without any obstacles. He arrived at an iron mountain that was a huge gandhola-stupa. He used the bridge to get across a swelling lake of poison and used the ladder to ascend the mountain. He came to the door of the temple, opened the latch, and went in. There were two destroyer dakinis, the receiving guard dakini, and the outer nirmanakaya devouring karma dakini, who said,

> I show various wrathful forms
> And make terrible roars.
> I am the devouring dakini.
> I like flesh and lust for blood!

He assumed a wrathful physical bearing, a lustful vocal expression, and a fearless mind. He later said,

> Going on, there were many terrifying dakinis.
> I did not move a tip of a hair in my pores.

The dakini fainted. Soon as she regained consciousness, she requested his forbearance, saying,

> Like a bee in a butter lamp, I was destroyed.
> Meditator, where are you from?
> I am like a subject, with little power.
> If I don't ask the intermediary female minister,
> My flesh and blood will be eaten and drunk.
> Therefore, Holy One, have pity on me!

After she said that, he asked to go inside. The sambhogakaya worldly karma dakini appeared again, and he countered with the three modes of body, speech, and mind, as before. It had the same result, after which she requested his forbearance and he asked to go in. Venerable Jnana Dakini covered her face with a clean red cloth and said, "Send the fortunate one in!"

When Tilopa went in he did not prostrate, so innumerable dakinis arose from their seats with the same thought, saying,

> This one showing disrespect to the Bhagavati
> Who is the Mother of the three times' buddhas:
> Why not destroy him?

The Venerable Mother herself then said,

> This is the Bhagavan, Protector of Beings,
> Father of the three times' Buddhas.
> His nature is Chakrasamvara.
> Even if violent vajra hail fell from the sky
> It could not deter him. Give him Dharma!

The dakinis asked, "What teachings do you want?" He would not accept, however, so the Venerable Lady asked, "Who are you? Who prophesied you? For what purpose have you come?"

> I am Panchapana. My sister Bestower of Bliss sent me.
> My intended purpose is ultimate truth.
> I request the supremely exalted
> Great secret of stainless great bliss.

He then saw a secret treasury of symbols of enlightened body, speech, and mind. The body symbol was that of the self-arising glorious innate-born Father-Mother in union. The speech symbol was a three-sided tetrahedron with self-risen letters of the seven-syllable mantra in lapis lazuli. The mind symbol was three self-risen five-pronged jewels.

She asked, "Did you see the three natures of this secret treasury of Dharma?"

"From the secret treasury of body, speech, and mind, I see the three wish-fulfilling jewels! I request instruction on view, meditation, conduct, results, commitment, and self-liberation." She said,

> To receive the secret treasury from me,
> I have three wish-fulfilling jewels,
> The innate born that clears the gloom of ignorance.
> If you understand this indication, I will give it to you.

He said,

> From the self-risen body treasury I receive the wish-fulfilling samaya.
> From the mantra-syllable speech treasury I receive the common
>   wish-fulfilling jewel.

From the hand-implement mind treasury I receive the wish-fulfilling
    jewel of ultimate truth.

The dakinis said,

Although you are fortunate because of being sealed
With the three wish-fulfilling jewels
From the secret treasury of body, speech, and mind,
As a samaya-bound, prophesied siddha,
Still, you will not open the door of glory!

The longer form of what they said was this:

In the self-risen treasury of body
Is the common wish-fulfilling jewel
Locked away by those with prophecy;
Without being prophesied, it will not open.

In the self-risen treasury of syllables and speech
Is the wish-fulfilling jewel of samaya,
Locked away by those with samaya;
Without samaya, it will not open.

In the hand-implement treasury of mind
Is the wish-fulfilling jewel of ultimate truth,
Locked away by those who are accomplished;
Without accomplishment, it will not open.

Tilopa said that he had those:

In the forest of sal trees the Dakini said,
"Samaya and prophecy endowed siddha!
You may take it if you will!"
I have the key of prophecy!

The dakinis clapped their hands and laughed, saying, "You have no prophecy! You've been deceived by mara!" They said,

The blind, looking, see no forms!
The deaf, listening, hear no sounds!
The mute, speaking, cannot be understood!
The crippled, running, get nowhere!
Since you've been deceived by mara, what you say is not true!

Tilopa replied,

Lies are faulty speech,
But with exhaustion of faults
No lie is spoken because there is no cause for it.
Since she never spoke a lie,
She is not a mara. It is true, she is a dakini!

They said, "Mara is not a dakini, therefore please instruct us!" In response, he sang of the meaning of having the key:

For the seals of the three secret treasuries
Use three keys of instructions.
Opening the three in succession
Is the meaning of the Chakrasamvara tantra.

Secret words of the Dakinis, the vow of mind,
Lamp of transcendent wisdom, clearing darkness of ignorance,
Intrinsic awareness, self-risen, self-luminous:
I have the key of this self-risen samaya.

I have the key of self-risen samaya,
That remains forever unborn.

I have the key of spontaneous experience
Of Mahamudra, nature of unborn elemental mind:
I am prophesied to attain the three bodies.

Not observing any object in mind,
Innate born, indivisible,
Without even a trace of mindfulness,

I have the key of a siddha's experience
Of nonabiding great bliss.

The dakinis were admiring and respectful and, in dependence upon the
secret sindhura vajra jnana mandala, introduced him to the four initiations
completely. With this, he attained the two siddhis. The Jnana Dakini said,

Bhagavan who is my father,
Supreme bliss, Heruka Chakrasamvara,
Buddha Tilopa, Protector of Beings,
I offer you the three wish-fulfilling jewels.

She then gave him the complete ear-whispered lineage with its blessings.
She also gave him the entire Shri Chakrasamvara tantra and its instructions.
She instructed him in the quintessential secret meanings. She gave him
many tantras such as the Six Ocean tantras, Union with the Four Dakinis
tantra, the Heruka Bhadra tantra, the Heruka Play of Compassion tantra,
the Shri Vajra Ocean Vajradakini tantra, the Samvara Vajra Garland and
Dakini Secret Treasury tantra, and the Self-Risen Vajradhara tantra, which
he brought with him to our world. With the attainment of Kechara siddhi
he flew away into space, saying,

Like a bird in space
Goes unimpeded, I, Prajnabhadra
Transcendent Wisdom Awareness,
Fly in the empty clarity of the luminous sphere!
All of the dakinis objected, saying,

Great Being, where are you going?
Please take care of us!

He would not accept, saying,

I am prevented because of my disciples,
Naropa, Riri, and Kasori.
I, the yogi, go to Crown Jewel Monastery.

Saying this, he left. In the sky, formless Jnana Dakini, without manifesting her body, aurally taught him nine rounds of Dharma:

> For conduct, pierce water with a sword!
> For samaya, look at the mirror of your own mind!
> For samaya substance, with the sun of realization,
> Destroy knots and seals on the ripening, liberating path.
> Turn the wheel of the channels, winds, and nets.
> Look at the lamp of transcendent wisdom awareness.
> Look at self-liberated Mahamudra.
> Look at the outer mirror of equal taste.
> Hold the jewel of the great bliss teachings.

He understood the instructions and, as he left for Crown Jewel Monastery, he said,

> In the stupa of the illusory body,
> I have understood the formless dakini's secrets.
> Controlling the hook of inexpressible speech,
> I go into the space of nondual clear light.

These were his qualities of overwhelming the dakinis and hearing teachings.

HIS QUALITY OF TEACHING WITHOUT A HUMAN TEACHER

Lord Tilopa is renowned to have heard teachings from the Jnana Dakini of Oddiyana and to have attained realization on that basis. His renown spread everywhere in India from East to West. Wanting to dispel their preconceptions about him, everyone asked what lamas he had met. He said,

> I have no human lama; my lama is the Omniscient One.

The dakinis, from space, said,

> Tilopa, you have manifested the meaning of the two truths
> And have mastered the five fields of knowledge.

You have no human lama whatsoever.
Who is your lama? The Omniscient One.

In order to dispel others' lack of faith,
He demonstrated having human gurus.
From four gurus of the four directions
He received four lineages.

From Master Charyapa, in dependence upon Chakrasamvara, he received the base, path, and result teachings on *tummo*, inner fire. From Master Nagarjuna, in dependence upon Guhyasamaja tantra, he received teachings of illusory body, clear light, and union as taught in father tantra. From Master Lawapa, in dependence upon the ear-whispered lineage of Hevajra, he received teachings on bringing the clear light of sleep onto the path, and the self-release of thought without foundation. In lineage from Padma Vajra, from Dakini Samantabhadri, in dependence upon the Ocean of Vows tantra, he received teachings on the blissful path of *phowa,* and bardo teachings. He said,

Charyapa, Nagarjuna, Lawapa,
And Samantabhadri are my gurus
Of the four transmission lineages,
And others, such as Indrabodhi.

Others list the teachings he received as illusory body, dream yoga, clear light, *phowa,* bardo, entering the corpse, *tummo,* and Mahamudra.

HIS QUALITY OF OVERWHELMING POWERFUL YOGIS

There was a great king who lived in that area who venerated his mother and would not allow her command to be disobeyed. When she was asked what was the most virtuous thing to do, she said that, in her opinion, if all the kingdom's pandits and sadhus were to gather and perform ganachakra, that would bring the ultimate merit. Because she said this, the king proclaimed to everyone that it must be done, and set the date.

They each came and erected their own mandalas. One of the most powerful yogis, acting as master, and asking if there was anyone of greater power present, took the throne. As soon as he did, the words, "Send in the ugly hag!"

were heard, and a wrathful woman appeared. She opened the door and told the powerful yogi not to take a seat at the head of the gathering.

"Who is more wrathful than I? Who will come?"

"My brother will come."

Asked where he lived, she replied, "He is playing in the great charnel ground called the Fiery One."

He said, "All right, have him come to the throne. We will compete and see who has greater power."

The invitation was made and a bluish man with bloodshot eyes wearing a cotton cloak came in and sat upon the throne in meditative absorption to compete in power. The other erected a mandala with deities and Tilopa did likewise. He could not destroy Tilopa's mandala, but Tilopa destroyed his. The other then summoned many fresh and old corpses, and transformed them into many ganachakra and other offerings. Tilopa gave it one glance and it collapsed back into being a charnel ground. Tilopa did the same, transforming charnel ground corpses into offerings, and the other yogi could do nothing to destroy them.

Then Tilopa turned his skin inside out to reveal the tantric deity and mandala with charnel grounds in every one of his body's pores, and many buddhas from many worlds with immeasurable emanations instructing and liberating sentient beings. Then he mounted a lion and brought it down on the sun and moon and rode them back and forth across the sky.

The other was unable to respond and was overcome with faith.

> *E ma!* This is incredible conduct!
> Such miraculous emanations!
> From what cause do they arise?
> From where does such a yogi come?

Tilopa acted as head master of the tsog gathering. The powerful yogis prostrated to him, circumambulated, offered mandala, and received instructions.

HIS QUALITY OF SUBDUING THE TIRTHIKA

In that region there was a tirthika, a non-Buddhist, who was very learned and powerful and sought to annihilate Buddha's teachings. Seeing that he needed to be controlled, Tilopa went where he was teaching and said, "They say you have an argument for me! Let's compete in power and debate!"

A time was set, the king to act as witness, and the loser to convert to the victor's teachings. The king and the two took their seats on three thrones. First they debated in language with scripture and logic and Tilopa was victorious three times. Then they competed in miracle powers. In such feats as the erection and destruction of mandalas with deities they were completely equal, but after they had both tethered the sun and brought it down, Tilopa held it back up in the sky so that the other could no longer bring it down.

Tilopa said, "Convert to my teachings!" and started to cut his topknot. This enraged the other and he emitted blazing fire from his mouth. Tilopa was not frightened. The tirthika asked,

> Who is this yogi who is not afraid of me,
> I, who make the three realms quake?

Tilopa emitted even more fire which stopped the other's fire and sent it back, burning him up to his hair knot. He said,

> I am completely free from danger!
> Therefore, I am Tilo!

He developed faith, and he and his entire retinue prostrated, offered mandala, circumambulated, and received instructions. All were liberated. One should learn the Nagpo Gewa Silwa Tsel instructions from the oral lineage.

His Quality of Subduing the Deceiving Magician

There was a maharaja and a magician who hated him. The magician invoked an illusory army which conquered the lands surrounding the king's palace. The king did not know it was an illusion. Everyone was afraid and wondering how to escape. An ugly woman with enlightened marks, leaning on a cane, appeared and asked, "What is happening to you?"

"They have seized all the other lands so we are fleeing!"

She said, "I need to speak to you! Get a message to the king!"

Subjects spoke to the outer ministers, they spoke to the inner ministers, and eventually the king got the message. He invited Lord Tilopa, who emanated an army that killed the entire opposing army. The magician knew it was Tilopa, and asked,

A holy being like you, who is based in Dharma!
How could you do something like this?

Tilopa answered,

Such things as killing illusory beings
Are not unwholesome because they lack minds!

With faith they requested instructions. The magician became known as the Deceiving Speaker of Truth in the Charnel Ground Sound of Laughter, according to the oral lineage.

HIS QUALITY OF SUBDUING THE BARMAID

Tilopa had gone to a region where there was a barmaid. He said, "I'm buying beer! Bring the beer!"
   "How will you pay for it?"
   "I'll make a drawing from the shade of the sun that will more than pay for the beer!" Then he emanated cats who drank the beer. Again, he emanated many yogis who drank the beer. Again, he, alone, drank the beer. He drank all of her beer and that of seven other barmaids. When they asked him for the money, he said, "Look at the containers!" The containers that had previously been empty were all more full than before. They developed overwhelming faith in him and asked him, "Holy One! From where have you come? Please care for us!"

I am Tilo, Protector of Beings!
The yogi who gives you sight!

She asked him to care for her and he gave her instructions. As a result, in that very lifetime she became a wisdom dakini, Sunlight Lamp Goddess, an immortal omniscient yogini.

HIS DIRECT TEACHING OF INTERDEPENDENCE AS THE MEANING OF KARMIC CAUSE AND EFFECT

When a non-Buddhist holding the view of a Charvaka Nihilist had infected everyone in a region with distorted views, even refuting true assertions about cause and effect made by a learned pandit, the debate had not yet been decided, with neither able to refute the other. Tilopa came to where they were debating. They asked him which debate was victorious and he replied that the debate asserting the existence of karmic cause and effect was victorious.

The other said, "Well, you and the birds may say so, but he could not refute my arguments with scripture and reasoning! It is not true, because I don't see it with my own direct perception!"

Tilopa said, "Close your eyes!" and snapped his fingers, at which point they could see all the abodes of hell, with many beings experiencing being cooked and burnt. There was an empty cauldron with molten liquid boiling in it and no one inside. He asked, "What is this empty one for?"

"There is a heretic, a forder, a tirthika, who asserts the nonexistence of the natural law of karmic cause and effect, who is engaging in much nonvirtuous activity of various kinds. Since he is actively engaging in propagation of views that distort reality, he will be cooked here after he dies."

He believed it, but said, "Alright, it is true that nonvirtuous conduct causes migration to hell, but there is no virtuous cause and effect, no need to practice virtue."

Tilopa said, "I will show you." In an instant he took him to the Heaven of the Thirty-three. In each of the palaces lived a divine couple. In one palace lived a solitary goddess.

He asked, "What about this one who lacks a companion?"

"In Jambudvipa there is someone who has changed his tenets to assert cause and effect, who has created great nonvirtue but by practicing virtue will take birth here."

The tirthika felt faith in that and Tilopa introduced him to the experience of realizing that appearances are one's own mind, saying,

> For the criminal propelled by his karma
> Hell is his own mind reflected back to him.
> For someone who has practiced the ten virtues
> His good migration is his own mind appearing to him.

Having been taught the effects of actions, he felt faith and received teachings. As a result he became the Liberated Mantrijnana of Radadi in the Southeast.

HIS QUALITY OF SUBDUING THE BUTCHER

There was a butcher who killed many living creatures. He would give the meat to his sole child, a son. At one point Tilopa saw that he should be subdued. The butcher was cooking a kettle of meat of many animals that he had killed. Tilopa emanated into the meat, at the same time making the butcher's son invisible. He transformed the meat into the flesh of the butcher's son. When the butcher took off the lid, looked inside, and saw his son, he was heartbroken, and wept. Tilopa said to him,

> If you give up killing and harming others
> I will bring your son back into existence.

Promising to give up harmful deeds, purify previous ones, and vowing not to repeat them in the future, the butcher developed faith in Tilopa and attained liberation. As he said,

> The results of harm created by karma
> Ripen upon oneself; abandon it.

After his liberation he was known as Jina Bodhi of Shriparvata, Glorious Mountain.

THE QUALITY OF MASTER TILOPA SUBDUING THE SINGER

In one region there was a master singer performing in a large bazaar. Tilopa asked him, "What are you crying about?"

The singer was angered and scornfully said it was a song.

"The sound *kye ma!* expresses crying and grief!"

They competed in singing. Tilopa said, "I only know the melodies of Brahma and songs that are beyond this world!"

Tilopa won and the other was overwhelmed. He developed faith and asked Tilopa to care for him, saying,

> Holy One, where are you from?
> You have overwhelmed me!

Tilopa replied,

> I have come here
> From the world of Brahma
> As a singer to protect one skilled in the branches of melody.
> I am Tilopa.
> Right now, I am wandering anywhere.

He became known as the Melodious Mute, who continues to live at Nagara.

His Quality of Subduing the Powerful One

There was a powerful sorcerer named Sun. All people had to bow to him. He killed those who remained upright. Even his entourage was fearful around him. Tilopa went before him and gave him a hostile look.

The sorcerer said, "I am going to put a spell on you!" and did his magic. Many ferocious Dharma protectors gathered, but Tilopa slew them with a glance. When his entourage arose, Tilopa also killed them with a look. The sorcerer was extremely sad and went before Tilopa.

Tilopa looked at him with love and he was happy. Tilopa said that if he refrained from harmful deeds in the future, there was a way to bring back his retinue. He hooked back the consciousnesses of the sorcerer's deceased entourage and returned them to life. The sorcerer felt intense faith. Tilopa said,

> I, Tilopa, who have realized the ultimate,
> Have never done what is called "killing" of anyone!

The sorcerer was liberated. He became known as Nyima-imi of Tsundhi Ling.

His Quality of Being Renowned as an Emanation of Chakrasamvara

On the banks of the River Salwen, near the Kedara Mountain pass, at the Blazing Charnel Ground, at the Temple called Sulakhatre, in the Sorrowless Grove, is where Tilopa took ordination and received bhikshu training. He became known as the Bhikshu Kalabha. There was a rule at that monastic abode, that in the morning you meditated and contemplated the teachings in your own room, and in the afternoon you circumambulated, and engaged in Dharma practices, or whatever deity practices everyone was participating in. If your conduct did not accord with this you were punished. Kalabha did just the contrary. In the morning he would go out killing many creatures on the road, separating their heads from their bodies and placing them in separate piles. He would go and feast on the barmaid's spent fermented barley.

His uncle, the sthavira Moonlight, Chandraprabha, could not bear the youth's behavior. If others saw, he would receive severe punishment. Saying that there was danger of his appearing biased, he met secretly with the abbots and masters.

"If we don't talk to Kalabha, I will have to say that we have failed our monthly confession." They spoke to Kalabha but he would not listen and kept on taking many lives.

One time the king was on the road for a periodic offering ceremony when Kalabha was acting this way. With abhorrence, the king asked him what his story was. In reply, he said,

> In the peaceful abode of the Sorrowless Grove,
> I am the disciple of the abbots and my uncle.
> I am Bhikshu Kalabha.
> For hundreds of millions of eons
> I have conversed with Buddha Shakyamuni,
> Nagarjuna, Aryadeva, and Vajradhara!
> I have been to hundreds of pure lands!
> I have seen the faces of hundreds of buddhas!
> I see the bhumi of the Very Joyful.
> I see the truth of interdependence and karma.
> I manifest dharmata dharmakaya.
> Even the great Saraha's realizations
> Do not compete with mine!
> As for me, I kill no sentient being!

Saying this, he snapped his fingers. All those creatures' heads and bodies rejoined and they flew off, radiating light. People said, "This is an emanation of Chakrasamvara." It was understood and became well known.

His Quality of Revealing Himself to Be Actual Chakrasamvara

At this time he would go before the palace of King Singhachandra, seeking alms. As he was stopped, venerated, and questioned about his conduct and teachings, one time the king was watching from the top of his temple. Noticing that there was a bhikshu who was peaceful, subdued, and admirable in conduct, when he investigated him he found that he was reciting many sutras and tantras that had never been heard before. Even when a learned pandit checked, he found him to be reciting a sutra he had never heard before, and was amazed.

The king felt faith in him and invited him to give teachings for many days. He would make prayers in accordance with Dharma for the king and then leave. The king invited him repeatedly to give teachings.

One time when the king inquired about his life in detail, he responded,

> Of Brahmin caste, I am Tilo,
> Who lacks a father and mother.
> I have no abbot or master at all.
> Because I am the self-risen buddha
> I do not train in teaching and listening.
> With logic of language and pramana
> You're just talking to yourself!
> I am inseparable from the body, speech, and mind
> Of Chakrasamvara. It is inexpressible.

At this time he became renowned as being actual Chakrasamvara.

His Quality of Revealing That He Embodies All Buddhas of the Three Times

One time a king named King Flower Islander had faith in the master and made requests to him with aspiration. Lord Tilopa took care of him also. He was asked to preside at a ganachakra gathering of many pandits and sadhus. In the chaos, they had visions of him in different mandalas. He said,

> My body is Hevajra,
> Speech is Mahamaya.

Mind is Chakrasamvara.
Senses are Guhyasamaja.
Limbs are Krishnayamari.
My fingers and toes are Vajra Bhairava.
In channels of Bodhgayas, four Vajra Seats,
Are energy-winds of Vajra Garlands.
My drops are the Treasure of Secrets
because my skull is the Ushnisha Buddha.
All is the nature of Kalachakra,
Great bliss of buddhas in union.
My pores are inseparable from the body,
Speech, and mind of all buddhas of the three times.

Then he left for the Crown Jewel Monastery. The yogis said that he was the nature of all buddhas of the three times, and this became well known.

Real emanation of Buddha, Protector of Beings,
Blessed by Tara, named Tilopa,
Endowed with five wisdoms, known as Prajnabhadra,
With secret names of Samvara Vajra,
Unobstructed Vajra, and Wheel of Bliss,
And renowned as Kalabha, O blissful, excellent lama,
Known as Venerable One of the Sesame,
Immortal Lord of Yogis, at your feet I bow.

This completes the Life of Tilopa.
ITHI

APPENDIX 2: A BRIEF ACCOUNT OF TILOPA AND NAROPA

BY GAMPOPA

Homage, Guru Vajradhara and the hosts of dakinis!

I shall briefly express some of the realized qualities
Of the precious Gurus of our Practice Lineage.

THERE ARE TWO instructions for practitioners: taking causes on the path, the Paramitayana, Vehicle of the Perfections, in lineage from Lord Atisha and so on; and taking results on the path, the Secret Mantra Vajrayana, in lineage from glorious Naropa and so on. Those who practiced in India and Tibet sought special lineages of these.

As for the teachers of the sutras and tantras, I shall express some of the qualities of the teacher Buddha and the commentators. By investigating the realized qualities of the gurus of the Practice Lineage, practitioners should develop conviction and make requests with heartfelt emotion, and in order to attain such qualities we should please the guru. The teacher of the Tantras is great Shri Vajradhara. For trainees of best and superlative faculties with pure appearances he emanates in sambhogakaya forms such as that of Vajradhara, and with that appearance fulfills their purpose. For those of middling and least faculties he emanates in forms suitable to each, such as that of Buddha Shakyamuni, and with that appearance fulfills their purpose, teaching the Vehicle of Logic and Dialectics. Emanating as Vajradhara for those of best and superlative faculties, he teaches the Secret Mantra Vajrayana. An emanation of his mind is the compiler of the teachings, Vajrapani. As said in the *Sambuta Tantra,*

I, myself, teacher of the great Dharma,
Am the teacher among the gathering,
And I am the compiler as well.

As for Tilopa, whom we speak of here, he was born in the eastern country of Zahor. He had fathomless realized qualities that are impossible to express. He was an emanated being. Sometimes he appeared as the Tilopa of our tradition but sometimes he appeared as a bhikshu. Sometimes he appeared in a single form and sometimes he emanated in many hundreds and thousands of forms. Sometimes he appeared as a naked yogi. He was a nirmanakaya who was indivisible from Vajrapani because, as he himself said,

Naropa who has attained the dharani of nonforgetfulness
Was my disciple for twelve years.
For those interested in later times
He has my biography.
If you want to know it, receive it from him.
With billions of emanations, I have conversed
With Buddha Shakyamuni, Nagarjuna,
Aryadeva, and others as well.
I see the truth of dharmata.

Tilopa's disciple Naropa was born in the western country of Srinagara. He was learned in the five fields of knowledge from the first. He had gone to practice the seven-syllable mantra[1] in a charnel ground. In the early dawn a dakini spoke to him in a dream:

Son of the Lineage! Go to the East! There is a yogi there named Tailo Prajnabhadra. Ask him for Mahamudra instructions!

Without asking the whereabouts of the country, Naropa set off to the East. He asked all the monks he met, "Have you seen a yogi named Tailo?" They replied that they had never seen a yogi named Tailo but that there was a destitute beggar named Tailo showing up everywhere. Then, at the door of the temple library an aged yogi with a dark red complexion appeared, in rags, shaking, holding four or five live fish in his left hand and a wood fire in his right. He sat down among the rows of Sangha receiving teachings from Naropa and cooked the fish on his stove. The monks had no faith in him and Naropa came holding a club and said, "You bring this into the ranks of my teachings?"

Tilopa replied, "If you don't like it . . . ," and snapped his fingers once, at which point the fish revived and flew up into space. Naropa then knew and was very embarrassed. He said he thought it was definitely Tilopa. All the monks then knew he was a mahasiddha and made three prostrations to him, and circumambulated him three times. Having been requested to forbear, the guru accepted their apology.

Then Naropa knew with certainty that he was Tilopa and, without doubt, made three prostrations and three circumambulations of the guru. Taking Tilopa's feet to his crown he said, "Since you were prophesied to me, please help me to escape from samsara!"

Tilopa left without saying anything and Naropa followed him. When they descended into one bamboo grove Naropa fell through an opening in the sand and was impaled on a bamboo stake. Tilopa glared into Naropa's face, then left. Naropa asked him to stay, but he left without saying anything.

Three days later he returned. He asked, "Are you in pain?" He waved his hand over Naropa, who was lying like a corpse covered in ashes. This made his wounds disappear, and he was healed. Tilopa gave him the name "Naropa," the "Corpse-like One," at that time.

As Naropa continued to follow Tilopa, at one time teachings were being given at a layperson's house. The monks sat down in rows and when food was distributed Tilopa said, "Naropa! I'm hungry but I can't receive any food! You go first and take some!"

Since Naropa had not been invited with the monks, they asked where he had come from and would not give him any food. Naropa in desperation scooped up what he could in a skull cup and ran, but they chased after him with clubs. Guru Tilopa saw and rendered the pursuers immobile, paralyzing them. Then he stopped the paralysis.

Naropa continued to follow him. Later they went up on to the balcony of a temple library. Tilopa said, "If there were someone who didn't break the guru's word, they would jump from this precipice!"

Naropa thought, "There's no disciple around here except me! He must be speaking to me!" and he jumped. It broke both his legs. The guru came to look at him and left. He came back a few days later and asked, "Are you in pain?" He waved his hand over Naropa who lay in the dust like a corpse, clearing and healing him.

Another time when he was accompanying the master, Tilopa gathered an exquisite garland of many flowers and gave them to Naropa. He told him that there would be two courtiers bringing their new bride through the crossroads and that he should hold the flowers up to her. When he did so the courtiers were pleased and started to make gifts to him. Then Tilopa told him not to take the gifts, but to massage the bride's breasts! When Naropa did this it enraged them and they beat him severely.

Tilopa then came and asked, "What's wrong?"

"I did as the guru said and they beat me! I'm at the brink of death!" Tilopa waved his hand over him and healed him.

Another time Indrabhuti's wife wished to invite him to preside over the ganachakra feast. She said, "Tilopa, Prajnabhadra! They say you have clairvoyance! I am inviting you to my ganachakra, requesting with conviction!" and Tilopa came, covering many days' journey in a single day. Naropa also attained miracle powers at that time. As they were staying in a house there someone said, "There are two beggars in this house!" Indrabhuti's wife said, "I've invited Tilopa to preside at the ganachakra so it may be him. I'm asking him." They participated in the ganachakra and other services.

Again, following him, one night they slept beside a large river. Tilopa said, "Naropa! I'm hungry! Go beg some food!" Naropa crossed the river, received some raw rice and came back. When he did, there was a bhikshu sitting on the guru's bed. He thought he was the guru's emanation and followed him, so the monk asked him, "Is this dreadful person soliciting a bhikshu in the evening?" Then he struck him in the forehead and left.

Naropa thought, "One with the ability to emanate as a monk is definitely a mahasiddha!" and when he followed after him he saw the monk in the forest, returning from the end of a path, reversing back, going back and forth, acting as if he was trapped. When Naropa looked, there was a stream about six feet wide that Tilopa could not jump or get across. There were many leeches in the water so Naropa asked the guru, "Shall I make a bridge for the lama to cross?"

Tilopa said, "Fine."

Naropa did so and Tilopa took a slow, leisurely stroll across his body that took a long time. Then Tilopa left. When Naropa got out of the water, leeches were sucking blood from every part of his body. He collapsed and remained there. After three days had passed the guru returned and asked, "Are you in pain?" He waved his hand over Naropa who had become like a corpse, healing him.

Another time, Naropa and the guru went to a charnel ground. Naropa returned from seeking alms. He had received some leftovers of worse quality than they had ever eaten before. He did not eat them himself but offered them to the guru because he felt that he must. The guru, for the purpose of helping Naropa to complete his accumulations, ate the dish with relish, smacking his lips, complimenting Naropa on the food he had obtained. Naropa was pleased thinking, "The guru very much enjoys whatever I bring him, no matter how distasteful!" He asked, "Should I seek some more?"

Tilopa answered, "Yes."

When Naropa searched, he could find no other place so he returned to the same one. There was nowhere in India a custom of seeking alms twice at the same place in a single day. Naropa knew this but still took some of the same food that had been put in his bowl before and ran. As before, he was chased, caught, and beaten to the point that he could not move. Again, the guru came, asked, "What's wrong?" and, as before, waved his hand over him, dispelled his wounds, and restored him.

Another time Tilopa said, "Naropa, don't rest in this big meadow. Go for a hike without eating or drinking." Naropa did so and, when he was close to death, Tilopa came, asked what had happened, waved his hand, and restored him.

Another time, from the midst of three huge fires, Tilopa asked, "Can anyone stay between these fires?" There was no one else there so Naropa thought he must be speaking to him. He stayed between the fires, causing all of his flesh and bones to turn white hot. He was about to die when Tilopa came, waved his hand over him, and restored him.

Another time Tilopa said to Naropa, "Seduce the king's queen!" Naropa went and, without choice, caught and seduced her. This resulted in her retinue giving him a crushing beating. He was revived and restored by the mere thought, "This is for the sake of the guru!"

Another time they encountered the palanquin of a minister's wife being carried. Tilopa asked, "Could anyone seize her?"

Naropa thought he was speaking to him so he grabbed her. The minister's retinue cut off all four of his limbs. This time, he thought there would be no recovery. Tilopa came and asked, "What's wrong?"

Naropa said, "I grabbed the minister's wife so he cut me!" Tilopa reconnected all four of his limbs, waved his hand over him, and restored him. During all of this Naropa said that he never lost faith in the guru being Buddha for even a moment.

Naropa stayed with Tilopa for twelve years. He underwent twelve austerities. Having served Tilopa, he thought that he must receive empowerment and instructions from him, so he offered Tilopa a mandala made from his own blood and made the request. Tilopa said,

> Your own awareness is transcendent wisdom realizing things as
>   they are!
> Tilopa has nothing at all to teach!

That was all he said.

Again, Naropa prostrated, circumambulated and beseeched the guru to take care of him. Tilopa glared this way and that. He spat, took some saliva, and anointed Naropa with it between his eyebrows. Naropa fainted. When he came to, all the words and meanings of the four classes of Tantra poured into his mind. In particular, he said that he directly received the instructions on the short AH inner fire meditation at that time.

Naropa thought, "I have had a chance to serve, and the guru has accepted me and blessed me, so I'll go somewhere else to accomplish the practice," but again he thought, "Shouldn't I ask whether I should teach or practice?" He returned and asked.

Tilopa poured a steaming heap of excrement into a skull cup, stuck a spoon made from a human rib bone into it, and gave it to Naropa. When he ate it, it was extremely delicious, with a hundred different flavors, such that he had never experienced before! Naropa thought, "Skull cups of human feces and spoons of human ribs are unclean things, but through blessings they are exquisitely delicious! Corresponding to this, nonpractice of Dharma is like filth, and meditation is like the blessing of unclean things! Tilopa is giving me a sign that I must meditate!"

The guru said, "That's only according to your understanding!"

Naropa made a prostration in departure and left. On the way, when he arrived at a large city, many people made offerings to him, saying that he was an excellent yogi. He received a basin full of pearls. Delighted with this, he took it into the guru's presence. He offered it thinking of the guru's great kindness and himself as an unimportant servant. Tilopa knew this, yet, to break Naropa's pride of still thinking of himself as a great yogi, he manifested himself sitting upon a huge throne of pearls. Naropa thought, "Guru Tilopa is endowed with such a wealth of property, what I have to offer is nothing amazing!" so he tossed away his pearls into the mandala and left.

When he arrived at a city on the path in the region where he left Guru Tilopa, he discovered it to be a city of blacksmiths. Having slept there, he rose early the next morning and entered meditation. The blacksmiths' wives thought that dawn had come and went to meet him, which made all of the blacksmiths go to seize him. They were not happy with his meditation; it made them angry. Thinking at length about the source of the problem, he realized the fault was his own. He severed the root of hatred, recognized ignorance, understood it to be unborn, and realized it was the kindness of the guru. It is said that he "severed the root of all phenomena" at that time.

Then he went to Nalanda monastery. It was necessary to have a guardian at each of the four doors of the monastery. At the east was He Renowned as Lord of Speech. At the south was Hidden Source of Wisdom. The west was guarded by Ratnakara Shantipa. There was no pandit guarding the northern door, so the king asked Naropa to take it. Naropa knew that his guru had said to him, "Don't be a four-door-guarding pandit for me!" but since it was for an important purpose he felt it wouldn't matter, so he accepted. The king became his disciple and he conferred initiation on him and gave teachings to him.

Then a non-Buddhist came to the north gate for debate. The first day Naropa could not handle him and he won. Afraid that the monks would lose their home, that night Naropa prayed to Tilopa and Tilopa came before him. Naropa said to his guru, "How small is your compassion! Yesterday you wouldn't help me in the debate!"

Tilopa replied, "I was beside you but the fault was that you broke my advice. Now, when you debate, first aim the threatening hand mudra at him. Then debate."

The next day when they gathered for the debate, by just aiming the threatening mudra, all the non-Buddhists trembled and became distracted. Many non-Buddhists were defeated and became Buddhists, it is said.

Another time an extremely large elephant had died in the northern sector. All the people were overcome with grief, saying that it would bring disease. Naropa had the villagers dig a grave big enough for the elephant at a comfortable distance away. Then, with his subtle mind-energy, he left his body and entered the body of the elephant and took it to the grave. It is said that he became the master of Nalanda at that time.

Another time when Naropa was bathing, his eight-spoked protection mandala amulet he had placed nearby was carried off by a crow. Naropa made the threatening mudra, gave one glance, and the crow was instantly paralyzed. This was a sign of his accomplishment of ritual activities.

Then he went to the forest monastery of Pushpahari and meditated there for twelve years. There arose in him the power to display the extraordinary conduct of rigpa-awareness.

On another occasion the master Shantipa and his assistants performed ganachakra. When one of the retinue was sent to carry out a torma, there was a naked ascetic seated on the torma platform. It so frightened him that he ran home. As a result of this appearance presenting itself, the master said, "He came to say he is like me. It was the great Naropa."

The entourage asked, "Why did he come here?" "He was giving an indication that if people like you wish to perform ganachakra you must have someone like me to preside as master at the ganachakra feast!"

Another time there was a pandit with his entourage in residence who was wise in all the five fields of knowledge. Naropa went there with a single assistant. That pandit received instructions from Naropa. Naropa said, "Although you are a great scholar, since I am accomplished, and since it was said that practitioners should instruct the scholars, I will teach you." The pandit was happy. At dusk the sound of a flute was heard, *di ri ri*. The pandit, in his dreams, thought that torma was being taken outside. In the morning Naropa had left. When it was asked where he went, people said, "He said his lama had gone somewhere, so he had to go there also, and he left!"

Later it is said that he enacted begging conduct holding a skull cup, begging from anyone he met. A fierce bandit put his knife into the skull cup. It is said that Naropa stirred it, it filled the bowl, and he drank it. He demonstrated many such miraculous feats, riding a lion into space, and so forth. He became endowed with immeasurable realized qualities because of his attainment of Mahamudra.

Appendix 3: The Mahamudra Prayer

---

by the Third Karmapa Rangjung Dorje

O Gurus and deities of yidam mandalas,
Buddhas and bodhisattvas of all space and time,
With affection for me, please grant your blessings
To bring the accomplishment of my prayers.

May the pure intentions and actions of myself
And infinite sentient beings, that river of virtue,
Running down from the snow mountains, unsullied in its three spheres,
Enter the ocean of the jinas' four kayas!

Up until that is attained,
In each and every one of our lives,
May we not even hear the words "harm" and "suffering"
But enjoy a glorious ocean of virtue and joy.

Attaining leisure and endowments with faith, perseverance, and wisdom,
Relying on the excellent spiritual guide, receiving the holy nectar,
And practicing correctly without any hindrance,
May we enjoy the sacred Dharma in all of our lives!

Hearing scripture and reasoning liberates from veils of ignorance,
Contemplation of the instructions dispels the darkness of doubt,
Light of wisdom from meditation illumines the way things are:
May illumination of the three wisdoms expand!

On the basis of the two truths, free of extremes of permanence
    and nihilism,
Through the path of two accumulations, free from extremes of reification
    and denial,
Attaining the fruit of enlightenment, free from the extremes of samsara
    and nirvana,
May we always meet with undistorted Buddhadharma!

In elemental mind, conjoined illumination and emptiness, the basis
    of purification,
Great yoga of tantric Mahamudra, the agent of purification,
Destroys adventitious stains of deception, that to be purified:
May we manifest the results of purification, the four kayas!

With confidence of the view that cuts through false projections
    about phenomena,
Precepts of meditation, practicing being undistracted from that view,
And supreme conduct enacting all of the aims of meditation,
May we have confidence of view, meditation, and action!

All phenomena are emanations of mind,
And mind is "no-mind," empty of identity,
Empty and unceasing, illuminating whatever appears:
By analyzing it, may we sever doubt from the root.

It does not exist—even jinas do not see it;
It is not nonexistent—it is the basis of samsara and nirvana;
It is not contradictory, the Middle Way path:
May I realize mind's true nature, dharmata, free from extremes.

Without the effort of any assertion to make,
Nor rejection of any object to deny,
May we ascertain perfect ultimate truth:
Unfabricated dharmata that is beyond intellect!

Not realizing just this, we cycle in samsara,
Realizing just this, Buddha is nowhere else.

May I realize alaya's true nature
That is free from assertion and rejection.

Appearance is mind; emptiness is also mind;
Realization and deception are both one's mind;
Whatever is produced or ceased in the mind is still mind:
May we cut through all reifications of the mind.

Undisturbed by winds of ordinary activities,
Through meditation free from effort of intellect,
May we master and practice the knowledge of naturally
Settling the mind in its innate unfabricated state.

Waves of gross and subtle thoughts pacified on the spot,
Remaining in the river of unmoving mind:
May we stabilize immutable oceanic shamata
Free from stains of sinking and fogginess.

By repeatedly viewing genuine mind, free from facsimiles,
May we gain special insight into Buddha's teaching of non-seeing.
Severing doubts about what is and is not,
May we know our own face without deception!

Viewing objects, objectless mind is seen!
Viewing the mind, it is nonexistent, empty of identity!
Looking at both, dual clinging is released on the spot;
May we realize the ultimate mode of existence of clear-light mind!

This freedom from mental activity is Mahamudra,
Great Madhyamaka, the middle way path, free from extremes,
And Dzogchen, the Great Perfection, as well, it is said:
By knowing one, may we attain confident knowledge of them all!

Free from concepts, great bliss experience never interrupted,
Not grasping things as real, clear light free from obscuring veils,
Nonconceptual, beyond intellect, existing spontaneously:
May we have uninterrupted effortless realized experience!

Perceptions of good and bad released on the spot,
Bad concepts and delusion purified in the natural sphere,
Ordinary awareness, free of accepting and rejecting:
May we realize ultimate truth free from fabrication!

Though beings by nature have always been buddha,
Not realizing it, they wander in endless samsara.
May we develop irresistible compassion for beings
Who are experiencing incessant suffering.

Within overpowering compassion's creative energy
Of unceasing love, emptiness of identity nakedly dawns:
Night and day, may we never be parted from meditation
On this supreme of paths, free from the pitfalls of duality.

Perfecting the "eyes" and clairvoyances that come from meditation,
Purifying the buddhafield that brings beings to maturity,
And perfecting all prayers to accomplish Buddhadharma,
Completing perfection, maturation and purification, may we become
     Buddha!

By power of the ten dimension's buddhas and bodhisattvas,
And the power of all pure virtue that exists,
May the pure prayers of myself and all sentient beings
Be accomplished just as they were made.

Appendix 4: The Vajradhara Lineage Prayer

by Bengel Jampel Zangpo[1]

Vajradhara, Tilopa, Naropa,
Marpa, Milarepa, Gampopa,
Karmapa Dusum Khyenpa,
Four major, eight minor lineages[2]—
Dri, Tag, Tsäl, the Drugpa, and so on—
Who've gained Mahamudra's profound path,
Beings' peerless guardians, Dagpo Kagyu:
Kagyu Lamas, bless us to uphold
Your lineage and your example!

Since detachment is the foot of meditation,
Detached from food, wealth, veneration,
Bless us to be great meditators
Who have fully given up this life!

Since aspiration and conviction are the head of meditation,
Bless us with the great meditators'
Unfeigned faith, always praying
To the guru who reveals the instructions!

Since nondistraction is meditation,
Bless us to not part from our object
Fixed right on the unfabricated
Original nature of all that appears.

Since thought's essence is dharmakaya,
Not being anything but appearing as anything,
Bless us to see whatever appears as its unceasing display
And that samsara and nirvana are nondual!

May we, in all lives, never be parted
From perfect gurus, enjoy Dharma,
Complete paths and stages' qualities,
And soon attain Vajradhara's state!

NOTES

Annotations by David Molk

TRANSLATOR'S INTRODUCTION

1. Tilopa, 988–1069.
2. Naropa, 1016–1100.
3. Marpa, 1012–1099.
4. Milarepa, 1052–1135.
5. Gampopa, 1079–1153.
6. *Ornament of Stainless Light: An Exposition of the Kalachakra Tantra,* by Khe-drup Norsang Gyatso, translated by Gavin Kilty (Boston: Wisdom Publications, 2004), p. 55.
7. This was originally Gampopa's position.
8. From the *Golden Garland of the Kagyu (bKa' brgyud gser gthreng),* fols. 5a–16b.
9. Dorje Dze Ö, a thirteenth-century disciple of dPal ldan Ri khrod dbang phyug, who was a disciple of 'Jig ten mgon po, founder of the Drikung Kagyu.
10. *The Great Kagyu Masters, The Golden Lineage Treasury,* translated by Khenpo Könchog Gyaltsen (Ithaca, N.Y.: Snow Lion Publications, 1990), pp. 33–45.
11. *The Life of the Mahāsiddha Tilopa,* by Mar-pa Chos-kyi bLo-gros, translated by Fabrizio Torricelli and Āchārya Sangye T. Naga (Dharamsala, India: Library of Tibetan Works and Archives, 1995). Torricelli and Naga list eight other Tibetan biographies (pp. viii–xi), including the one by Dorje Dze Ö.
12. Tibetan 'Khor lo sdom pa, the "mandala bound together," meaning the gathering of all phenomena within bliss-void wisdom. The deity practice of Chakra-samvara focuses on developing bliss in the subtle body to induce corresponding subtler levels of awareness, and ultimately the subtlest clear light awareness.
13. *The Life of Tilopa and the Ganges Mahamudra,* by Khenchen Thrangu Rinpoche (Auckland, New Zealand: Namo Buddha Publications and Zhyisil Chokyi Ghatsal Trust Publications, 2002).
14. This is the origin of Tilopa's name, "The Sesame Pounder."
15. The sesame metaphor doha is also included in the biography by Dorje Dze Ö.

16. Translated by Khenpo Konchog Gyaltsen; see note 10.
17. Crafts, medicine, Sanskrit, logic, and Dharma.
18. For a detailed account, see *The Life and Teaching of Naropa* by Herbert V. Guenther (London and New York: Oxford University Press, 1963).
19. A symbolic offering of the entire universe held in the hands.
20. *The Blue Annals,* trans. by George N. Roerich (Delhi: Motilal Banarsidass, 1988), pp. 399–402.
21. sPyi ther pa.
22. Paindapatika.
23. Marpa's nine wives are said to symbolize the nine goddesses of the Hevajra mandala. Marpa is renowned for having been able to integrate profound realization with the life of a householder.
24. *The Blue Annals,* a simplified narrative. Other accounts relate that Naropa sent Marpa to Maitripa to learn the essence of Mahamudra.
25. *The Blue Annals,* p. 402.
26. Citations of the *Jewel Ornament of Liberation* from oral commentary by Sangyes Nyenpa Rinpoche translated by David Molk, unpublished manuscript.
27. As I am translating the compound Tibetan term *mos gus.*
28. Threefold faith: convinced, clear, and aspiring faith.
29. Four reliances: rely not upon the guru but upon their teaching; rely not upon the words of the teaching but upon their meaning; rely not upon a provisional meaning but on the definitive meaning; and rely not on ordinary mind but upon transcendent wisdom consciousness.

DISCOVERY OF SACRED SECRETS ON THE BANKS OF THE GANGES

1. The eight great chariots, or practice lineages, as categorized by Jamgön Kongtrul in his *Treasury of Instructions* are the Nyingma lineage, the Kadampa lineage, the Lamdré or Sakya lineage, the Marpa Kagyu lineage, the Shangpa Kagyu lineage, the Pacification and Chöd lineages, the Kalachakra or Jordruk (Yoga of Six Branches) lineage, and the Orgyen Nyendrup or Three Vajras lineage of Orgyen Rinchen Pal.
2. The author, Sangyes Nyenpa Rinpoche, in his previous incarnation was Kyabje Dilgo Khyentse's brother.
3. Arya attainment: direct insight into ultimate reality.
4. The Sakya monk Wangchug Gyaltsen's biography of Naropa lists twelve acts of austerity: (1) jumping off the temple roof, (2) jumping into fire, (3) being beaten by the almsgivers, (4) going into the water with the leeches, (5) contact with burning hot sharp reeds, (6) running himself to exhaustion, (7) being beaten by the wedding party, (8) being beaten by the king and ministers, (9) being beaten by the prince's army, (10) striking his erect penis with a stone in self-castigation, (11) giving his consort to Tilopa, and (12) exhaustion from chasing Tilopa. Each of the hardships is said to have occurred after the period of a year, and each

resulted in receiving instructions from Tilopa. These instructions were (1) purification, guru yoga, gathering of merit, generation and completion stages, and yogas of daily life; (2) single taste; (3) commitments; (4) *tummo,* inner fire; (5) illusory body; (6) dream; (7) clear light; (8) *phowa;* (9) entering a corpse; (10) eternal innate great bliss; (11) mahamudra; and (12) bardo. See *The Life and Teaching of Naropa* by Herbert V. Guenther (London and New York: Oxford University Press, 1963).

5. The state of unification of Heruka-Vajrayogini's pure land.

6. The four extremes (*mtha' bzhi*) are the extremes of existence (of true unimputed existence), nonexistence (of conventional existence), both, and neither. The eight extreme projections are the extremes of production, cessation, coming, going, permanence, nihilism, singularity, and plurality.

7. This nonverbal "indication" is said to have ignited Naropa's ultimate realization.

8. *rgyal ba:* victor, conqueror. A title synonymous with buddha.

9. *rang sems phyag rgya chen po.*

10. *The Vajradhara Lineage Prayer.* See appendix 4 for the full prayer.

11. Dagpo Rinpoche refers to Gampopa, Sönam Rinchen.

12. *bla ma la gsol ba phur tshugs su btab,* making a strong "driving" request with the same objective repeatedly.

13. *The Vajradhara Lineage Prayer,* cited with and without identification several times throughout. See appendix 4 for the full prayer.

14. *sems 'tshol mkhan po,* "abbot instructor of the mind-quest," the teacher who introduces a student to the nature of mind.

15. *lo mnyam,* equal age.

16. Also found in *The Vajradhara Lineage Prayer,* appendix 4.

17. *rtsam pa,* roasted barley flour.

18. Generating the deity in stages corresponding to the five wisdoms.

19. *snying po'i lugs,* a reference to these Mahamudra instructions, in particular the Essence Mahamudra System in which the deepest import is imparted directly to the trainee, forcefully causing simultaneous realization and liberation.

20. Birth from an egg, a womb, heat and moisture, and miraculous birth.

21. *lam rgyud lnga,* another counting of the six realms in which demigods are not counted separately. Upper demigods are included within gods, and lower demigods within animals.

22. *rang bab.*

23. *gdod nas.*

24. *ka dag.*

25. *ye nas dag pa.*

26. *'dro ba 'di dag ma lus sangs rgyas rgyu,* literally, "All beings without exception are causes of buddhas," meaning the substantial cause that will become a buddha.

27. *dal ba.*

28. *btsan sa zin.*

29. Tib. *rlung,* Skt. *vayu,* wind, the subtle energies of the body.

30. The five sense consciousnesses and the mental consciousness.
31. *ldog pa.* Isolates are related to the generic images used by conceptual thought. Thought's image is not of the object itself but of that which is "not not the object," an "isolate" of the object. In this instance the image would be that of a fabrication, something nonexistent.
32. *shin tu mthar thug pa.*
33. *gtad so.*
34. *zag bcas.* The contamination is by ignorance and other delusions.
35. *chos nyid,* reality; in this context, union of ultimate subject and object.
36. Technical note on Great Madhyamaka and "Emptiness of Other":

    In the first round of teaching, Buddha taught the Four Noble Truths, a description of two cause and effect relationships: resultant bondage in suffering, and its causes; and resultant liberation in bliss, and its causes. It was a consummate description of base, path, and result: our situation, what could be done about it, and where that could lead.

    In the middle round of teachings, in order to reveal and destroy the reifying ignorance which is at the root of all problems, Buddha taught the illusory nature of all things, their emptiness, their "not existing in the manner they appear," their shunyata. This was not a negation of the first round, but a refinement, a deeper and vaster explanation. The cause and effect relationships described in the Four Noble Truths would not function as they do unless all phenomena lacked true or inherent existence. Form is emptiness, emptiness is form. Emptiness is no other than form, form is no other than emptiness. All phenomena from form to omniscience were revealed to be empty of inherent existence.

    The third and final stage of Buddha's teachings, according to some, was intended for those who were unable to understand the profound implications of the middle round. This view holds that the final round of teachings presents a Chittamatra (Mind Only) system, that does not completely accord with reality, a provisional teaching that is ultimately refuted by the logic presented in the middle round of the teachings. In Great Madhyamaka, however, the third round of Buddha's teachings, while accepted as Chittamatra in general, is also viewed as a final definitive teaching, a further refinement of the second round's teachings. That is because, for ultimate realization, the shunyata that is explained in the middle stage of the teachings must be realized, not by an ordinary mind, but by a specific state of mind, the elemental mind of clear light as explained in Tantra. This clear light mind, this "luminous empty transcendent wisdom," besides being empty of its own inherent existence, is also empty of all other adventitious conceptual states of mind grosser than itself, and so is termed "empty of other." It is not a contradiction of the self-emptiness of the Middle Way, but a term for the clear light mind that must realize that emptiness in order for complete nondual realization to occur. The Emptiness-of-Other system is therefore called the Great Middle Way, the Mahamadhyamaka.

    It is not just a philosophical system, but the experience of yogis, contemplatives, those who work with the mind, that all phenomena of samsara and nirvana arise out of clear light mind; that all phenomena are the nature of mind. Buddha gave the final round of teachings in order to more fully explain how phenomena that are empty of inherent existence arise and appear. They depend upon the subtlest mind of clear light, the mind "basis-of-all." Although it lacks inherent existence, Buddha called it "fully established," an "unexcelled continuum," and "primordial purity." Realization of clear light as explained in highest yoga tantra surpasses all other realizations and makes the third round an expansion and refinement of the earlier teachings.

Related to this, Rinpoche makes a case for the greatness of Asanga, asking why his teachings are not considered to be as profound as Chandrakirti's with respect to describing ultimate truth. For the Great Madhyamaka, or Maha-madhyamaka, the second round's import is a temporary ultimate, whereas the clear light mind of the third round is the final ultimate. When clear light mind manifests, it, and only it, can completely merge with shunyata. Whether that experience is described from the point of view of the experienced object, a space-like "absence of inherent existence," which is a non-affirming negation, or from the point of view of the experiencing subject, "a clear light mind that is empty of inherent existence," which is an affirming negation, the experience that is being described is the same. An interesting confirmation of this by H. H. the Fourteenth Dalai Lama as translated by Alexander Berzin appears in *The Gelug/Kagyü Tradition of Mahamudra* (Ithaca, N.Y.: Snow Lion Publications, 1997), pp. 234–35:

> regarding the topic of madhyamaka the great Rendawa was the best of all learned, erudite masters with whom Tsongkapa could have a direct relationship. On the face value of Rendawa's writings, however, concerning the decisive understanding of the madhyamaka view, we would have to say that he does not assert voidness as a non-affirming nullification. But Kaydrubjey, in his *Miscellaneous Writings,* has asserted that although Rendawa's and Tsongkapa's writings on the topic have different manners of expression, they come down to the same thing.

37. *dis theg pa.*
39. *dir theg pa.*
39. *sems kyi ngo bo.*
40. *stong nyid.*
41. *sems kyi gnas lugs.*
42. *de kho na nyid.*
43. *bde ba chen po.*
44. *yid la mi byed pa'i don.* As the name of this dharmachakra, I capitalize it for the most part, translating it as "Free of Mental Activity" or "No Mental Activity." It could also be translated as "Nonattention," etc. I also capitalize it to signify that the meaning is not encapsulated by the literal English words, i.e., it is not a

simple nonaffirming negation. It refers to the principal "essence-meaning" that is being pointed out in these instructions: our own primordial elemental clear light mind "free of mental activity."

45. *zhe 'dod.*

46. Ritual from the *Sarvadurgatiparisodhana Tantra,* an aspect of Buddha Vairochana.

47. Vasubandhu.

48. Go rams pa bsod nams seng ge, 1429–1489.

49. In normal terminology, *sems can,* "sentient being," by definition indicates a being who is still limited, that is, all beings from ordinary beings up to bodhisattvas on the verge of becoming buddhas. This is in contrast to a buddha, a fully purified, awakened being.

50. The fivefold Mahamudra instructions, *phyag rgya chen po lnga ldan gyi man ngag,* were the principal meditation of the supreme Desheg Pagmo Drupa (1100–1170). Then, the great Gyalwa Drigungpa Rinchen Pal, Kyobpa Jigten Sumgön, "Protector of the Three Worlds" (1143–1217), composed them as doha. The fivefold Mahamudra practice is

1. bodhicitta Mahamudra to enter the path of the Mahayana;
2. deity's form Mahamudra to abandon ordinary appearance and grasping;
3. esteem and devotion Mahamudra to receive blessings;
4. true nature Mahamudra to resolve the nature of samsara and nirvana; and
5. dedication Mahamudra to increase virtue inexhaustibly.

51. *dad pa.*

52. *mos gus.*

53. *tshwa tshwa,* small reliquaries cast of plaster, cement, etc. of buddhas and other sacred images, an art form traditionally made as offerings for shrines, sometimes enshrining ashes of deceased lamas or relatives to memorialize them and bless living beings. Naropa's mind became the same as Tilopa's, as if cast from the same mold.

54. The vajra with a thread tied to it extending to a vase by which dharanis, mantric syllables, are visualized as passing along during tantric ritual.

55. See appendix 4 for translation.

56. *gzer.*

57. Sung by Milarepa in praise of the blessed site in Nepal by that name.

58. *gsal.*

59. In Madhyamaka, under intense investigation of their ultimate nature, basis, path, and result cannot stand up to analysis and do not appear. To such awareness there is no basis, path, or fruit to be attained. To awareness that is not analyzing, or that is lightly analyzing, conventionally existent basis, path, and result may appear. In any case, mere, or general, existence is not denied.

60. The basis of having already viewed the luminosity of one's own mind; having already ceased mental reification.
61. *rtsad bdar bcad,* or *rtsad bdar chod,* usually translated as "investigate" or "examine." Literally, "investigate and cut the root."
62. The five sense consciousnesses and mental consciousness.
63. *cog ger bzhag.*
64. Drubtob Nyemowa Samten Puntsok, founder of the Elephant Trunk monastery near Lake Manasarovar.
65. The metaphor is that of a stick with a burning ember on the end which, if spun in the dark, creates an illusion of circles and shapes that the eye is drawn to follow.
66. *spros pa brgyad kyi mtha'.* On the four and eight extremes, see note 6 above.
67. *bar rlung.*
68. Oral instructions are required for further explication.
69. *rig pa'i thog brdzis btang.*

Appendix 1: Tilopa, from the *Golden Garland of the Kagyu*

1. 1284–1339.

Appendix 2: A Brief Account of Tilopa and Naropa

1. Chakrasamvara's seven-syllable mantra, OM HRI HA HA HUM HUM PHAT.

Appendix 4: The Vajradhara Lineage Prayer

1. Bengel Jampel Zangpo (Ban sgal 'jam dpal bzang po) was a student of the Eighth Karmapa Mikyö Dorje.
2. The four greater lineages are Karma Kagyu, Barom Kagyu, Tshalpa Kagyu, and Phagdru Kagyu; the eight minor lineages are Drigung Kagyu, Taklung Kagyu, Throphu Kagyu, Drukpa Kagyu, Martshang Kagyu, Yelpa Kagyu, Yazang Kagyu, and Shugseb Kagyu.

WORKS CITED IN THE COMMENTARY

Ascertaining the Three Vows: sDom pa gsum gyi rab tu dbye ba'i gzhung, sDom gsum rab dbye by Sakya Pandita. English translation: *A Clear Differentiation of the Three Codes* by Sakya Pandita Kunga Gyaltshen. Translated by Jared Douglas Rhoton; edited by Victoria Scott. Albany: State University of New York Press, 2002. Also: *Perfect Conduct: Ascertaining the Three Vows* by Ngari Panchen Pema Wangyi Gyalpo with commentary by His Holiness Dudjom Rinpoche. Translated by Khenpo Gyurme Samdrub and Sangye Khandro. Boston: Wisdom Publications, 1996.

Autocommentary on Entering the Middle Way: dBu ma la 'jug pa'i bshad pa/ dBu ma la 'jug pa'i rang 'grel; Madhyamakāvatārabhāṣya by Chandrakirti.

Bodhisattva Pitaka: Byang chub sems dpa'i sde snod kyi mdo; Bodhisattvapiṭakasūtra.

Chakrasamvara Tantra: bDe mchog 'khor lo'i rgyud.

Chöd: Taking Appearances on the Path: gCod snang ba lam khyer by Jamgön Kongtrul Lodrö Taye.

Commentary on Valid Cognition: Tshad ma rnam 'grel gyi tshig le'ur byas pa; Pramāṇavārttikakārikā by Dharmakirti.

Discriminating Dharmata: Chos nyid rnam 'byed; Dharmadharmatāvibhāga by Asanga/Maitreyanatha. English translation: *Distinguishing Phenomena from Their Intrinsic Nature: Maitreya's Dharmadharmatavibhanga with Commentaries by Khenpo Shenga and Ju Mipham.* Translated by Dharmachakra Translation Committee. Boston: Snow Lion, 2013.

Drigung Doha of the Fivefold [Mahamudra Practice]: 'Bri gung lnga ldan mgur by Jigten Sumgön.

Entering the Middle Way: dBu ma la 'jug pa; Madhyamakāvatāra by Chandrakirti. English translation: *Introduction to the Middle Way: Chandrakirti's Madhyamakavatara, with Commentary by Ju Mipham.* Translated by Padmakara Translation Group. Boston: Shambhala Publications, 2005. Also: *Ocean of Nectar: The True*

Nature of All Things. Translation and commentary by Geshe Kelsang Gyatso. London: Tharpa Publications, 1995.

Expressing the Names of Manjushri: 'Jam dpal mtshan brjod; Mañjuśrīnāmasaṃgīti.

Four Hundred Verses on the Middle Way: bsTan bcos bzhi brgya pa zhes bya ba'i tshig le'ur byas pa; Catuḥśatakaśāstrakārikā by Aryadeva. English translation: *Aryadeva's Four Hundred Stanzas on the Middle Way,* by Gyel-tsap, with commentary by Geshe Sonam Rinchen. Translated and edited by Ruth Sonam. Ithaca, N.Y.: Snow Lion Publications, 2008.

Four Seats Tantra, Tantra of the Four Vajra Seats: rDo rje gdan bzhi'i rgyud; Catuḥpitha.

Great Cloud Sutra: sPrin chen po'i mdo; Mahāmeghasūtra.

Great Drum Sutra: rNga bo che chen po'i leu'i mdo; Mahābherīhāraka-parivarta-sūtra.

Guhyagarbha Tantra: gSang ba snying po'i rgyud. English translation: *Luminous Essence: A Guide to the Guhyagarbha Tantra* by Jamgon Mipham. Translated by the Dharmachakra Translation Committee. Ithaca, N.Y.: Snow Lion Publications, 2009.

Guide to the Bodhisattva's Conduct: Byang chub sems dpa'i spyod pa la 'jug pa; Bodhicaryāvatāra by Shantideva. English translation: *The Way of the Bodhisattva.* Translated by Padmakara Translation Group. Boston: Shambhala Publications, 2008. Also: *A Guide to the Bodhisattva Way of Life.* Translated by Vesna A. Wallace and B. Alan Wallace. Ithaca, N.Y.: Snow Lion Publications, 1997. Also: *The Bodhicaryavatara.* Translated by Kate Crosby and Andrew Skilton. Oxford and New York: Oxford University Press, 1996. Also: *A Guide to the Bodhisattva's Way of Life.* Translated by Stephen Batchelor. Dharamsala, India: Library of Tibetan Works and Archives, 1979. Also: *Guide to the Bodhisattva's Way of Life: A Buddhist Poem for Today.* Translated by Geshe Kelsang Gyatso and Neil Elliot. Ulverston: Tharpa, 2002.

Hitting the Essence in Three Words: Tshig gsum gnad rdeg mkhas pa shri rgyal po'i khyad chos rtsa ba dang 'grel pa (Hitting the Essence in Three Words, Special Teachings of the Wise and Glorious King, Root Text and Commentary), by Dza Paltrul Rinpoche. English translation: *Dzogchen: The Heart Essence of the Great Perfection,* by H. H. the Fourteenth Dalai Lama. Ithaca, N.Y.: Snow Lion Publications, 2000. Also: *Golden Letters,* translation by John Myrdhin Reynolds. Ithaca, N.Y.: Snow Lion Publications, 1996.

Jewel Ornament of Liberation: Dvag po thar rgyan/ Dam chos yid bzhin gyi nor bu thar pa rin po che'i rgyan, by Gampopa. English translation: *The Jewel Ornament of Liberation: The Wish-Fulfilling Gem of The Noble Teachings,* translated by Khenpo Konchog Gyaltsen Rinpoche. Ithaca, N.Y.: Snow Lion Publications, 1998.

Kalachakra Tantra: Dus 'khor.

Lamp on the Path: Byang chub lam gyi sgron ma; Bodhipathapradīpa by Atisha. English translation: *Atisha's Lamp for the Path to Enlightenment,* commentary by Geshe Sonam Rinchen, translated by Ruth Sonam. Ithaca, N.Y.: Snow Lion Publications, 1997.

Mahamudra Prayer: Phyag chen smon lam by the Third Karmapa Rangjung Dorje.

Mahaparinirvana Sutra: 'Phags pa yongs su mya ngan las 'das pa chen po'i mdo.

Ocean of Definitive Meaning of Mahamudra: Phyag chen nges don rgya mtsho by the Ninth Karmapa Wangchuk Dorje.

Ornament of Sutra: Theg pa chen po'i mdo sde'i rgyan gyi tshig le'ur byas pa; Mahāyānasūtrālaṃkārakārikā by Asanga.

Perfection of Definitive Meaning of the Fivefold [Mahamudra]: Nges don rdzogs pa lnga ldan by Jetsun Milarepa.

Praise of the Teachings on Mind and Mental Factors: Sems sems byung bstan pa'i bstod pa by Khenpo Tsultrim Gyamtso.

Precious Garland of the Middle Way: dBu ma'i rin chen phreng ba; Ratnāvali by Nagarjuna. English translation: *Nagarjuna's Precious Garland: Buddhist Advice for Living and Liberation,* translated by Jeffrey Hopkins. Ithaca, N.Y.: Snow Lion Publications, 1997.

Questions of King Dharanishvara Sutra: gZungs dbang gi zhus pa'i mdo/ gZungs kyi dbang phug rgyal pos zhus pa'i mdo/ De bzhin gshegs pa'i snying rje chen po bstan pa'i mdo; Dhāraṇīśvararājaparipṛcchasūtra/ Tathāgata-mahākaruṇā-nirdeśa-sūtra.

Root Wisdom: Fundamental Treatise on the Middle Way, Called 'Wisdom'; dBu ma rtsa ba'i tshig le'ur byas pa shes rab ces bya ba; Prajñā-nāma-mūlamadhyamakakārikā by Nagarjuna. English translation: *The Fundamental Wisdom of the Middle Way: Nagarjuna's Mulamadhyamakakarika,* translated by Jay Garfield. New York: Oxford University Press, 1997. Also: *Nagarjuna's Middle Way,* translated by Mark Siderits and Shoryu Katsura. Somerville, Mass.: Wisdom Publications, 2013.

Samadhiraja Sutra: King of Meditative Stabilizations Sutra; Ting nge 'dzin rgyal po'i mdo.

Sambuta Tantra: rGyud sam pu ta.

Seven Points of Mind Training: Theg pa chen po'i gdams ngag blo sbyong don bdun ma'i rtsa ba by Geshe Chekawa. English translation: *Enlightened Courage: An Explanation of the Seven-Point Mind Training,* commentary by Dilgo Khyentse Rinpoche. Translated by the Padmakara Translation Group. Ithaca, N.Y.: Snow Lion Publications, 2006. Also: *Seven Points of Mind Training,* commentary by Khenchen

Thrangu Rinpoche. Auckland: Zhyisil Chokyi Ghatsel Publications, 2006. Also: *The Great Path of Awakening: A Commentary on the Mahayana Teaching of the Seven Points of Mind Training* by Jamgon Kongtrul. Translated by Ken McLeod. Boston: Shambhala Publications, 1987. Also: *Training the Mind and Cultivating Loving-Kindness* by Chogyam Trungpa. Boston: Shambhala Publications, 2003. Also: *The Practice of Lojong: Cultivating Compassion Through Training the Mind* by Traleg Kyabgon. Boston: Shambhala Publications, 2007.

Seventy Verses on Emptiness: sTong pa nyid bdun cu pa'i tshig le'ur byas pa; Śūnyatāsaptatikārikā by Nagarjuna. English translation: *Nagarjuna's Seventy Stanzas: A Buddhist Psychology of Emptiness,* translated by David Ross Komito. Ithaca, N.Y.: Snow Lion Publications, 1999.

Sixty Verses on Reasoning: Rigs pa drug cu pa'i tshig le'ur byas pa; Yuktiṣaṣṭikākārikā by Nagarjuna.

Sukhavati Prayer: bDe smon by the Fifth Karmapa Dezhin Shegpa.

Sutra of the Ten Grounds: mDo sde sa bcu pa; Daśabhūmikasūtra. English translation: *An Annotated Translation of the Dasabhumika.* Studies in Southeast and Central Asia, ed. by D. Sinor. Satapitaka Series 74. New Delhi: 1968.

Tantra of the Two Examinations: rGyud brtag pa gnyis, a condensed version of the Hevajra Tantra.

Ten Suchnesses: De kho na nyid bcu pa by Maitripa.

Thirty-seven Practices of Bodhisattvas: rGyal sras lag len so bdun ma by Ngulchu Togme (dNgul chu thog med). English translation: *The Thirty-seven Verses on the Practice of a Bodhisattva,* commentary by Dilgo Khyentse Rinpoche. Translated by the Padmakara Translation Group. Boston: Shambhala Publications, 2007. Also: *The Thirty-Seven Practices of Bodhisattvas: An Oral Teaching,* by Geshe Sonam Rinchen, translated by Ruth Sonam. Ithaca, N.Y.: Snow Lion Publications, 2001. Also: *Transforming Adversity into Joy and Courage: An Explanation of the Thirty-seven Practices of Bodhisattvas* by Geshe Jampa Tegchog. Ithaca, N.Y.: Snow Lion Publications, 2005. Also: *The Thirty-seven Practices of a Bodhisattva.* Commentary by Khenpo Tsultrim Gyamtso Rinpoche. The Marpa Foundation, 2001.

Treasury of Dohas: Do ha mdzod ces bya ba spyod pa'i glu; Dohakoṣanāmacaryāgīti by Saraha. English translation: "Saraha's Treasury of Songs," translated by David Snellgrove. Pp. 224–239 in *Buddhist Texts Through the Ages.* Edited by Edward Conze. New York: Harper and Row, 1964.

Treasury of Instructions: gDams ngag mdzod by Jamgön Kongtrul Lodrö Tayé. Detailed catalog at http://gdamsngagmdzod.tsadra.org/

Treasury of Knowledge: Shes bya mdzod by Jamgön Kongtrul Lodrö Tayé. English translation: *Treasury of Knowledge.* Translated by the Kalu Rinpoché Translation

Group. 10 vols. Ithaca, N.Y.: Snow Lion Publications, 2003–2011; Boston: Snow Lion, 2012.

Treasury of the Supreme Vehicle: Theg mchog mdzod by Longchen Rabjampa. A commentary on the seventeen tantras of the Men Ngag De division of Atiyoga.

Victory Banner of Siddhi: dNgos grub rgyal mtshan gi gsung mgur by the Drigung master Mahasiddha Nyemowa Samten Phuntsog.

Uttaratantra: Mahayana Treatise on the Highest Continuum; Theg pa chen po rgyud bla ma'i bstan bcos; Mahāyānottaratantraśāstra by Maitreya/ Asanga.

Yeshe Lama (Ye shes bla ma) by Jigme Lingpa. English translation: *Yeshe Lama,* by Vidyādhara Jigmed Lingpa. Translated by Lama Chönam and Sangye Khandro. Ithaca, N.Y.: Snow Lion Publications, 2009.

ABOUT THE AUTHOR

SANGYES NYENPA RINPOCHE was recognized as the tenth of his line by H. H. the Sixteenth Karmapa, who prophesied his birthplace, the name of his parents, and the year of his birth. Born into a family of practitioners who lived at the temple of Guru Rinpoche, Tiger's Nest, Tagtsang, Bhutan, he was invited to Rumtek Monastery, where he was enthroned by H. H. Karmapa. Receiving instructions from H. H. Dilgo Khyentse Rinpoche as well as Khenchen Tsultrim Gyamtso Rinpoche, Khenchen Dzogchen Dazer Rinpoche, and Geshe Lharam Menla from Drepung Monastery, he received the novice and bodhisattva vows, many empowerments of highest yoga tantra, instructions such as Moonbeams of Mahamudra, Eliminating the Darkness of Ignorance, and Pointing the Finger at Dharmakaya, and was thus introduced to ultimate realization. He attained the title of acharya and taught for three years at the Nalanda Institute in Rumtek. Nyenpa Rinpoche is one of the most learned of his generation in both philosophy and tantric ritual. He lives in his monastery Benchen Phuntsok Dargyeling, Kathmandu, giving teachings to the monks and other disciples and spending the rest of his time in retreat. For more information, please see www.sangyenyenpa.com.